A+chieve
Tutorials
LLC
Academic and Testing Excellence

MAximum SAT

ISBN 1-4116-2385-1

Visit Achieve Tutorials on the web at www.AchieveTutorials.com and www.MaximumSAT.com

Written by Pete Edwards
Special thanks to Kerith Dilley, Larrilyn Edwards, Sarah Gallivan, Jack Miller, Adam Rodgers, and Traci Sexton

While every effort is made to ensure this manual is complete and error free, mistakes do occasionally occur. If any errors are discovered, they will be posted in an errata sheet available at www.MaximumSAT.com and www.AchieveTutorials.com. If you find an error, please let us know by emailing errors@MaximumSAT.com. Updates to this text and additional resources for book owners will also be posted on the above websites.

Book Code:AT 05-2400-0102

GETTING THE MOST FROM THIS MANUAL

Maximum SAT is designed for both individual and classroom use. This manual fully explains everything students need to know to maximize SAT scores – whether they are working on their own, with a tutor, or in a classroom. (Tutors can use the manual as a valuable resource, targeting tutorial sessions to each student's individual strengths and weaknesses.)

PICK UP A COPY OF THE OFFICIAL SAT STUDY GUIDE!

If you are taking one of Achieve Tutorial's *Maximum SAT* courses, or working with one of our tutors, we will provide you with the *The Official SAT Study Guide for the New SAT*™. **If you plan to use this manual on you own or with another tutor, you should buy a copy of *The Official SAT Study Guide*.**

You may note that this manual is not overflowing with sample tests. We *have* created sample questions, examples, and timed drills to help you learn the material and techniques. However, we STRONGLY believe that REAL SAT problems are your best resource. No matter how good any test prep company may be, (and no one is better than we are) nobody writes questions *exactly* like the SAT test writers. For this reason, the manual and workbook contain pointer boxes to real SAT questions.

In most sections, after material has been introduced, you will see a pointer box in the right margin:

Try real examples ➡	PT1 S2 Q16, 19; S4 Q15
	PT2 S3 Q21; S6 Q8

For instance, this pointer box tells you that you will find examples of a particular question type in Practice Test 2, Section 2, Questions 16 and 19; Section 4, Question 15, as well as Practice Test 2, Section 3, Question 21, and Section 5, Question 8. (All references to *The Official SAT Study Guide* published in 2004.)

> If you are taking a *Maximum SAT* class or working with an Achieve Tutorials tutor, please don't work ahead in this guide or in *The Official SAT Study Guide* unless you clear it with your instructor or tutor first. The last four tests in *The Official SAT Study Guide* are often used as practice tests.

PRACTICE!

If you want to see real improvements in your score, you must practice. There is no substitute for time spent diligently working on SAT materials.

Whenever you do homework or use practice materials, take the work seriously. Don't rush through just to get the work done, because that won't help much. Don't work in front of the TV, with music playing, or with your computer on. These are all too distracting.

When you miss questions, spend some time trying to figure out what mistakes you made and how to get that type of question right the next time you see one.

LEARN SOME NEW WORDS!

Vocabulary is still important on the New SAT, even though the old vocabulary-driven Analogies questions have been eliminated. Sentence Completion and Reading Comprehension questions are often vocabulary-based. Time spent improving your vocabulary can only help. Start with the lists we provide in the Vocabulary Lists section at the end of the manual. They are filled with words we deem likely to appear on the SAT. We've provided dictionary-style definitions, because that's what it tested on the SAT. Don't put this off! **You should spend some time every day improving your vocabulary.** That's right, every single day. It will pay off in school and on the New SAT. For more information on vocabulary, see the Vocabulary section of the Critical Reading chapter.

SYLLABUS

What follows is a recommended Syllabus based on five weeks of preparation for the SAT.

Each week, expect to spend at least six hours covering the material in this manual, as well as additional time completing homework and drills. Also, make sure to schedule time to take the practice tests as indicated!

You can, of course, develop your own syllabus. If you have more than five weeks, stretch it out. Spend more time on the particular skills and techniques that you need to improve.

If you are using this manual to teach a class, two three-hour sessions per week, plus time for practice tests, should be enough to cover all the material and allow some time for drills.

Practice tests are essential. Don't expect to improve if you don't practice. Full, timed practice tests are the only way you can really assess your improvement. **Take practice tests seriously!** Here are some tips to help you maximize the value of practice tests:

❶ Take full tests in one sitting. You can take a 10 to 15-minute break after completing the first five sections. (The tests in *The Official SAT Study Guide* are shorter than the actual test by 25 minutes. They are missing an unscored experimental section that the College Board uses to test future SAT questions, among other things.)

❷ Make the practice tests you take as realistic as possible. Find a setting that closely mimics real test conditions. Libraries are excellent places to take practice tests. They are relatively quiet, but provide some of the distractions you may experience in a real test. Definitely do not take tests in front of the television or with music playing.

❸ Time yourself carefully. Timing is a huge factor on the SAT. Make sure you give yourself exactly the right amount of time for each section. (After you have scored the test, you may wish to complete any questions you didn't get to.)

❹ Use the answer sheets. Rip them out of the book or copy them. You'll need to use them on the real test, so get used to them.

❺ Use the same calculator you'll use on the real SAT. Learn how to use it efficiently. You certainly don't want to waste time fiddling with an unfamiliar calculator during the SAT.

Recommended Syllabus

Take Practice Test 5 **(In *The Official SAT Study Guide*)**		Before you begin preparing for the SAT, it is important to know where you stand. Because this manual assigns Practice Tests 1-4 as homework, take Practice Test 5 as a diagnostic test. Score the test carefully and note your strengths and weaknesses.
Week 1	Introduction	Some of the biggest tricks and techniques are in these first lessons. Learn them well so you can practice them over the next few weeks. **Make sure you spend time every day learning vocabulary!**
	Math Lesson 1	
	Writing Lesson 1	
	Math Lesson 2	
	Writing Lesson 2	
	Critical Reading Lesson 1	
Week 2	Math Lesson 3	This week delves deeper into specific information that will buy you points on the test. Keep working! **Make sure you spend time every day learning vocabulary!**
	Writing Lesson 3	
	Critical Reading Lesson 2	
	Math Lesson 4	
	Writing Lesson 4	
	Do Some Extra Vocabulary	
Take Practice Test 6 **(In *The Official SAT Study Guide*)**		Focus on using the techniques you've learned over the past two weeks, especially *Making Up Numbers*, *Using the Answers*, Sentence Completion, and Reading Comprehension techniques
Week 3	Test Review	Take some serious time to analyze the practice test. Review every question you missed and figure out how you could have gotten it right. **Make sure you spend time every day learning vocabulary!**
	Math Lesson 5	
	Writing Lesson 5	
	Math Lesson 6	
	Writing Lesson 6	
	Critical Reading Lesson 3	
Take Practice Test 7 **(In *The Official SAT Study Guide*)**		Start to work on pacing and timing for each section. Remember, you need to get as many of the easy and medium questions correct as possible, and then worry about the hard ones. Look for the easy way to do every question, and use the techniques!

Week 4	Test Review	You've learned a lot, and now you're getting into some of the nitty-gritty. Stay focused on the material and try to put everything you've learned together. Take some serious time to analyze the practice test. Review every question you missed and figure out how you could have gotten it right. **Make sure you spend time every day learning vocabulary!**
	Math Lesson 7	
	Writing Lesson 7	
	Math Lesson 8	
	Begin Timed Drills	
Take Practice Test 8 (**In** *The Official SAT Study Guide*)		Now it's time to really put it all together! Focus on pacing for each section so you get as many questions correct as possible without going too fast. Look for alternative approaches to tougher questions, or questions that would take too long to do "the right way."
Week 5	Final Assignments Lesson	Now it's time to review anything that's been giving you a hard time. Take some serious time to analyze the practice test. Review every question you missed and figure out how you could have gotten it right. Do the timed drills from the manual and any uncompleted sections from *The Official SAT Study Guide*. **Make sure you spend time every day learning vocabulary!**
	Review	
	Finish Timed Drills	

THE BASICS

The College Board changed the SAT for the March 2005 test and beyond. The test was changed for a variety of reasons, most notably pressure from the University of California. In a 2001 speech to the American Council on Education, UC President Richard C. Atkinson announced his recommendation that the university no longer require the SAT I for admission to any of the eight UC campuses. The University of California is one of the nation's largest users of the SAT, so it is generally assumed that this pressure forced the College Board to make some changes.

The changes are not drastic. Analogy questions and Quantitative Comparison questions were eliminated. Short Reading Comprehension passages were added. Some higher-level math was added. The old SAT II Writing test, including its essay, was rolled into the New SAT.

The New SAT has 10 sections. There are 9 scored sections — 3 Math, 3 Critical Reading and 3 Writing (1 Writing section is an essay) — and 1 "experimental" section. The experimental section will probably look just like one of the Math, Critical Reading or Writing sections, but it will not count toward your score in any way. Don't waste your time trying to figure out which one is experimental. Just take the whole test as if it counted. The sections break down like this:

Section	Time	Questions
Math		
Math 1	25 minutes	20 questions (All Multiple Choice)
Math 2	25 minutes	18 questions (8 Multiple Choice; 10 Fill-In)
Math 3	20 minutes	16 questions (All Multiple Choice)
Critical Reading		
Critical Reading 1	25 minutes	24 questions (8 Sentence Completions; 16 Reading Comprehension)
Critical Reading 2	25 minutes	24 questions (5 Sentence Completions; 19 Reading Comprehension)
Critical Reading 3	20 minutes	19 questions (6 Sentence Completions; 13 Reading Comprehension)
Writing		
Writing 1	25 minutes	Writing Sample (1 Essay question)
Writing 2	25 minutes	35 questions (11 Sentence Improvement; 18 Error Identification; 6 Paragraph Improvement)
Writing 3	14 minutes	14 questions (All Sentence Improvement)
Experimental		
Experimental Section	25 minutes	(Could look like any section)

The sections may not appear in this order.

Most question types on the SAT are presented in approximate order of difficulty. For example, the nine Sentence Completion questions at the beginning of one of the Critical Reading sections will start with three relatively easy questions, followed by three medium questions, and then three harder questions. The exceptions are the Reading Comprehension and Paragraph Improvement sections, which do not appear in order of difficulty. Knowing this can help you manage your test strategy, avoid simple mistakes, and get the right answer more often.

Always be aware of the level of difficulty of the problem you're working on. If you are working on a hard problem, be VERY wary of any answer choices that seem too easy. If any blockhead walking down the street would choose (A) on a hard question, it is highly unlikely (A) is the right answer.

Here's an example that might appear as question 17 out of 20... definitely a hard question:

17) If the population of bacteria in a Petri dish is reduced by 30 percent, and then reduced again by 50 percent, these two reductions would reflect a single reduction of what percent?

(A) 20
(B) 50
(C) 65
(D) 80
(E) 85

Answer choice D, 80 percent, is way too easy. Any bozo could add 30 and 50, so that CAN'T be the right answer. Not on a hard question.

In general:

- **Easy questions have easy answers**
- **Medium questions require more work**
- **Hard questions rarely have easy answers**

Keep in mind that level of difficulty is a relative thing. You might know some hard vocabulary that the average student doesn't, but you might not know a word the SAT folks think almost everyone should know.

Furthermore, we're going to learn some math techniques that make hard problems easy. Don't assume that since you know how to get the right answer quickly, the question isn't "hard." Just be aware of each section's increasing level of difficulty, and don't pick an answer that's too easy for a hard question.

YOUR BEST SAT FRIEND

So what is your best SAT friend? A #2 pencil? Your calculator? No!

Process of Elimination is your best SAT friend!

You should tackle most problems by eliminating wrong answer choices before trying to find the "correct" answer. It is interesting to note that the "correct" answer is the answer that earns you points. It is not always the "right" answer. Sometimes the correct answer is *the answer that stinks the least.* You might not even like the "correct" answer, but if it's the best of the choices, then it must be the "correct" answer according to the test writers.

Many questions on the SAT have two, three or even four answers that are obviously wrong, but they hang about mucking up the works, getting in the way. If you can quickly eliminate those wrong answers by crossing them off, you'll be able to focus on the one, two or three answers that might actually be right.

This is extremely helpful on more difficult problems. With practice, you'll find that you can get the right answer to a question you don't know how to solve simply by eliminating answers that cannot be correct.

PACE YOURSELF

The SAT is a long test. It is designed to make you rush through. The people who write this test are counting on you to make mistakes just because you are going too fast. Don't fall into their trap. *It is **essential** that you get all or most of the easy and medium questions correct in order to get a good score.* So slow down and be extra careful on the easy and medium questions.

If you spend too much time on the hard questions, you are probably wasting time you could have spent getting more of the easy and medium questions right.

Here's the real secret to pacing: **Slowing down can actually speed you up!** Crazy? Weird? Impossible? Not really. Most students rush through the problems so fast that they misread a significant number of questions or rush into an approach that will take too long. If you take your time, read carefully and check your work, you'll avoid lots of time-consuming errors.

So slow down and really focus on each question.

Here's another secret: You probably don't have to finish the test! You should only finish the sections if you think you can score above a 700 on the Critical Reading, above a 670 on the Math, and above 670 on the Writing. Otherwise, you should slow down, answer fewer questions and get more right.

How do you know whether to finish the test? When taking practice tests, make a realistic assessment of your likely score. If your score is below the 700 / 670 / 670 range, try slowing down and not finishing. As you improve, you may want to tackle a couple more questions. Eventually, you may or may not finish any of the sections, but you should find your own optimal pace that reduces or eliminates careless errors but doesn't waste too much time.

SHOULD YOU GUESS?

Correct answers on the SAT improve your score. Incorrect answers lower your score (except on the Student-Produced Response section, also called the Fill-In section).

Scoring on the SAT is done first by a "raw score." Each correct answer adds 1 "raw score" point, each incorrect answer subtracts $\frac{1}{4}$ "raw score" point. Raw scores are converted to the familiar 200 – 800 point scale for Math and Critical Reading sections. The Writing raw score is converted to a 20-80 point sub-score, and then combined with the Essay score to give a scaled score of 200 – 800.

If you guess randomly, odds are that you will not help or hurt your score. For example, if you guess on five questions, you are likely to get one out of five correct. So, you would add 1 point for the correct answer and subtract $\frac{1}{4}$ for each incorrect answer, for a total of 1 point subtracted. Therefore, your score doesn't increase or decrease. *We don't recommend that you randomly guess...* **however:**

If you can eliminate at least one incorrect answer choice, always guess between the remaining choices! Odds are that this will improve your overall score.

Also, you should always guess on the Student-Produced Response (Fill-In) questions. There is no penalty for guessing on these questions.

A computer scores the SAT answer sheets. You must carefully and completely fill in ovals on the answer sheet using a #2 lead pencil. If you fill in two answers for the same question, or if you do not completely fill in an oval, it will be counted as no answer at all.

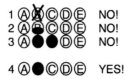

1 Ⓐ Ⓧ Ⓒ Ⓓ Ⓔ   NO!
2 Ⓐ ⬤ Ⓒ Ⓓ Ⓔ   NO!
3 Ⓐ ⬤⬤ Ⓓ Ⓔ   NO!

4 Ⓐ ⬤ Ⓒ Ⓓ Ⓔ   YES!

For the Student-Generated Response (Fill-In) questions, you need to fill in the corresponding ovals below your handwritten answers. Handwritten answers are NOT scored.

← You can write your answer here, but it won't be scored

← You must fill in your answer here to get credit

There is no partial credit! SO, if you worked out the problem correctly, got the correct answer, but then a) marked the wrong answer, b) circled or checked the right answer or c) wrote in the correct answer but didn't fill in properly, you're out of luck. You should be extremely careful filling in the correct ovals. If you choose not to answer a question, be sure to *leave that answer blank* on the answer sheet and move on to the next question on the answer sheet. DON'T fill in the right answer to the wrong question!

Some students prefer to fill in the answer to each question as soon as they finish the problem. Others prefer to finish an entire page of the test and then fill in answers to all of the questions on the page at the same time. (This technique might reduce the chance that you'll fill in bubbles for a question you actually skipped, *but during **the last five minutes** of the test switch to filling in after each question.*)

Choose whichever method you are most comfortable with. You may want to experiment during practice tests.

MATH

MATH INTRODUCTION

You may find this hard to believe, but most of the math on the SAT is not very difficult.

Let's say that again: **most of the math on the SAT is not very difficult**. The SAT tests very basic concepts that the Educational Testing Service thinks you should have learned sometime between 1st grade and 11th grade, with a couple of tougher concepts thrown in for fun.

So what makes it HARD to get a good score on the SAT math? It's the way the questions are asked. **The math is *NOT* difficult, but it can be *VERY TRICKY***. Once you learn *how* the cruel, heartless people who write this test make questions tricky, you will be able to get a lot more questions right.

The real key here is to always look for the **EASY WAY** to solve every problem. Sometimes the easy way is going to involve simply doing the math, but quite often a different approach will get the answer more quickly and more accurately.

So, you still need to know the basic math concepts that the SAT tests. This manual will both refresh your understanding of the basic material and teach you how to spot the traps that the SAT sets for you. We'll also focus on finding the easy way to approach math problems. Plus, you'll learn a few tricks of our own that the folks at the SAT don't want you to know.

MATH LESSON 1

CALCULATOR TIPS

You are allowed to use a standard calculator on the SAT math sections. A calculator is a great tool, but **beware**!

❶ A calculator is *never* necessary! It can be very helpful, but don't dive right for your calculator before you really understand what the problem is asking. This not only wastes precious time, but also can lead to wrong answers. So use your calculator, but make sure it's going to help you first!

❷ Be careful entering long calculations! It is very easy to leave out parentheses, misplace symbols or mistype numbers. Your calculator follows very strict rules for order of operations. For example, $-2^2 \neq (-2)^2$ and $12 \times 3 \div 5 \times 2 \neq 12 \times 3 \div (5 \times 2)$. It is always a good idea to take smaller steps with your calculator, and double check the results if they seem too big, too small, or too complex. Jot down the intermediate steps on the page so you can see the work.

❸ You should not need to use any formulas or programs on your calculator. The math on the SAT is not that complicated. If you are particularly well-versed in using the more complex capabilities of your calculator, by all means use them if it will help. **But don't waste any time trying to figure out some complex function during the test.** There will always be a simpler way to answer the question.

❹ Put fresh batteries into your calculator before you take the SAT. If your batteries die during the test, you need to finish without it. Note: It is possible that changing batteries will erase any formulas or programs you have entered or loaded into your calculator. Be sure to check your calculator instruction manual, which should explain how to avoid loss of data.

❺ Finally, **make sure your calculator model is allowed**. Most standard calculators are fine. However, you are **not** allowed to use: Palm Pilots; Pocket PCs; cell phones; handheld computers; or calculators with full alphabet keyboards, paper tape, or power cords; or those that make noise. You **are** allowed to use the ubiquitous* TI-83 graphing calculator.

---

* That's an SAT word! If you don't know it, look it up!

There are two basic math question types on the SAT: Multiple-Choice questions and Student-Produced Response questions, or what we like to call "Fill-In" questions. The math topics covered are the same in both sections; only the formats of the questions are different.

MULTIPLE-CHOICE SECTIONS

Most of the Math is in standard Multiple-Choice format. Each question is followed by five possible answer choices labeled (A) – (E). There are two special sub-types you need to know about.

INFORMATION FOR MORE THAN ONE QUESTION

Some questions start with information that pertains to two or three questions that follow. For instance, a question may start with a heading such as "**Questions 6-8 refer to the following information.**" It is easy to miss this heading, so keep an eye out for it. These questions typically have their own order of difficulty.

For example, if questions 6-8 refer to the same information, question 6 will probably be relatively easy, question 7 will be trickier, and question 8 will be the trickiest of the three.

I, II, III QUESTIONS

I, II, III questions give you some basic information followed by three mathematical statements. Your job is to figure out which of the three statements "must be true", "could be true", "must be false" or "could be false" (depending on the wording of the question). These are really three questions in one, but you'll see some great ways to solve them later in the manual.

STUDENT-PRODUCED RESPONSE (FILL-IN) SECTION

There are no answer choices to choose from on the Student-Produced Response questions. You have to come up with your own answers. You should fill them in by hand on the answer sheet, just to help you avoid mistakes. Then you **must** fill in the corresponding ovals below your handwritten answers. (Your handwritten answers don't actually count. You must fill in the correct ovals to get credit for a correct answer.)

Answer formats are fairly restricted, however. You can only fill in positive integers, improper fractions or decimals. You **cannot** fill in negatives, variables, exponents, square roots, etc. If you get a negative, variable, exponent or square root as an answer, you've made a mistake and need to go back to the problem!

Fractions must be bubbled in as improper fractions. $3\frac{1}{3}$ must be bubbled in as $\frac{10}{3}$ or 3.33. If you enter…

3	1	/	3

… and bubble in 3 1 / 3, it will be interpreted as $\frac{31}{3}$.

You must fill in as much of a decimal as you can. If you want to enter $\frac{1}{3}$ as a decimal, you must enter as many digits as possible. If you enter…

	.	3	3

…or…

		.	3

… you will not get credit. You need to enter

.	3	3	3

Always start your entries in the leftmost box. If you start in the leftmost box, you will be more likely to fill in all the digits you need.

If your answer doesn't fill in all four boxes, you can place it wherever it fits:

2			

	2		

		2	

			2

… are all acceptable… but *start with the leftmost box*, just to be consistent.

> **Don't forget!** Numbers you write in by hand don't count! You **MUST** fill in the corresponding ovals below or you won't get credit for the answer! The space provided for you to write the answer is only there for your convenience.

Yes, even the math section of the SAT is a vocabulary test. You have to know the following terms to answer some questions accurately:

INTEGER

Any positive or negative whole number or zero. Everything except decimals and fractions. Integers include 100, 34, 2, 1, 0, -1, -5, -35.

Try real examples ➔	PT3 S8 Q1

REAL NUMBER

Any positive or negative number or zero, *including* fractions and decimals.

IMAGINARY NUMBER (i)

Imaginary numbers appear when you violate one of the basic rules of math: *You can't take the even root of a negative number.* The letter i is used to represent the value of $\sqrt{-1}$. For more on imaginary numbers, see the Imaginary Numbers section in The Weird Stuff section.

DIGIT

Digits are single integers, 0 through 9. The number 124 is a 3-digit number. (See Digits under The Weird Stuff section for tips on tackling SAT digit problems.)

EVEN / ODD

Even numbers are evenly divisible by 2. Odd numbers are not. Zero is even. For example, even numbers include -6, -2, 0, 2, 4, 10, etc. Odd numbers include -9, -7, -1, 1, 3, 7, etc.

POSITIVE / NEGATIVE

Positive numbers are greater than zero. Negative numbers are less than zero. Positives and negatives include decimals and fractions. Zero is neither positive nor negative.

CONSECUTIVE

Consecutive means "in a row in ascending order." Consecutive integers might include -2, -1, 0, 1, 2. Some questions might ask about consecutive even integers (ex. 2, 4, 6, 8) or consecutive odd integers (ex. 5, 7, 9, 11).

SUM

The result of addition. No rocket science required.

DIFFERENCE

The result of subtraction... not to be confused with "What's the difference between dogs and cats?" (Dogs have owners. Cats have staff.)

PRODUCT

The result of multiplication.

QUOTIENT

The result of division.

REMAINDER

Remember third grade, before you knew about fractions and decimals? Then you may remember remainders. A remainder is the amount left over when a number cannot be evenly divided by another number. For example:

$$
\begin{array}{r}
1\ R\ 2 \\
7\overline{)9} \\
-7 \\
\hline
2
\end{array}
$$

The remainder is 2.

PRIME

This is an important one. Any number that is only evenly divisible by 1 and itself is prime. **2 is the lowest prime number and the only even prime number.** The first few primes (which you should memorize) are:
2, 3, 5, 7, 11, 13, 17, 19, 23, 29 and 31.

Beware! 0 and 1 are NOT prime!

FACTOR / DIVISOR

A number that divides evenly into another number is a factor or a divisor. For example, 1, 3, 7 and 21 are factors of 21. There are two ways you may have to deal with factors: prime factors or all factors.

PRIME FACTORS

To find *prime factors* use a Factor Tree Diagram. For example, to find the prime factors of 70:

Keep reducing until everything at the end of an arrow is prime. So, the prime factors of 70 are 2, 5 and 7.

ALL FACTORS

To find *all factors* of a number, use factor pairs. Start with 1 and the number, then work your way up the integers, pairing two factors together.

All factors of 75:

1	75	$(1 \cdot 75 = 75)$
3	25	$(3 \cdot 25 = 75)$
5	15	$(5 \cdot 15 = 75)$

You will note that as the first number in the pairs gets larger (1, 3, 5), the second gets smaller (75, 25, 15). When the first number gets close to the second number and you have checked all the numbers in between as possible factors, you should have all the factors.

Try real examples ➡ PT1 S3 Q8

DISTINCT

Distinct simply means "different" with no repeats. 2 and 3 are the only "distinct" prime factors of 12, though all the prime factors are 2, 2, and 3.

MULTIPLE

On the SAT, the term multiple refers to positive integer multiples, unless otherwise stated. Multiples are the original number multiplied by any positive integer (including 1). Multiples of 13 are 13, 26, 39, 130, 13,000,013…

ABSOLUTE VALUE ($|x|$)

By definition, the absolute value tells how far a number is from zero on the number line. For all practical purposes, it just means "get rid of any negative sign."

SETS { }

A set is a collection of numbers, terms or elements. Sets with finite or limited number of elements can be written as a list between brackets, for example {2, 4, 6, 8}. Sets are usually named using capital letters. For example, set B = {2, 3, 5}. **Sets contain NO repeats! For example, {2, 2, 4, 5, 6, 6} is written <u>incorrectly</u> and should be written as {2, 4, 5, 6}.** (Groups of numbers in between parentheses **CAN** have repeats: (2, 3, 3, 5, 7) but are not sets.

The order of the things in the set doesn't matter. For example,

{2, 9, 13, 14} = {13, 14, 2, 9}

You probably won't see this on the test, but sets can also be named using "Set Builder" notation that looks like this:
K = {y | y is an even integer}, which can be read as "K is the set of all y such that y is an even integer." Annoyingly wordy, but basically, all it means is that y can be any even integer. Just remember that the part on the right just defines the value(s) of the variable.

AN ELEMENT OR MEMBER OF A SET

… is simply one of the things in a set. The set {2, 3, 7, 9} has four elements or members.

You may not remember these symbols that deal with sets, but they occasionally appear on the SAT.

THE UNION (∪)

… is the smallest set that consists of all the elements of two or more given sets combined. Basically, you just join or merge two groups of numbers, but don't duplicate any number that overlaps.
{2, 3, 5, 6, 8} ∪ {2, 5, 7, 10, 15} = {2, 3, 5, 6, 7, 8, 10, 15}.

THE INTERSECTION (∩)

… is the set that consists of all of the elements common to two or more other sets. Basically, the intersection is the overlap of two sets of numbers.
{2, 3, 5, 6, 8} ∩ {2, 5, 7, 10, 15} = {2, 5}.

THE EMPTY SET ({} OR ∅)

If a set contains no members, it is called the "Empty Set" and uses one of two symbols: {} or ∅.

OTHER SET SYMBOLS ($\in$ AND $\notin$)

The symbol $\in$ indicates that a number IS a member of a particular set.
The symbol $\notin$ indicates that a number is NOT a member of a particular set.

For example, if K is the set of all odd integers, then:

$3 \in K$

$2 \notin K$

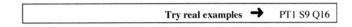

Try real examples ➔ PT1 S9 Q16

X AND Y VARIABLES

Most equations use the variables x and y. Variables are simply a way of representing possible values. In equations, a variable sometimes represents only one possible value (for example: $3y = 24$, so y can only equal 8). Other times, a variable can represent a whole wide array of values (for example: $2x + 7y = 37$, in which x and y could be any real number).

x and y values are often represented on the standard coordinate grid in which x is always the horizontal axis and y is always the vertical axis:

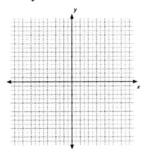

DOMAIN

The Domain of a function is the set of all possible x values of the function. Domains are typically restricted by two basic rules of math: *you can't divide by zero* and *you can't take the even powered root of a negative number.* For example, in the equation $y = \dfrac{3}{x}$, the value of x cannot be zero, so the domain of x would include all real numbers except zero.

RANGE

The range of a function is the set of all possible y values of the function.

Okay, here we go. The biggest, most useful technique for scoring well on the SAT is right here at the beginning.

MAXIMUM MATH TIP ①

MAKING UP NUMBERS

Which of the following problems is easier?

If you have 100 apples and you fill 3 boxes that can hold 2 dozen apples each, how many apples do you have left over?

A)   94
B)   72
C)   56
D)   28
E)   6

If you have x apples and you fill y boxes that can hold z dozen apples each, then in terms of x, y, and z, how many apples do you have left over?

A) $12x - yz$

B) $\dfrac{x}{12} - yz$

C) $x - yz$

D) $x - 12yz$

E) $x - \dfrac{yz}{12}$

Yup, the one on the left is definitely easier. That's because it deals with real numbers, not variables. Algebra problems like the one on the right can be pretty tricky… unless you know that you can just **make up your own numbers** to solve the problem, in which case the problems become much easier.

Here's the good news: *Making Up Numbers* is one of the most powerful tools you can learn for solving SAT math problems. And here's the better news: *Making Up Numbers* works best on hard math problems. That's right, the ones you were likely to miss are the ones that you'll be able to get just by *Making Up Numbers*. The only bad news: You have to practice the technique you're about to learn.

On some problems, you can use just about any number. On other problems you have to be more careful. Below we talk about how to make up your own numbers for different question types.

MAKING UP NUMBERS ON MULTIPLE-CHOICE: *IN TERMS OF*

If a math question on the SAT has variables in the answer choices, and especially if it has the phrase *in terms of* in the question, it's usually a great candidate for *Making Up Numbers*. Here's a simple example:

Ex) Jackie has *x* photo albums which contain photos of his iguana and his tapir. If each photo album contains *i* photos of his iguana and *t* photos of his tapir, then how many total photos, in terms of *x*, *i*, and *t* does he have?

(A) (i+x)t
(B) (t+x)i
(C) (i+t)x
(D) (ix)+t
(E) (tx)+I

Here's how to solve it:

❶ First *Make Up Numbers*, and write them down. Let's say that Jackie has 4 photo albums that each contains 3 photos of his iguana and 2 photos of his tapir. So:

$x = 4$

$i = 3$

$t = 2$

❷ Now just solve the problem. Each album contains 5 photos, and there are 4 albums, so 20 total photos. The answer we're looking for is 20:

Answer = 20

❸ Now we just have to stick the numbers we made up into the answer choices and see which one gives us 20:

(A)	(i+x)t	(3+4)2	= 14
(B)	(t+x)i	(2+4)3	= 18
(C)	(i+t)x	(3+2)4	= 20
(D)	(ix)+t	(3*4)+2	= 24
(E)	(tx)+I	(2*4)3	= 14

So, only answer choice (C) gives us the answer we're looking for.

Notice that even though we got the right answer after only trying answer choices (A), (B) and (C), we checked ALL the answers. Always check all the answers... or at least do enough math to make sure another answer won't work. If another answer does work, simply *Make Up Numbers* again and try the answers that worked the first time.

There is a fine art to choosing the right numbers. What numbers should you make up?

Try very *simple numbers*, like 2, 3, 4, 5, 10, 100, etc.

Sometimes the specifics of a question might mean a weird number like 39 is easy in the problem. Often it is useful to make up numbers that are simple multiples or factors of the numbers that appear in the problem.

There are some numbers you should almost always avoid for Multiple-Choice *Making Up Numbers*:

Avoid making up 0, 1 and any number you see in an answer choice or in the problem itself.

Why? It's quite possible that more than one answer choice will work if you don't choose numbers carefully. However, even if more than one answer choice works, you haven't wasted too much time. Here's what you do next:

First, cross off all the answer choices that didn't work with your first made-up number.

Second, simply make up a slightly different number and try the answer choices that you haven't crossed off.

You can't *Make Up Numbers* for all the variables in every problem. Sometimes *Making Up Numbers* for one variable fixes the value of one or more other variables. For example, if you have the equation $y = 4x + 2$, when you make up a value for x, the value for y is fixed by the equation. If you choose $x = 3$, then $y = 14$. You don't have a choice.

Let's take a look at another problem:

Ex) In a science class, Tammy is measuring the absorption capacity of two types of sponges that absorb different amounts of water. She has y ounces of water, and finds that it takes 22 sponges of one size to absorb all the water, but it only takes 11 sponges of another size to absorb all the water. In terms of y, how many ounces of water can one of the more absorbent sponges absorb?

(A) $11y$

(B) $\dfrac{y}{2}$

(C) $\dfrac{y}{11}$

(D) $\dfrac{y}{22}$

(E) $\dfrac{22y}{11}$

❶ In this case, we only have one variable, y. So let's make up a number that's easy to work with. The numbers in the problem make things a little more difficult. We need to find a number that works well with both 11 and 22. Why not make up 44, a simple multiple of both 11 and 22?

$$y = 44 \text{ ounces}$$

❷ Now we simply solve the problem with our made-up number. The first size of sponge took 22 sponges to absorb all 44 ounces. So each sponge absorbed $\dfrac{44 \text{ ounces}}{22 \text{ sponges}}$, or 2 ounces per sponge. The second size of sponge took 11 sponges to absorb all 44 ounces. So each sponge absorbed $\dfrac{44 \text{ ounces}}{11 \text{ sponges}}$, or 4 ounces per sponge. So the second was more absorbent, and the answer we're looking for is 4:

$$\text{Answer} = 4$$

❸ Now let's just pop our made-up number into the answer choices:

(A) 11×44 (which is way too big... don't even do the math)

(B) $\dfrac{44}{2} = 22$ Too big.

(C) $\dfrac{44}{11} = 4$ That's it!

(D) $\dfrac{44}{22} = 2$ Too small.

(E) $\dfrac{22 \times 44}{11} = 88$ Again, too big.

So the answer is (C)!

Try real examples ➜	PT1 S3 Q17; S6 Q7
	PT2 S3 Q18
	PT3 S2 Q8

MAKING UP NUMBERS FOR PERCENTS AND FRACTIONS

Quite often you can make up numbers for problems that don't even have a variable in the problem or the answer choice. Percent, fractional part and probability problems are the most common of these.

Percent problems that are good candidates for *Making Up Numbers* don't deal with actual values, only percents. For percent problems, try making up the number 100: $100 or 100 items or 100 choices, depending on the question. This may seem too obvious, but 100 will work well in almost all percent problems that use no real values.

> Ex) Starting in 1992, Reggie spent 10% of the money in his bank account each year for three years. If he never put more money in the account, what percent of his original amount does he have after three years?

Notice that there are no variables actually written in the problem, but there is an unknown quantity: the original amount of money in Reggie's account. Here's how to solve it:

Simply say Reggie has $100 in 1992.

He spends 10% of $100, or $10, so he has $90 left in 1993.
In 1993, he spends 10% of $90, or $9, so he has $81 left.
In 1994, he spends 10% of 81, or $8.10, so he has $72.90 left after 3 years.

$$\frac{72.90}{100} = 72.9\%.$$

(Not the number you expected? For more information on percents, see the Percent section of the Algebra and Arithmetic chapter.)

For **fractional part problems**, look for questions that don't deal with actual values, but only fractions. *Multiply the denominators of each of the fractions in the problem.* Use the product as your made-up number.

> Ex) Joan spends 1/3 of her salary on rent, 2/5 of her remaining salary on hair care products for her goldfish, and 1/4 of what's left on chocolate. If these are her only expenses, what fractional part of her salary does she have left over?

Here's how to solve it:

Multiply all of the denominators together, $3 \times 5 \times 4 = 60$. Assume her salary is $60. Make a tree showing how she spends her salary:

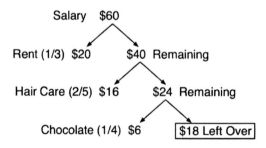

So she has $18 out of $60, which is $\dfrac{18}{60} = \dfrac{3}{10}$.

You can even use this method to solve difficult fractional part problems that have real numbers in them. Just ignore the numbers until the end and then set up a proportion using the answer you get. So, if the problem above had included a change in the final sentence:

> Ex) Joan spends 1/3 of her salary on rent, 2/5 of her remaining salary on hair care products for her goldfish, and 1/4 of what's left on chocolate. If these are her only expenses, and she has $54 left over, what is Joan's salary?

To solve the problem, ignore the $54 until the end. Complete the problem as above, getting the answer 3/10 of her salary is left over. Then set up a simple proportion:

$$\frac{3}{10} = \frac{54}{x}$$

Solve for x to get $180.

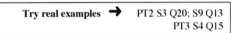

Try real examples ➜	PT2 S3 Q20; S9 Q13
	PT3 S4 Q15

MAKING UP NUMBERS FOR I, II, III; AND MUST BE TRUE / FALSE

I, II, III and *Must Be True / False* problems can be tougher than most Making Up Numbers questions for one very specific reason: *Making up one set of numbers won't always get you the right answer!* These questions are all about process of elimination. *You'll have to make up more than one set of numbers* and cross off the wrong answers.

• I, II, III Questions

These questions give you some mathematical statements or rules for the problem, and then ask you which of three following statements must be true or could be true. There could be one, two, three, or even no correct answers. Here's an example:

> Ex) If x is an even integer, which of the following must be an odd integer?
>
> I. $\dfrac{x+1}{2}$
> II. $3x + 7$
> III. $\dfrac{9-12x}{5}$
>
> (A) I only
> (B) II only
> (C) III only
> (D) II and III
> (E) I, II, and III

Here's how to solve it:

❶ Make up a relatively simple number that satisfies the requirements of the problem. In this case, x must be an even integer, so choose an easy number like 0, 2, or 4 and try it out. Let's use 2:

$$\text{I. } \frac{2+1}{2} = \frac{3}{2} = \cancel{1.5} \text{ (1.5 isn't an integer)}$$

$$\text{II. } 3(2) + 7 = 6 + 7 = 13 \text{ (Works!)}$$

$$\text{III. } \frac{9 - 12(2)}{5} = \frac{9 - 24}{5} = \frac{-15}{5} = -3 \text{ (Works!)}$$

❷ Eliminate any answer choices that include the statements I, II, or III that don't work:

(A) ~~I only~~
(B) II only
(C) III only
(D) II and III
(E) ~~I, II, and III~~

❸ Make up other numbers and try them. Try some weird numbers, like 0 or negatives.

> Note: Problems come in many different varieties. The problem type itself can help determine which weird numbers to use. When dealing with exponents, for example, it's often helpful to try fractions, because fractions between 0 and 1 get smaller when they are raised to powers.

Let's try 0 in the remaining statements:

$$\text{II. } 3(0) + 7 = 0 + 7 = 7 \text{ (Works!)}$$

$$\cancel{\text{III. } \frac{9 - 12(0)}{5} = \frac{9 - 0}{5} = \frac{9}{5}} \quad (\frac{9}{5} \text{ isn't an integer.})$$

❹ Eliminate more of the remaining answer choices:

(A) ~~Already eliminated~~
(B) II only
(C) ~~III only~~
(D) ~~II and III~~
(E) ~~Already eliminated~~

In this example, we're only left with answer choice (B).

You may have to repeat steps **❸** and **❹** more than once.

Note: Often, using your *Made-up Numbers* will help you to figure out what math rule or concept the question is testing. So, if you can figure out the theory behind the question, you can frequently eliminate wrong answers and get the right answer fairly quickly.

- **Must Be True / False**

  These questions are similar to I, II, III questions, except they have only one correct answer among the 5 answer choices. For a Must Be True, four of the answers may work some of the time, but only one will work **all of the time**. Here's an example:

  If $b \geq -1$ and $a < 2$ which of the following must be true:

  (A) $ab > 0$
  (B) $a - b > 0$
  (C) $a - b < 0$
  (D) $(b+1) \times |a| \geq 0$
  (E) $-b \times |a - 2| \leq 0$

  ❶ Make up a relatively simple number that satisfies the equation:

  Let's try $b = 1$ and $a = 0$:
  (A) $(1)(0) > 0$ (False!)
  (B) $1 - 0 > 0$ (True!)
  (C) $0 - 1 < 0$ (True!)
  (D) $((1+1) \times |0| \geq 0) \Rightarrow ((1)(0) \geq 0)$ (True!)
  (E) $(-1 \times |0 - 2| \leq 0) \Rightarrow ((-1)(-2) \leq 0) \Rightarrow (2 \leq 0)$ (False!)

  ❷ Eliminate answer choices that didn't work:

  (A) ~~$ab > 0$~~
  (B) $a - b > 0$
  (C) $a - b < 0$
  (D) $(b+1) \times |a| \geq 0$
  (E) ~~$-b \times |a - 2| \leq 0$~~

  ❸ Make up some weird numbers (like 0, 1, fractions, negatives, very large numbers, very small numbers) and try to eliminate more wrong answers:

  Let's try $b = 0$ and $a = -1$ in the remaining answer choices:
  (A) Already eliminated
  (B) $(-1 - 0 > 0) \Rightarrow (-1 > 0)$? False!
  (C) $(-1 - 0 < 0) \Rightarrow (-1 < 0)$? True!
  (D) $((0+1) \times |-1| \geq 0) \Rightarrow (1 \times 1 \geq 0) \Rightarrow (1 > 0)$? True!
  (E) Already eliminated

❹ Eliminate answer choices that didn't work:

(A) ~~Already eliminated~~
(B) ~~$a = b > 0$~~
(C) $a - b < 0$
(D) $(b+1) \times |a| \geq 0$
(E) ~~Already eliminated~~

Well, looks like we got a little unlucky, and we have to try steps **❸** and **❹** again. How about $a = 0$ and $b = 0$? (There's no reason they can't be the same number unless the problem specifies they are different or distinct!)

(A) ~~Already eliminated~~
(B) ~~Already eliminated~~
(C) $0 - 0 < 0$? False!
(D) $\left((0+1) \times |0| \geq 0\right) \Rightarrow (1 \times 0 \geq 0) \Rightarrow (0 \geq 0)$? True!
(E) ~~Already eliminated~~

Great! We're down to just one answer choice: (D)

After making up a number or two, you may have noticed that $b + 1$ in answer choice (D) was always going to be greater than or equal to 0, and $|a|$ was always going to be greater than or equal to 0. That always makes (D) true. If you do notice the math concept the question is testing, it might save you some time, but if not, you can still get the right answer!

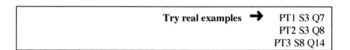

Try real examples ➡ PT1 S3 Q7
PT2 S3 Q8
PT3 S8 Q14

POWERING THROUGH: TRYING SIMPLE NUMBERS

Some problems require you to find specific, fairly simple numbers, but the math is fairly involved. For example, a question might involve two non-linear equations with two variables, and solving for one variable would be difficult. Usually, the answers to these questions are simple integers, so why not just try a few easy integers?

Often, powering through a problem is the fastest, most accurate way to solve it. Let's look at an example:

Ex) If x and y are positive integers, how many (x, y) ordered pairs satisfy the equation $4x + 3y \leq 15$?

The best way to attack this problem is to simply power through. Let's just try some numbers:

If $x = 1$, y could equal 1 or 2 or 3, but not 4 or more.
So $(1, 1)$, $(1, 2)$ and $(1, 3)$ are possible.

If $x = 2$, y could equal 1 or 2, but not 3 or more.
So now $(1, 1)$, $(1, 2)$, $(1, 3)$, $(2, 1)$ and $(2, 2)$ are possible.

If $x = 3$, y could equal 1, but not 3 or more.
So now $(1, 1)$, $(1, 2)$, $(1, 3)$, $(2, 1)$, $(2, 2)$, and $(3, 1)$ are possible.

That gives us 6 possible ordered pairs!

Try real examples ➡	PT3 S2 Q14; S8 Q7

Review the chapter and focus on *Making Up Numbers* before trying these Math problems.

Remember to look for the **EASY WAY** to solve these problems.

Practice with these problems from *The Official SAT Study Guide:*

Practice Test	Section	Questions
1	3	5, 7, 8, 12, 17, 19
	6	7, 8
	9	3, 8, 10, 11, 12, 13, 16
2	3	8, 15, 18, 20
	9	13, 16
3	2	7, 8, 16, 18
	4	1, 6, 15
	8	1, 14

All test, section, question and page numbers refer to *The Official SAT Study Guide* (2004)

Be sure to carefully score the sections from *The Official SAT Study Guide* and review the questions you miss. Figure out why you missed each question and how you can get it right the next time!

Additional Practice:

Math Homework Drill 1

Note: Each question is numbered to indicate where the question would most likely appear in a math section, and therefore shows relative level of difficulty. Questions with no answer choices are Fill-Ins.

Solve each of the following problems and choose the best of the choices given. Use any available space for scratch work, if necessary.

7. If $ab = -4$ and $ac = 7$, which of the following must be a negative number?

(A) ac
(B) bc
(C) abc
(D) $c - ab$
(E) $c + ab$

7.1. A factory produces b TVs per hour. Of this number produced each hour, c have 20-inch screens and the rest have 24-inch screens. In terms of b and c, how many hours does it take the factory to make 200 24-inch screen TVs?

(A) $\dfrac{200}{b - c}$

(B) $\dfrac{100}{c}$

(C) $\dfrac{200}{bc}$

(D) $\dfrac{b + c}{200}$

(E) $200bc$

8. If x is a negative number with an absolute value between 0 and 1 and y is a negative integer, which of the following could be the product of x and y?

(A) -5

(B) $-\dfrac{5}{3}$

(C) $-\dfrac{1}{2}$

(D) 0

(E) 1

12. If w, x, y, and z are four consecutive negative integers, which of the following statements must be true?

(A) $y - x > z$

(B) $x + y > w$

(C) $-w < -z$

(D) $w + z < x + y$

(E) $x - y = w - z$

13. A soccer team scored a total of x points during its first three games of a season. If $\dfrac{1}{3}$ of the points were scored in the first game and the team scored half as many points in the second game as it had in the first, how many points did the team score in the third game, in terms of x?

(A) $\dfrac{x}{2}$

(B) $x - 3$

(C) $\dfrac{2x}{9}$

(D) $2x - \dfrac{x}{6}$

(E) $\dfrac{x}{6}$

16. A large basket of apples contains l apples. A small basket contains s apples. Ms. Kumar purchased one small basket and one large basket and then found that each basket contained exactly r rotten apples. In terms of r, l, and s, how many non-rotten apples did Ms. Kumar purchase?

(A) $(l + s) + r$

(B) $(l + s) + 2r$

(C) $l + (s - 2r)$

(D) $l + (s - r)$

(E) $2(l + s + r)$

Answers:

MATH LESSON 2

MAXIMUM MATH TIP ②

USING THE ANSWERS

Using the Answers is a lot like *Making Up Numbers*, except the answers give you a choice of only five numbers to try. It is often easy to simply pop the answer choices back into the problem to see which one works out.

The best questions for *Using the Answers* are Multiple-Choice questions that have real numbers in the answer choices and wordy, confusing questions. Here's an example:

> Ex) Bob and his father have a combined weight of 280 pounds. If Bob weighs 3/4 of his father's weight, how much, in pounds, does his father weigh?
>
> (A) 90
> (B) 120
> (C) 150
> (D) 160
> (E) 200

Real number answer choices are usually in order from largest to smallest or smallest to largest. This is a great help! It gives you a starting point that can limit the amount of work you do.

Note: *Using the Answers* questions usually have two parts. We're going to use one part to find the answer and one part to check if the answer is right. In algebra terms, these questions really set up simultaneous equations, but we're not going to worry about that for the moment.

Here's how to solve them:

❶ ORGANIZE AS A CHART

Keeping organized is a key to solving questions by *Using the Answers*. The answer choices represent something in the problem, so write a heading that indicates what they represent above the answer choices. To the right, mark down headings for the other unknowns in the problem.

❷ **ELIMINATE OBVIOUSLY WRONG ANSWERS**

Try to eliminate any answer choices that are obviously wrong. Sometimes these answers will be too big or too small, or multiples of the wrong number. Cross them off!

❸ **TRY THE MIDDLE ANSWER CHOICE**

Try the *middle value* of the answer choices that are left. Pop it back into the problem, and write down the other values that you can figure out in beneath the headings you wrote. Check to see if it works. If you're lucky, you will have the correct answer and you'll be done. If not...

❹ **CROSS OFF MORE WRONG ANSWERS**

Cross off the answer that didn't work. If it's easy to see, determine if the number you tried is too big or too small. If you're sure it's too big, cross off anything larger and try a smaller number. If you're sure it's too small, cross off anything smaller and try a bigger number.

❺ **TRY WHAT'S LEFT**

Try the middle value of the remaining answer choices. Repeat steps ❹ and ❺ if necessary.

On most problems, you'll have to do this two or three times to get the answer.

Let's see how to do it in this example:

Ex) Bob and his father have a combined weight of 280 pounds. If Bob weighs 3/4 of his father's weight, how much, in pounds, does his father weigh?

(A) 90
(B) 120
(C) 150
(D) 160
(E) 200

Here's how to solve it:

❶ Set up a chart using the answer choices. The answers represent the father's weight. Bob's weight is also unknown:

```
Father          Bob        Total weight
(A) 90
(B) 120
(C) 160
(D) 180
(E) 200
```

❷ Eliminate obviously wrong answers if you can.

Bob weighs less than his father, so his father must weigh more than half of the total weight. That means that answer choices (A) and (B) are too small.

❸ Start with the middle of what's left, answer choice (D).

```
Father          Bob        Total weight
(A) 90
(B) 120
(C) 160
Start here →    (D) 180     135        315
(E) 200
```

If Bob's father weighs 180 pounds, Bob must weigh 3/4 of 180, so $\frac{3}{4} \cdot 180 = 135$ pounds. Their combined weight, therefore, would be $180 + 135 = 315$ pounds, which is too high. So the father's weight must be lower.

❹ & ❺ Cross off answer choices (D) and (E) (since they are too large). The only choice we have left is (C) 160. A quick check shows us it is the correct answer.

```
Set up a chart using the answer choices:
Father          Bob        Total weight
(A) 90
(B) 120
(C) 160         120        280
(D) 180         135        315
(E) 200
```

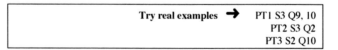

Try real examples ➡ PT1 S3 Q9, 10
PT2 S3 Q2
PT3 S2 Q10

MAXIMUM MATH TIP ③

ESTIMATING

Don't underestimate the values of estimating on the SAT. A quick and dirty estimation can often eliminate most of the answers or even eliminate all but the right answer. Some problems even require you to estimate.

When estimating, look at the answer choices first:

> If the answers are spread out and quite far from one another, it's probably a good question on which to estimate.

> If the answers are close together, it's probably a bad choice for estimating. Here are examples of good and bad choices:

Good question for estimating:	Bad question for estimating:
(A) 12	(A) 1.2
(B) 24	(B) 1.35
(C) 30	(C) 1.5
(D) 55	(D) 1.55
(E) 75	(E) 1.6

The most useful way to estimate on the SAT is to round hard-to-work-with numbers to easily manageable numbers close to the value in the problem. The closer the better, but you don't have to be *that* close if the answers are far apart. For example:

> Ex) What is the product of 1.95 and 6.14?
>
> (A) 8.43
> (B) 9.973
> (C) 10.037
> (D) 11.973
> (E) 13.214

> If you simply round 1.95 to 2 and 6.14 to 6, you can see that the product must be pretty close to 12. Answer choice (D) is the only one that's really close.

You can also estimate on geometry problems, but be *very careful*, especially when the figure is not drawn to scale. If the figure is not to scale, try to redraw it so that it is to scale. If there are several ways you could redraw the figure based on the given information, then redraw it several ways.

Try real examples ➜ PT2 S9 Q3

PEMDAS: THE ORDER OF OPERATIONS

Know how to use PEMDAS because you'll need it! PEMDAS is an acronym for the proper order in which to solve algebraic and mathematic expressions.

Parentheses	Deal with things inside parentheses first.
Exponents	Resolve exponents next.
Multiplication **D**ivision	The only tricky thing here is that you have to do multiplication and division LEFT to RIGHT. If division comes first, do the division first.
Addition **S**ubtraction	Do these last in any order.

DIVISIBILITY RULES

There are some nice little tricks to check whether a large integer is divisible by some common smaller integers. This is extremely helpful, for instance, when trying to reduce large fractions. Here are some divisibility rules:

A number is divisible by:	If:
2	If the number is even, it's divisible by 2
3	*This is the most useful rule:* First add the <u>individual</u> <u>digits</u> of the number. If the resulting sum is divisible by 3, then the number is divisible by 3. For example, the sum of the digits of 5283 is 5 + 2 + 8 + 3 = 18, which is divisible by 3, therefore 5283 is divisible by 3.
4	Look at the last two digits of the number as a 2-digit number. If this 2-digit number is divisible by 4, then the whole number is. For example, 6788 is divisible by 4 because 88 is divisible by 4.
5	If a number ends in 5 or 0, it is divisible by 5.
6	Combine the rules for 2 and 3. If the number is even *and* divisible by 3, then it is divisible by 6.

A number is divisible by:	If:
7	*You won't really EVER need this, but hey, it's fun in a sick sort of way:* To determine if a number is divisible by 7, take away the last digit of the number, double the digit and subtract the doubled number from the remaining number. If the result is evenly divisible by 7 (e.g. 14, 7, 0, -7, etc.), then the number is divisible by seven. This may need to be repeated several times. Told you it was sick.
9	Same as the rule for divisibility by 3. First add the digits of the number. If the resulting sum is divisible by 9, then the number is also. For example, the sum of the digits of 6219 is 18, which is divisible by 9, therefore 6219 is divisible by 9.
10	If a number ends in 0, it is divisible by 10.

CONVERTING UNITS

Converting units (for example converting *miles per hour* to *feet per second*) is all about canceling units. The first thing to think about is what kind of unit(s) the answer is looking for. Is it distance over time (like mph) or volume (like quarts or liters). Let's assume you're looking for feet per second. Distance over time. On the left, write down the number that is given in the problem in the format of distance over time. Write down the units you're looking for on the right. Your diagram should look something like this:

Ex) How many feet per second are in 36 miles per hour?

36 Miles		Feet
1 Hour		Second

Now it's just a matter of canceling units using basic 1 to 1 conversions. Let's start with miles to feet. Miles are on the top, so we need to cancel miles by placing miles on the bottom. We know there are 5280 feet in a mile (on the SAT, they'll tell you) so put 5280 feet over 1 mile. The mile units cancel:

36 ~~Miles~~	5280 Feet		Feet
1 Hour	1 ~~Mile~~		Second

Now let's convert hours to seconds. It's easier to go from hours to minutes, then minutes to seconds. Hours is on the bottom, so we want to cancel with hours on the top: place 1 hour over 60 minutes. Hours cancel.

36 ~~Miles~~	5280 Feet	1 ~~Hour~~		Feet
1 ~~Hour~~	1 ~~Mile~~	60 Minutes		Second

Then to cancel minutes, place 1 minute over 60 seconds. Minutes cancel.

36 ~~Miles~~	5280 Feet	1 ~~Hour~~	1 ~~Minute~~	Feet
1 ~~Hour~~	1 ~~Mile~~	60 ~~Minutes~~	60 Seconds	Second

So we're left with exactly the units we're looking for, feet per second, and a fairly simple math problem:

$$\frac{(36)(5280)}{(60)(60)} = 52.8$$

So:

36 ~~Miles~~	5280 Feet	1 ~~Hour~~	1 ~~Minute~~	52.8 Feet
1 ~~Hour~~	1 ~~Mile~~	60 ~~Minutes~~	60 Seconds	Second

THE NUMBER LINE

The Number Line is a simple concept, but actually drawing it out is extremely useful on the SAT, even on very difficult problems. The tricky issues tend to be dealing with negative numbers and fractions, and often deciding which number or fraction is bigger than which. Just remember, anything to the right on the number line is bigger, anything to the left is smaller.

<table>
<tr><td>Try real examples ➡ PT2 S3 Q3
PT3 S4 Q17</td></tr>
</table>

FRACTIONS

MIXED AND IMPROPER FRACTIONS

Mixed fractions are non-integer fractions greater than 1 or less than −1 that show a value using a whole number and an additional fractional part. For example, $1\frac{1}{2}$ is a mixed fraction.

Improper fractions have only a numerator and a denominator with no leading integer. For example, $\dfrac{24}{5}$.

Remember, Fill-In questions don't allow mixed fractions! If you need to refresh your skills converting mixed fractions to improper fractions, or visa versa, please ask your tutor or teacher at school.

FRACTION IN THE DENOMINATOR

If there is a fraction in the denominator of another fraction, simply remove the fraction from the denominator, flip it over and multiply it by the numerator:

$$\dfrac{\dfrac{2}{5}}{\dfrac{4}{7}} = \dfrac{2}{5} \times \dfrac{7}{4} = \dfrac{7}{10}$$

Note that fractions in the numerator are **not** flipped.

FRACTION X: ADDING, SUBTRACTING, AND COMPARING

The Fraction X is an excellent method for adding, subtracting and comparing fractions without converting fractions to common denominators first. You actually get a common denominator just by following a simple process. But note: You must start with improper fractions.

To use the Fraction X:

❶ Set up the addition or subtraction problem.

$$\dfrac{2}{5} + \dfrac{1}{7} = \dfrac{?}{?}$$

❷ Multiply **up and across**, the denominator of the left with the numerator of the right.

$$\dfrac{2}{5} \nearrow \overset{5}{\underset{7}{\dfrac{1}{}}} = \dfrac{?}{?}$$

❸ Multiply **up and across**, the denominator of the right with the numerator of the left. Bring the + or − sign up.

$$\overset{14 \quad + \quad 5 = 19}{\dfrac{2}{5} \searrow \dfrac{1}{7}} = \dfrac{?}{?}$$

❹ Add or subtract the numbers at the top and then multiply across the bottom.

$$\frac{2}{5} \overset{+}{\rightarrow} \frac{1}{7} = \frac{19}{?}$$

And you get:

$$\frac{2}{5} + \frac{1}{7} = \frac{19}{35}$$

Occasionally you will have to reduce the fraction to put it in its simplest terms.

To figure out which fraction is larger, do steps ❷ and ❸ above… simply multiply up and across. The larger product will appear over the bigger fraction.

Ex)   Which is bigger, $\frac{9}{10}$ or $\frac{100}{111}$?

$$\overset{1000}{\underset{❷}{\frac{9}{10} \nearrow \frac{100}{111}}}$$

$$\overset{999 \quad 1000}{\underset{❸}{\frac{9}{10} \nwarrow \frac{100}{111}}}$$

So, $\frac{100}{111}$ is larger, since 1000 is larger than 999.

If you're comparing negative fractions, move the negative sign up to the numerator in both fractions to avoid confusion.

REDUCING / SIMPLIFYING / COMMON DENOMINATORS

Reducing fractions wisely can save a lot of time and effort. Most intricate fractions or products of fractions on the SAT can be simplified shrewdly by following some basic guidelines:

To reduce a fraction, divide the numerator and denominator by the same number:

• Cancel zeros on the top and bottom first.

• Reduce by small numbers: divide the top and bottom by values such as 2, 3 and 5 first.

- If you have 10, 100, 1000, etc. in the denominator and no zeros in the numerator, DON'T break up the 10, 100, 1000, etc. You can just move the decimal point of the numerator when all the other reducing is done.

- When multiplying (and only multiplying) fractions, ANY numerator can cancel with ANY denominator.

- NEVER reduce fractions across a + (plus), - (minus), or = (equal) sign. Use the Fraction X or cross multiply first.

For example, in this incorrect problem, someone tried to cancel the 4 in the denominator with 8 in the numerator, but you **can't** cancel across a + sign:

$$\text{Wrong: } \frac{5}{4} + \frac{8}{7} = \frac{5}{1} + \frac{2}{7}$$

Use the Fraction X to see that:

$$\text{Correct: } \frac{5}{4} + \frac{8}{7} = \frac{67}{28}$$

DECIMALS

You may choose to use your calculator for most decimal problems. Just be sure to enter carefully! If you want to manipulate decimals by hand, follow these tips:

ADDING / SUBTRACTING DECIMALS

The rule here is pretty simple. Line up the decimal points. Add and subtract as normal, carrying the decimal point directly down. If decimals have a different number of digits to the right of the decimal point, add zeroes to the end of the decimals that are shorter, so that they all have the same number of digits to the right of the decimal point.

MULTIPLYING DECIMALS

To multiply decimals by hand, set up and complete a multiplication problem ignoring the decimals. Then count the **total** number of digits to the right of the decimal points of the numbers you are multiplying and move the decimal point in the answer the same number of spaces to the left:

$$
\begin{array}{r}
2.25 \\
\times \quad 0.04 \\
\hline
0.0900
\end{array}
$$

DIVIDING DECIMALS

To divide decimals by hand, set up a long division problem with the decimals in place. Move the decimal in the divisor to the right until there are no more digits to the right of the decimal point. Move the decimal in the number being divided the same number of spaces to the right. Add zeros if necessary. Carry the decimal point straight up, then do the division problem as normal.

$$.02\overline{)12.4} = 2\overline{)1240}$$

PERCENTS

Percents are simply another way of writing a value that could be expressed as a fraction or a decimal. In fact, they are just like fractions, but with 100 always used as the denominator. For example, 23% just means $\frac{23}{100}$.

100% $\left(\frac{100}{100}\right)$ basically means "the whole thing."

COMPLEMENTARY PERCENTS

Sometimes it is easier to use "complementary percents" when trying to solve a problem. For example, if an item is discounted by 30%, you could take 30% of the price of the item, and then subtract that 30% from the original price. However, it is often easier to just take 70% of the original price. A 30% discount leaves 70%.

In general, if you are taking a discount, subtract the percent from 100%. If you are increasing by a percent, add the percent to 100%.

20% more = 120%

So take 120% of the original number.

23% less = 77%

So take 77% of the original number.

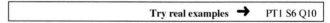

Try real examples ➡ PT1 S6 Q10

DECIMAL, FRACTION, PERCENT CONVERSION

Try filling in all the missing values in the following table. For some, you may need to do some basic division. Feel free to use your calculator.

Calculator tip: Many calculators, including the TI-83, have a function that can display rational answers as reduced fractions instead of decimals. On the TI-83, enter a decimal or a math expression and then press the MATH button and select choice "1: ▶Frac" to display as a fraction. Check your calculator manual to see if it will return answers as fractions instead of decimals.

Decimal, Fraction, Percent Conversion Table

Fraction	Decimal	Percent
$\dfrac{1}{2}$		
	$.3\bar{3}$	
		25%
	.2	
$\dfrac{1}{6}$		
		$12\dfrac{1}{2}\%$ or 12.5%
$\dfrac{2}{3}$		
		10%
		35%
$\dfrac{1}{100}$		
	.6	
		37.5%

PERCENT PROBLEM TRANSLATION

Lots of percent problems on the SAT are word problems, and it is sometimes difficult to convert the words into the proper math formula. The chart below gives some basic English to Math translations that you can use to simplify a percent problem.

English	Math
"Percent" or "%"	$\dfrac{}{100}$ (divide by 100)
"What" or "what number"	x, y, z (any variable)
"of"	$\times$ or $\cdot$ (multiply)
"is, are, were, equals"	$=$

Ex) 42 percent of what is 60 percent of 80 percent of 70 percent of 600?

Here's how you translate it:

$$\frac{42}{100} \times x = \frac{60}{100} \times \frac{80}{100} \times \frac{70}{100} \times \frac{600}{1}$$

Try real examples ➡ PT1 S9 Q10
PT3 S8 Q12

PERCENT INCREASE OR DECREASE

Percent Increase or Decrease problems (percent change problems) often add a layer of difficulty to percent problems. Try the example below:

Ex) If a equals the percent increase from 12 to 15, b equals the percent decrease from 15 to 12 and c equals the percent decrease from 5 to 4, then which of the following must be true?

(A) $a > b > c$
(B) $a < b < c$
(C) $a = b = c$
(D) $a = b > c$
(E) $a > b = c$

Many people look at the problem above and choose answer choice (D). They think that the percent decrease from 15 to 12 is the same as the percent increase from 12 to 15. They are wrong, of course.

The formula for percent increase / decrease (percent change) is:

$$\text{Percent Change} = \frac{\text{The Difference Between Two Numbers}}{\text{The Starting Number}} \times 100$$

When there is a **Percent Increase** or **Percent Greater**, the Starting Number is the LOWER of the two numbers.

When there is a **Percent Decrease** or **Percent Less**, the Starting Number is the HIGHER of the two numbers.

Let's look again at our example from above:

Ex) If *a* equals the percent increase from 12 to 15, *b* equals the percent decrease from 15 to 12 and *c* equals the percent decrease from 5 to 4, then which of the following must be true?

(A) $a > b > c$
(B) $a < b < c$
(C) $a = b = c$
(D) $a = b > c$
(E) $a > b = c$

Here's how to solve it: For the value of *a*, 12 is the starting number and 3 is the difference, therefore:

$$a = \frac{3}{12} \times 100 = \frac{1}{4} \times 100 = 25\%$$

For the value of *b*, 15 is the starting number and 3 is the difference, therefore:

$$b = \frac{3}{15} \times 100 = \frac{1}{5} \times 100 = 20\%$$

For the value of *c*, 5 is the starting number and 1 is the difference, therefore:

$$c = \frac{1}{5} \times 100 = 20\%$$

So, answer choice (E) $a > b = c$ is the correct answer.

Note! The "Starting Number" is not necessarily the number that started off the whole problem. It is the Starting Number for that particular section of the problem. Here's a particularly difficult example that combines elements of normal percents with percent increase / decrease:

Ex) If the price of an item is decreased by 20%, and then the discounted price is reduced by 25%, by what percent would this new price have to be increased to return the item to its original price?

Are you temped to say 45%? That's way too easy! Can't be true! Not on a hard problem like this. Here's how to solve it:

First, you don't know what the price of the item actually is, so why not *Make Up Numbers*? It's a percent problem, so use $100.

The easiest way to do this is by using complimentary percents. A decrease of 20% means the result will equal 80%. Translate: 80% of $100 is:

$$\frac{80}{100} \times \$100 = \$80$$

$80 decreased by 25% (using the same method):

$$\frac{75}{100} \times \$80 = \$60$$

Now the tricky part. The problem asks what percent would the new price have to be increased to return the item to its original price, which was $100. Well, the starting number here is actually the $60! The difference is $40, so:

$$\frac{\$40}{\$60} \times 100 = 66.\overline{6}\%$$

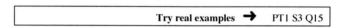

| **Try real examples** ➡ | PT1 S3 Q15 |

WORD PROBLEM TRANSLATION

One of the hardest things on the SAT is reading word problems correctly. They can be long and convoluted with lots of potential pitfalls. We've already seen how some simple translations can help with percent problems. Here's a more complete chart of words and their math translation:

English	**Math**
"Percent" or "%"	$\frac{\overline{}}{100}$
"Per" or "for"	÷ (divide by or ratio)
"What" or "what number"	x, y, z (variable)
"of"	× or · (multiply)
"is, are, were, equals"	=
x is y more than z	$x = z + y$
x is y less than z	$x = z - y$ (Note the order!)
the sum of x and z	$x + z$

The best way to handle complicated word problems is to take small steps. Read one sentence, or half a sentence, and pause. Get comfortable with that section of the question before you move on. Proceed through the whole question this way, and then put all those small, manageable pieces together at the end.

| **Try real examples** ➡ | PT1 S3 Q10 |
| | PT2 S9 Q14 |

Review the chapter and focus on *Using the Answers* and percent problems before trying these Math questions.

Remember to look for the **EASY WAY** to solve these problems.

Practice with these problems from *The Official SAT Study Guide:*

Practice Test	Section	Questions
1	3	9, 10, 15
	6	3, 10
	9	5, 6, 7, 10
2	3	1, 2, 3
	6	1, 10
	9	1, 3, 14
3	2	6, 10
	4	4, 9, 16, 17
	8	2, 3, 12

All test, section, question and page numbers refer to *The Official SAT Study Guide* (2004)

Be sure to carefully score the sections from *The Official SAT Study Guide* and review the questions you miss. Figure out why you missed each question and how you can get it right the next time!

Additional Practice:

Math Homework Drill 2

Note: Each question is numbered to indicate where the question would most likely appear in a math section, and therefore shows relative level of difficulty. Questions with no answer choices are Fill-Ins.

> Solve each of the following problems and choose the best of the choices given. Use any available space for scratch work, if necessary.

8.   Mr. Kwan spent $48 on groceries. If 10 percent of the bill was for produce, one half of the bill was for canned goods, 25 percent was for meat, and the remainder was for dairy products, how much did Mr. Kwan spend on dairy products?

(A) $1.92
(B) $4.80
(C) $7.20
(D) $12.00
(E) $16.40

15.   At a track meet in March, Michael ran the 400m race in 72 seconds. In June, he ran the 400m race in exactly one minute. By what percent did Michael reduce his time for the 400m race from March to June?

(A) 12%
(B) 15%
(C) $16\frac{2}{3}\%$
(D) 20%
(E) $22\frac{1}{3}\%$

1. If the expression $y\dfrac{y}{5}$ is equivalent to $\dfrac{18}{5}$, what is the value of y?

    (A) $\dfrac{3}{5}$

    (B) $\dfrac{5}{3}$

    (C) 3

    (D) 15

    (E) 18

10. In a school charity drive, the 7th grade class raised $850. If the 6th grade class raised 20 percent less than the 7th grade class, how much, in dollars, did the 6th grade class raise? (Ignore the dollar sign when filling in your answer.)

10.1 If $\dfrac{1}{3}$ of $\dfrac{1}{6}$ of a certain number is one half of $\dfrac{1}{4}$ times x times that same number, what is the value of x?

    (A) $\dfrac{1}{18}$

    (B) $\dfrac{1}{6}$

    (C) $\dfrac{2}{9}$

    (D) $\dfrac{1}{3}$

    (E) $\dfrac{4}{9}$

Answers:

MATH LESSON 3

ALGEBRA AND ARITHMETIC PART III

MANIPULATING AN EQUATION

A mathematical equation is like an old balance scale. In order to properly manipulate an equation, you must keep the two sides of an equation equal, or balanced. If you perform a mathematical function on one side of the equation, you must also perform it on the other. Just remember, you have to do it to the entire side of the equation! You can add the same number to both sides, subtract a number from both sides, multiply both sides by the same number, divide both sides by the same number, etc.

DON'T DO TOO MUCH MATH

On the SAT, you may not have to actually solve an equation that appears in a problem. You may just be able to manipulate it, depending on the question.

$$\text{Ex)} \quad \text{If } 4x + 2y = 3 \text{, then what is } 12x + 6y = ?$$

You don't need to know what x and y are, you just need to notice that $12x + 6y$ is 3 times bigger than $4x + 2y$, therefore $12x + 6y = 3(4x + 2y) = (3)3$, and the answer is 9.

Try real examples ➜ PT2 S6 Q9

SOLVING FOR A VARIABLE OR RATIO

Solving for a variable or ratio simply refers to manipulating an equation so the variable or ratio that you are solving for is alone on one side of the equal sign, and everything else is on the other side. You spent a large part of your Algebra class learning how to solve for variables, so this manual assumes that you have a basic set of skills. If you need further help, see your teacher or tutor.

To solve for a variable, you need to get it all alone on one side of the equation. Here are some tips for solving an equation for a variable:

- **Get rid of fractions and decimals first.**

  To get rid of fractions, multiply both sides of the equation by the lowest common denominator. To get rid of decimals, multiply both sides of the equation by multiples of 10 until the decimals are gone.

- **Isolate the variable.**

  Move all of the terms that contain the variable to one side of the equation and all the terms that don't contain the variable to the other side of the equation by adding or subtracting.

- **Factor out variables if necessary.**

  Sometimes the variable you're solving for will appear in two or more terms raised to the same power. If you can't combine the terms, factor out the variable.

- **Get rid of the numbers "attached" to the variable…**

  … by multiplying and dividing. If the variable is multiplied by a number, then divide both sides of the equation by the number. If the variable is divided by a number, multiply both sides by the number.

To solve for a ratio, $\dfrac{x}{y}$ for example, get all the x terms on one side of the equation and all the y terms on the other side of the equation. Then divide both sides by y and get rid of any numbers attached to the x.

Try real examples ➜ PT1 S3 Q1
PT2 S3 Q6

DISTRIBUTING

When you simplify expressions in math, you may have to use the Distributive Property, which is the rule for multiplying through parentheses. It's pretty simple: multiple the value outside the parentheses by each term inside the parentheses. Here are two examples:

$$2(x+4) = (2)(x) + (2)(4) = 2x + 8$$

$$-x^2(3x - 5) = (-x^2)(3x) + (-x^2)(-5) = -3x^3 + 5x^2$$

F.O.I.L.

F.O.I.L. is an acronym for multiplying two polynomials with two terms, such as $(4x + 2)(2x - 3)$. F.O.I.L. stands for:

$(\text{first} \times \text{first}) + (\text{outer} \times \text{outer}) + (\text{inner} \times \text{inner}) + (\text{last} \times \text{last})$

For example:

$$(4x+2)(2x-3) \text{ means:}$$

$$(4x)(2x)+(4x)(-3)+(2)(2x)+(2)(-3)$$
$$=8x^2-7x+4x-6$$
$$=8x^2-3x-6$$

Notice that the two middle terms can usually be combined into one term. Occasionally they cancel each other out, as in $(x-y)(x+y)=x^2-y^2$.

FACTORING

Factoring commonly occurs in two ways on the SAT: Factoring out common terms and factoring simple quadratic equations.

FACTORING COMMON TERMS

If each term that you are adding or subtracting on one side of an equation has some of the same pieces, you can factor out those pieces. It's basically the opposite of distributing. For example, $4xy-3y=y(4x-3)$. Both terms contained a y, so you can factor it out of both terms.

FACTORING QUADRATIC EQUATIONS

A quadratic equation has one or more terms raised to the second power. They usually look something like: x^2+6x+8. Factoring a quadratic is just doing the opposite of F.O.I.L.ing. Typically, if you have to actually do the factoring, it will be on a difficult problem, but the factoring itself won't be too difficult. They just want to know you can do it.

The first step is to break the equations into two pieces. The term that is squared goes on the left of both pieces (unsquared):

$$x^2+6x+8$$
$$\big(x \quad \big)\big(x \quad \big)$$

The numbers that go on the right must be factors of +8 (the last term), and add together to give you +6 (the middle term). The only integer factors of 8 are $(1,8)$ and $(2,4)$, so…

$$\big(x \quad 4\big)\big(x \quad 2\big)$$

Since both 6 and 8 are positive:

$$\big(x+4\big)\big(x+2\big)$$

You may have to use trial and error and check your answer using F.O.I.L.

If there is a number in front of the x^2, breaking up the middle term is more difficult. Here is a trickier example:

$$2x^2 - 2x - 4$$
$$(2x \quad)(x \quad)$$
$$(2x \quad 4)(x \quad 1) \; or \; (2x \quad 1)(x \quad 4) \; or \; (2x \quad 2)(x \quad 2)$$
$$(2x - 4)(x + 1)$$

You should look for these three of the common quadratic equations that are easy to solve:

$$x^2 + 2xy + y^2 = (x + y)(x + y) = (x + y)^2$$
$$x^2 - 2xy + y^2 = (x - y)(x - y) = (x - y)^2$$
$$x^2 - y^2 = (x + y)(x - y)$$

Try real examples ➡ PT2 S6 Q12

EXPONENTS

Exponents consist of a base and an *exponent* (or *power*). In x^2, the x is the base and the ^{2} is the exponent. This expression just means that x is multiplied by itself 2 times:

$$x^1 = x$$
$$x^2 = x \cdot x$$
$$x^3 = x \cdot x \cdot x$$
$$x^4 = x \cdot x \cdot x \cdot x$$

One tricky exponent to remember is that any number or variable raised to the zero power equals 1:

$$1^0 = 1$$
$$5^0 = 1$$
$$78^0 = 1$$
$$999^0 = 1$$
$$x^0 = 1$$
and so on.

Exponent problems on the SAT don't have to be difficult if you remember a few basic rules.

When in doubt, think about a very simple version of the exponent problem, and apply the same rule to the more difficult problem.

Try real examples ➡ PT2 S9 Q7

EXPONENTS AND PARENTHESES

Be wary of exponents and parentheses. The exponent only affects the number or variable it is above, unless it is above parentheses, and then it affects everything in parentheses.

$$2y^2 = 2 \times y \times y = 2(y^2)$$
$$(2y)^2 = 2y \times 2y = 4y^2$$

RAISING FRACTIONS TO EXPONENTS

Exponents work the way you expect them to in most cases. When you square something, it gets bigger. But fractions between 0 and 1 are different. When you raise these fractions to exponents, they get *smaller*.

$$\left(\tfrac{1}{2}\right)^2 = \tfrac{1}{4}$$
$$\left(\tfrac{1}{3}\right)^2 = \tfrac{1}{9}$$
$$\left(\tfrac{2}{5}\right)^2 = \tfrac{4}{25}$$
$$\left(\tfrac{1}{2}\right)^4 = \tfrac{1}{16}$$

The higher the exponent, the smaller they become. It is often important to remember this when *Making up Numbers*.

ADDING OR SUBTRACTING EXPONENTS

In order to add or subtract expressions with exponents, the expressions have to have the same base and the same exponent. The exponent doesn't change:

$$x^2 + x^2 = 2x^2$$
$$4x^3 + 3x^3 = 7x^3$$
$$7y^5 - 5y^5 = 2y^5$$

You can't add or subtract expressions with different bases and/or different exponents. The following cannot be simplified:

$$x^2 + x^3 = ??$$
$$4y^3 + 3x^3 = ??$$
$$7y^5 - 5y^2 = ??$$

MULTIPLYING OR DIVIDING EXPONENTS

You can multiply and divide exponential expressions with different exponents and the same base. First, remember to treat the numbers in front of the exponents separately. Then add the exponents if you're multiplying and subtract if you're dividing.

If you're confused, think of the simple case:

$$y^2 \times y^3 = (y \times y) \times (y \times y \times y) = y^{(2+3)} = y^5$$
$$y^5 \div y^2 = \frac{y \times y \times y \times y \times y}{y \times y} = y^{(5-2)} = y^3$$

Here are a couple of slightly more complex examples:

$$3y^2 \times 4y^7 = (3 \times 4) \times y^{(2+7)} = 12y^9$$
$$\frac{8z^7}{2z^3} = \frac{8}{2} \times z^{(7-3)} = 4z^4$$

RAISING TO POWERS

When you raise exponents to further exponential powers, you simply multiply the exponents:

$$(q^2)^3 = (q \times q) \times (q \times q) \times (q \times q) = q^{(2 \times 3)} = q^6$$
$$(t^4)^{13} = t^{(4 \times 13)} = t^{52}$$

REDUCING TO THE SAME BASE

In order to compare exponential expressions, or to add and subtract them, you might have to reduce them to the same base. Look at this problem and note that some of the values are purposefully too big for most calculators:

Ex) Which value is largest?

(A) 4×3^{1199}

(B) 1200^3

(C) 27^{400}

(D) $\left(3^{300}\right)^3$

(E) $\left(12^{1200}\right)^0$

You may note that answer choice (B) is probably not too big for your calculator, so it is definitely NOT the largest. Eliminate it. You should also note that answer choice (E) = 1, since any number raised to the 0 power equals 1. Eliminate that, too.

It is difficult to compare exponents with different bases, so convert (C) to an exponent with base 3. ($27 = 3^3$) Then combine exponents and look more closely at (A), (C) and (D):

(A) 4×3^{1199}

~~(B) 1200^3~~

(C) $27^{400} = \left(3^3\right)^{400} = 3^{1200}$

(D) $\left(3^{300}\right)^3 = 3^{900}$

~~(E) $\left(12^{12}\right)^0 = 1$~~

At this point, you can probably tell that (D) is also too small, but we'd still like a better comparison of (A) and (C). To do this, try to get the exponents themselves to be the same by pulling a single 3 out of 3^{1200}:

(A) 4×3^{1199}

(B) ~~1200^3~~

(C) $27^{400} = \left(3^3\right)^{400} = 3^{1200} = 3 \times 3^{1199}$

(D) ~~$\left(3^{300}\right)^3 = 3^{900}$~~

(E) ~~$\left(12^{12}\right)^0 = 1$~~

And finally we can see that answer choice (A) is the largest!

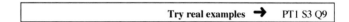

Try real examples ➜ PT1 S3 Q9

SCIENTIFIC NOTATION

Scientific notation is a very specific format for displaying numbers. It consists of a number in decimal form, with **one and only one** digit left of the decimal, multiplied by some power of 10.

6.02×10^{23} *is* in scientific notation.

60.2×10^{22} has the same value, but it *is not* in scientific notation because it has two digits to the left of the decimal.

To convert a number to scientific notation, move the decimal right or left until there is only one digit to the left of the decimal.

If you have to move the decimal *left* a certain number of spaces (making the number itself smaller) you have to add that number to the exponent of 10 (making the 10 larger to compensate for the smaller number).

$$6203 = 6.203 \times 10^3$$

If you have to move the decimal *right* a certain number of spaces (making the number itself larger) you have to subtract that number from the exponent of 10 (making the 10 smaller to compensate for the larger number).

$$.00013023 = 1.3023 \times 10^{-4}$$

You should familiarize yourself with the scientific notation function of your calculator. On most scientific calculators, the "EE" key puts numbers into scientific notation. If you enter "1.5 EE 4", your calculator will probably display "1.5E4" which means 1.5×10^4.

Multiplying and dividing numbers in scientific notation is most easily done on your calculator, but you can do it by hand. Treat the decimals separately from the powers of 10, then move the decimal and adjust the power of 10 if necessary to maintain scientific notation.

NEGATIVE EXPONENTS

Negative exponents rarely appear on the SAT. They are a little strange. For all practical purposes, negative exponents mean "put the exponent on the other side of the fraction bar and get rid of the negative." Here are some examples:

$$z^{-3} = \frac{1}{z^3}$$

$$\frac{1}{x^{-2}} = x^2$$

$$\frac{x^2 y^{-3} z^{-4}}{x^{-3} y^2 z^{-5}} = \frac{x^2 x^3 z^5}{y^2 y^3 z^4} = \frac{x^5 z}{y^5}$$

It might help you to think of this in a somewhat backwards progression from positive to negative exponents. To drop down an exponent, for example to go from x^4 to x^3, you just need to divide by x. Look what happens when you get to exponents of 0 and below:

$$x^3 = x \cdot x \cdot x$$

$$x^2 = \frac{x^3}{x} = \frac{x \cdot x \cdot x}{x} = x^2$$

$$x^1 = \frac{x^2}{x} = \frac{x \cdot x}{x} = x$$

$$x^0 = \frac{x^1}{x} = \frac{x}{x} = 1$$

$$x^{-1} = \frac{x^0}{x} = \frac{1}{x}$$

$$x^{-2} = \frac{x^{-1}}{x} = \frac{\frac{1}{x}}{x} = \frac{1}{x^2}$$

Achieve Tutorials *MAximum SAT*

FRACTIONAL EXPONENTS

Fractional exponents rarely appear on the SAT. A fractional exponent simply tells us a root is involved. The bottom number of the fraction tells us which root, and the top number of the fraction tells us what power the expression is raised to:

$$x^{\frac{1}{2}} = \sqrt{x}$$

$$x^{\frac{3}{4}} = \sqrt[4]{x^3}$$

Fractional exponents can be negative, too:

$$x^{-\left(\frac{2}{7}\right)} = \frac{1}{\sqrt[7]{x^2}}$$

Try real examples ➜	PT1 S9 Q14

SQUARE ROOTS AND CUBE ROOTS

The square root function ($\sqrt{}$) simply reverses the squared function.

For example, if $3^2 = 9$ then $\sqrt{9} = 3$.

Square roots (and all even roots) are positive by definition!

For example, $(-3)^2 = 9$ but $\sqrt{9} = 3$, **not** -3.

SIMPLIFYING

If the expressions under the square root symbol are perfect squares, simplifying is easy:

$$\sqrt{16} = 4$$
$$\sqrt{x^2} = x$$
$$\sqrt{4x^6} = \sqrt{(2x^3)^2} = 2x^3$$

If the expressions under the square root symbol are not perfect squares, you can often simplify by factoring out perfect squares. Here are two ways to do that:

❶ Simply factor out perfect squares under the square root symbol. Take the square root of the perfect squares and leave the rest under the square root symbol:

$$\sqrt{32x^5} = \sqrt{16x^4 \times 2x} = 4x^2\sqrt{2x}$$

Or...

❷ You can use a prime factor tree to factor the expression under the square root symbol. Two of the same factor under the square root symbol become one factor on the outside of the square root symbol. Single factors stay under the square root symbol:

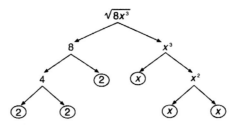

There are three 2s: A pair of 2s and a single 2. So the pair becomes a single 2 outside and we leave the single 2 under the square root. There are also three x's, a pair of x's and a single x. So the pair becomes a single x outside and we leave a single x under the square root. Therefore:

$$\sqrt{8x^3} = 2x\sqrt{2x}$$

	Try real examples ➡ PT2 S6 Q7

CUBE ROOTS

You usually won't see anything more difficult than a simple cube root. The cube root simply undoes raising to the 3rd power:

$$2^3 = 8 \quad \text{so} \quad \sqrt[3]{8} = 2$$
$$\sqrt[3]{x^6} = \sqrt[3]{\left(x^2\right)^3} = x^2$$

Cube roots (and all odd roots) of negative numbers are negative:

$$\sqrt[3]{-8} = \sqrt[3]{(-2)^3} = -2$$

HIGHER ROOTS (RADICAL EQUATIONS)

The New SAT might take roots above cube roots. Often the best way to deal with higher roots is to use your calculator's root functions or convert the roots to fractional exponents.

ADDING AND SUBTRACTING ROOTS

In order to add or subtract roots, the bases under the root and the number of the root must be the same. The square root doesn't change:

$$4\sqrt{2x} + 3\sqrt{2x} = 7\sqrt{2x}$$

MULTIPLYING AND DIVIDING ROOTS

You can break apart or combine square roots by multiplying or dividing the numbers under the square root symbol. You can break up a fraction under a square root to be a square root in the numerator over a square root in the denominator.

$$\sqrt{2} \times \sqrt{3} = \sqrt{2 \times 3} = \sqrt{6}$$

$$\sqrt{\frac{5}{4}} = \frac{\sqrt{5}}{\sqrt{4}} = \frac{\sqrt{5}}{2}$$

Try real examples ➡	PT1 S9 Q14

RAISING ROOTS TO POWERS

The most frequent "root raised to a power" questions on the SAT involve a square root being squared:

$$\left(\sqrt{x}\right)^2$$

When squaring the square root, the operations cancel each other out. Goodbye square root, goodbye square. So:

$$\left(\sqrt{x}\right)^2 = x$$

You are unlikely to see these on the SAT, but on more difficult root raised to powers questions, change the root to a fractional exponent first, then simply multiply exponents:

$$\left(\sqrt[4]{x^3}\right)^5 = \left(x^{\frac{3}{4}}\right)^5 = x^{\frac{15}{4}} = \sqrt[4]{x^{15}} = x^3\sqrt[4]{x^3}$$

Review the chapter before trying these Math problems.

Remember to look for the **EASY WAY** to solve these problems.

Practice with these problems from *The Official SAT Study Guide:*

Practice Test	Section	Question
	3	1, 9
1	6	1
	9	1, 14
	3	2, 6
2	6	7, 9, 12
	9	7
3	2	1

All test, section, question and page numbers refer to *The Official SAT Study Guide* (2004)

Be sure to carefully score the sections from *The Official SAT Study Guide* and review the questions you miss. Figure out why you missed each question and how you can get it right the next time!

Additional Practice:

Math Homework Drill 3

Note: Each question is numbered to indicate where the question would most likely appear in a math section, and therefore shows relative level of difficulty. Questions with no answer choices are Fill-Ins.

Solve each of the following problems and choose the best of the choices given. Use any available space for scratch work, if necessary.

1. If $4y - 2 = 10$, what is $6y + 2$?

   (A) 14
   (B) 16
   (C) 18
   (D) 20
   (E) 22

5. If $2x + 4y = 6$ and $3x + 6y + 9z = 36$, what is the value of z?

   (A) 3
   (B) 5
   (C) 6
   (D) 9
   (E) 18

9. If $4^{x-2} = 64$, what is the value of x?

   (A) 1
   (B) 2
   (C) 3
   (D) 4
   (E) 5

17. A line in the xy-coordinate plane is described by the equation $y = (a+1)x - 8$. What is $a + 1$ in terms of x and y?

   (A) $\dfrac{y+4}{x}$

   (B) $\dfrac{8y}{x}$

   (C) $\dfrac{4y}{x}$

   (D) $y - \dfrac{8}{x}$

   (E) $\dfrac{y+8}{x}$

9.1 If $3 - m = \dfrac{m}{3} + \dfrac{3}{5}$, what is the value of m?

1.1. If $m + n = 4$ and $3n + 3 = 12$, what is the value of m?

(A) -1
(B) 0
(C) 1
(D) 3
(E) 5

3. If $4x - 2y = 6$, what is the value of $6x - 3y$?

(A) 9
(B) 10
(C) 12
(D) 18
(E) 24

14. If $x^2 + 2xy + y^2 = (x - y)^{-2}$ and $x + y = 2$, what is the value of x?

(A) $\dfrac{1}{2}$

(B) $\dfrac{3}{4}$

(C) $\dfrac{5}{4}$

(D) 2

(E) 4

Answers:

MATH LESSON 4

ALGEBRA AND ARITHMETIC PART IV

INEQUALITIES

Inequalities show that something is greater than or less than something else. The chart below shows the symbols you need to know.

>	Greater than
<	Less than
≥	Greater than or equal to
≤	Less than or equal to

Manipulating an equation with an inequality is just like dealing with an equation with an equal sign. For example:

$$7x - 3 \leq 3x + 5$$
$$7x - 3 + 3 \leq 3x + 5 + 3 \quad \text{(add 3 to both sides)}$$
$$7x \leq 3x + 8$$
$$7x - 3x \leq 3x + 8 - 3x \quad \text{(subtract } 3x \text{ from both sides}$$
$$4x \leq 8$$
$$\frac{4x}{4} \leq \frac{8}{4} \quad \text{(divide both sides by 4)}$$
$$x \leq 2$$

You can add to both sides, subtract from both sides, multiply both sides or divide both sides, *with one extra rule:*

 Caution!

If you multiply or divide by a negative number, the direction of the inequality switches:

$$-x > 5$$
$$x < -5$$

On a harder problem, the SAT might try to trick you into thinking you can multiply or divide by a variable when you really can't. Take a look at this question:

If $x > yz$, then which of the following is also true?

I. $\dfrac{x}{y} > z$

II. $\dfrac{x}{z} > y$

III. $\dfrac{x}{yz} > 1$

(A) I only
(B) I and II
(C) III only
(D) I, II and III
(E) none

The answer is (E), none of the above! Here's why:

I. You don't know whether the y is positive or negative. If it is positive, then $\dfrac{x}{y} > z$ is true, but if it is negative (and you are therefore dividing by a negative), you have to switch the sign, so in that case $\dfrac{x}{y} < z$. They can't both be true!

II. Likewise, if z is positive, then $\dfrac{x}{z} > y$. If z is negative, then $\dfrac{x}{z} < y$. They can't both be true!

III. Likewise , if yz is positive, then $\dfrac{x}{yz} > 1$. If yz is negative, then $\dfrac{x}{yz} < 1$. Again, they can't both be true!

So, in general, if you don't know whether a variable is positive or negative, you can't multiply or divide by that variable in an inequality!

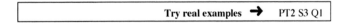

Try real examples ➡ PT2 S3 Q1

ABSOLUTE VALUE EXPRESSIONS (| |)

Most absolute value problems will simply deal with the definition of an absolute value, which basically says, "get rid of any negative signs." For example:

$$|-2| = 2$$
$$|3.4| = 3.4$$

If you have a fairly sophisticated calculator, it should have an absolute value function, probably called ABS.

These problems can get trickier when dealing with algebraic expressions. For example:

> It would seem that:
> $$|a| = a$$
>
> But this is not always true! It is true if $a \geq 0$:
> $$a = 3$$
> $$|3| = 3$$
>
> But what if $a < 0$?
> $$a = -3$$
> $$|-3| = 3$$
>
> This seems all well and good until you try to solve the equation in terms of a again:
> $$a = -3$$
> $$|-3| = 3$$
> $$3 = -a$$
>
> Therefore, if $a < 0$, then:
> $$|a| = -a$$
>
> So, if you don't know whether a is positive or negative, then:
> $$|a| = a \text{ or } |a| = -a$$
>
> … depending on a's value.

This can get even trickier when dealing with variables within inequalities. For example:

> $$|x + 2| > 4$$
>
> You need to consider two possibilities: Possibility ❶, when $x + 2 \geq 0$, in which case you can just drop the absolute value symbol, and possibility ❷, when $x + 2 < 0$, in which case you need to make the $(x + 2)$ negative. Remember that when you multiply or divide by zero, the sign flips:

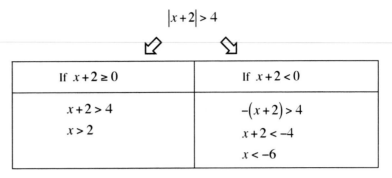

If $x+2 \geq 0$	If $x+2 < 0$
$x+2 > 4$ $x > 2$	$-(x+2) > 4$ $x+2 < -4$ $x < -6$

On the number line, this would look like:

Try real examples   ➜   PT1 S3 Q19

LINEAR EQUATIONS

Linear equations on the SAT appear as equations involving one or two (very occasionally three) variables that are not raised to exponents, under roots, or in the denominator. Here are some examples:

$$x = 5$$
$$y = -3$$
$$y = 5x + 2$$
$$\frac{1}{2}x - \frac{3}{4}y = 8$$
$$4a + 5b - 3c = 2$$

Linear equations, as the name suggests, represent straight lines on the xy (or xyz) coordinate plane. For more on linear and coordinate geometry, see the Geometry section.

SIMULTANEOUS LINEAR EQUATIONS

In general, if you have a linear equation with a single variable, you can solve for that variable. If you have two variables, you need two different linear equations to solve for the two variables.

You can think of "solving" a system of linear equations in two ways. On a graph, the "solution" to two linear equations is the coordinates of the point where the two lines cross. From a mathematical point of view, the solution is the x and y pair that works in both equations.

There are two common methods for solving these "systems of equations" or "simultaneous equations": the substitution method and the addition / subtraction method.

THE SUBSTITUTION METHOD

To use the substitution method:

❶ **Solve for one variable.**

You need to solve one equation for one of the two variables. In other words, get one variable by itself on one side of the equation.

❷ **Substitute.**

In the other equation, replace that variable with all the junk on the other side of the equal sign.

❸ **Solve for the remaining variable.**

Now you've created an equation with only one variable, so solve for the variable.

❹ **Use the value for the first variable.**

Take that value for the variable you figured out and pop it back into the first equation.

❺ **Solve for the second variable.**

Solve the equation for the second variable.

Here's what it should look like:

Ex) If $3x + y = 11$ and $2x + 4y = 24$, then what are the values of x and y?

Equation A

$3x + y = 11$ $\Longleftarrow$ *1) Solve for y*

$y = 11 - 3x$ *2) Replace the y* $\Longrightarrow$

          3) Solve for x $\Longrightarrow$

$\Downarrow$

$y = 11 - 3(2)$ $\Longleftarrow$ *4) Plug 2 in for x*

$y = 11 - 6$ $\Longleftarrow$ *5) Solve for y*

$y = 5$

$x = 2$ *and* $y = 5$

Equation B

$2x + 4y = 24$

$2x + 4(11 - 3x) = 24$

$2x + 44 - 12x = 24$

$-10x + 44 = 24$

$-10x = -20$

$x = 2$

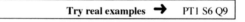

Try real examples ➜	PT1 S6 Q9

THE ADDITION / SUBTRACTION METHOD

To use the addition / subtraction method (also called the elimination or linear combination method) you first need to get the two equations in the same basic format. Put all the terms with variables in the same order on one side of each equation and all the terms with only numbers on the other side. Then:

       Achieve Tutorials *MAximum SAT*

❶ Balance one of the variables.

You need to get the same number (positives and negatives don't matter) in front of one of the variables, so multiply one or both equations to get the same number in front of one variable. (Often the equations on the SAT will already have the same number in front of a variable and you won't have to do this.)

❷ Line up the equations.

Copy one equation directly under the other with like terms right below each other.

❸ Add or subtract to solve for one variable.

Add or subtract straight down to eliminate one of the variables.

❹ Use the value for the first variable.

Take that value for the variable you figured out and pop it back into the first equation.

❺ Solve for the second variable.

Solve the equation for the second variable.

Here's what it should look like:

$$
\begin{array}{ll}
\textit{Equation A} & \\
3x + y = 11 & \Longleftarrow 1)\ \textit{Multiply by 4} \\
4(3x + y) = 11(4) & \quad (\textit{to match } y \textit{ terms}) \\
12x + 4y = 44 & \\
-(2x + 4y = 24) & \Longleftarrow 2)\ \textit{Copy equation over} \\
\hline
10x + = 20 & \Longleftarrow 3)\ \textit{Subtract \& solve} \\
x = 2 & \quad 4)\ \textit{Plug 2 in for } x \Longrightarrow \\
& \quad 5)\ \textit{Solve} \Longrightarrow
\end{array}
$$

$$
\begin{array}{l}
\textit{Equation B} \\
2x + 4y = 24 \\
\\
\Downarrow \\
2x + 4y = 24 \\
\\
\\
2(2) + 4y = 24 \\
4 + 4y = 24 \\
4y = 20 \\
y = 5
\end{array}
$$

$x = 2$ *and* $y = 5$

Sometimes you have to create two linear equations from a word problem.

Ex) Ryan has 11 coins, some dimes and some quarters. If he has $1.40 in change, how many dimes does he have?

Here's how you solve it:

Let's pick two variables to use. Let d represent the number of dimes and q represent the number of quarters. Now we have to figure out two equations:

Well, Ryan has 11 coins, so $d + q = 11$. (This may be the harder equation to spot in the problem, even though it is mathematically pretty simple.)

His total money is $1.40 (or 140¢), so the number of dimes times 10 plus the number of quarters times 25 must add up to 140. (Notice we converted from dollars to cents right at the beginning to avoid confusion.) So the second equation becomes: $10d + 25q = 140$.

Now just solve as above. The substitution method is easy here because you can solve the first equation for a variable without much work:

$$
\begin{array}{lll}
\underline{\textit{Equation A}} & & \underline{\textit{Equation B}} \\
d + q = 11 & \Longleftarrow 1)\ \textit{Solve for } d & 10d + 25q = 140 \\
d = 11 - q & 2)\ \textit{Replace the } d \Longrightarrow & 10(11 - q) + 25q = 140 \\
& 3)\ \textit{Solve for } q \Longrightarrow & 110 - 10q + 25q = 140 \\
\Downarrow & & 15q + 110 = 140 \\
& & 15q = 30 \\
d = 11 - (2) & \Longleftarrow 4)\ \textit{Plug 2 in for } q & q = 2 \\
d = 9 & \Longleftarrow 5)\ \textit{Solve for } d & \\
q = 2 \textit{ and } d = 9
\end{array}
$$

> You may remember that these linear equations represent straight lines. When you "solve" a system of linear equations, you're really finding the coordinate of the point where the two lines cross. For more on linear equations, see the Coordinate Geometry section.

RATIONAL EXPRESSIONS

Rational Expressions on the SAT can involve more sophisticated algebraic expressions. A Rational Expression is basically a polynomial fraction. In other words, a fraction that has variables in the denominator is a rational expression. Here are a couple of examples:

$$
\frac{5}{2x} \quad \text{or} \quad \frac{(x+2)}{(x^2 + 7x + 10)}
$$

The main rule to remember for rational expressions is that you **CANNOT DIVIDE BY ZERO!** So, any number that makes the denominator of a fraction equal to zero is not a possible answer, and is therefore out of the Domain.

The next rule is to simplify the expression by factoring and canceling anything you can in the numerator and denominator.

In the first example, $\dfrac{5}{2x}$, x cannot equal 0, because that would make the denominator 0. Pretty easy, right?

The second example is a bit more difficult. We need to factor the denominator first:

$$\frac{(x+2)}{(x^2+7x+10)} = \frac{(x+2)}{(x+2)(x+5)}$$

At this point, *before* you cancel, you should note that x can't equal -2 or -5.

To simplify further, cancel the $(x+2)$:

$$\frac{(x+2)}{(x+2)(x+5)} = \frac{1}{(x+5)}$$

> Rational Expression problems are GREAT candidates for *Using the Answers*!

DIRECT AND INVERSE VARIATION

Direct and Inverse Variation is just a fancy way to describe fairly simple equations.

DIRECT VARIATION

Direct Variation between two values basically means that if one value goes up, the other goes up as well. For example, if your furnace is in working order and you turn the thermostat up, the temperature in the house goes up as well.

If the two values went up at an equal rate, the equation would be pretty simple:

$$y = x$$

Unfortunately, the two values don't necessarily go up at the same rate; they usually just go up proportionally. For every inch you move the thermostat, the temperature might increase 20 degrees.

So, there has to be a number, a constant number in fact, that tells us how much faster one of the values rises. That constant value is represented by the letter k. Let's take a look at an example:

"y varies directly as x" translates to $y = kx$

"y varies directly as the square of x" becomes $y = kx^2$

"y is directly proportional to the cube of x" is $y = kx^3$

The k represents some constant value. If the problem gives you x and y values that work in the equation, you can figure out what k is:

> Ex) If y varies directly as x, and y is 12 when x is 2, what is the direct variation equation?

Write out the equation with k:

$$y = kx$$

Then use 12 for y and 2 for x and solve for k:

$$12 = k \times 2$$

$$k = 6$$

The direct variation equation becomes:

$$y = 6x$$

You could then use that equation to solve for any y value when given an x value:

> Ex) If y varies directly as x, and y is 12 when x is 2, what is the value of y when x is 3?

Solve as above to get the equation $y = 6x$. Then replace x with 3:

$$y = 6(3) = 18$$

Try real examples ➜ PT1 S6 Q6

INVERSE VARIATION

Inverse Variation is very similar to Direct Variation. It also relates two values, except that when one value goes up, the other goes down. Here's how you translate it:

"y varies inversely as x" translates to $y = \dfrac{k}{x}$

"y varies inversely as the square of x" becomes $y = \dfrac{k}{x^2}$

"y is inversely proportional to the cube of x" is $y = \dfrac{k}{x^3}$

You can solve Inverse Variation problems just like Direct Variation problems, by solving for k first.

AVERAGE

You may remember that the formula for an average is:

$$\text{Average} = \frac{\text{Total (sum) of all items}}{\text{Number of items}}$$

There is, however, an easier way to think about averages. Let's look at the Average T:

THE AVERAGE T

The Average T is just a simple way of arranging the average equation:

$$\frac{Total}{\text{\# of items} \mid Average}$$

To find the *Total*,
multiply the *# of items* and the *Average*.

To find the *# of items*,	To find the *Average*,
divide the *Total* by the *Average*.	divide the *Total* by the *# of items*.

Most average problems on the SAT require that you do the Average T two or three separate times. Usually, you will have to worry about adding and subtracting the *Totals* and adjusting the # *of items*. Here's an example:

> Ex) Franz averaged a score of 80 on seven tests. If he averaged 90 on his last two tests, what did he average on his first five tests?

Here's how you solve it:

We need to set up three different Average T's. Let's start with all seven tests:

$$\frac{Total}{7 \mid 80} \implies \frac{560}{7 \mid 80}$$

So, he scored a total of 560 points on all seven tests. Next, let's look at the last two tests:

$$\frac{Total}{2 \mid 90} \implies \frac{180}{2 \mid 90}$$

So he scored a total of 180 points on the last two tests. Well, that means he had to have scored 380 points on the first five tests, the 560 total points minus the 180 on the last two tests:

$$\frac{Total}{5 \mid ?} \implies \frac{560 - 180}{5 \mid ?} \implies \frac{380}{5 \mid ?} \implies \frac{380}{5 \mid 76}$$

So, Franz averaged 76 on his first five tests.

Try real examples ➡	PT1 S9 Q13

MEAN / MEDIAN / MODE / RANGE

This section really could have been put in the Math Vocabulary section, because the SAT mostly tests whether or not you know what the Mean, Median, Mode and Range are.

MEAN

The Mean, or arithmetic mean, is exactly the same as the average. See the Average section in the preceding pages.

MEDIAN

The Median is just the middle number in a group of numbers. To find the Median, you must put all the numbers in order.

- **Odd number of numbers.**

   If there is an odd number of numbers, the Median is just the one in the middle. 7 is the Median of (1, 1, 4, 7, 8, 8, 34)

- **Even number of numbers.**

   If there is an even number of numbers, average the two middle numbers. 5 is the Median of (4, 4, 6, 7) because it's the average of 4 and 6.

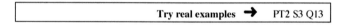

Try real examples ➡ PT2 S3 Q13

MODE

The Mode is the most commonly occurring number in the list.

9 is the Mode of (2, 2, 4, 5, 5, 7, 9, 9, 9, 11).

There can be more than one Mode in a list of numbers.

The list (2, 5, 12, 3, 2, 17, 77, 3, 17, 35) has three Modes: 2, 3, and 17. Note that it really helps to order the numbers before looking for the Mode: (2, 2, 3, 3, 5, 12, 17, 17, 77, 35).

RANGE

The Range is the biggest number minus the smallest number in a group. 20 is the Range of (2, 19, 19, 20, 22), since 22 – 2 = 20.

To avoid the SAT's Mean, Median, Mode, and Range traps, here are two tips:

Achieve Tutorials *MAximum SAT*

> If you only know *one thing* (Mean, Median, Mode or Range and NOT any of the numbers) you can't know anything else about the others!

> If the numbers in the group are all evenly spaced, the median and the mean have the same value!

RATIOS AND PROPORTIONS

Ratios come in several different forms ("1:3", "the ratio of 1 to 3", or even "$\frac{1}{3}$"), but it is important to note that ratios and fractions are NOT the same thing. A fraction is $\frac{\text{a part}}{\text{the whole}}$ while a ratio is $\frac{\text{a part}}{\text{a part}}$. For example, if you have a total of 11 animals — 4 cats and 7 dogs — the ratio of cats to dogs is 4:7 or $\frac{4}{7}$ but the fraction of animals that are cats is $\frac{4}{11}$.

When dealing with ratios, it is always important to keep the total in mind.

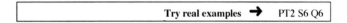

Try real examples ➡ PT2 S6 Q6

RATIO CHART

The Ratio Chart, shown below, is a useful tool for solving many ratio problems.

Ratio Chart	Object 1	Object 2	Total
Ratio			
Times			
Real numbers			

The *Ratio* goes in the top row and any *Real numbers* go in the bottom row. *Totals* go in the rightmost column. To find the *Times* number, divide any *Real number* by its corresponding *Ratio*. **All the Times numbers are the same all the way across.** Just fill them in, then multiply down.

Ex) In a cup of hot cocoa, the ratio of mix to water is 2 to 5. If there are 35 ounces of cocoa in a mug, how much mix was used?

First fill in the information you know:

Ratio Chart	Mix	Water	Total
Ratio	2	5	
Times			
Real Numbers			35

Now add the *Ratios* to get the ratio *Total*:

Ratio Chart	Mix	Water	Total
Ratio	2	5	7
Times			
Real Numbers			35

Find the *Times* by dividing the real total (35) by the ratio total (7). The *Times* is 5, so fill that in across the entire *Times* row.

Ratio Chart	Mix	Water	Total
Ratio	2	5	7
Times	5	5	5
Real Numbers			35

Now just multiply down:

Ratio Chart	Mix	Water	Total
Ratio	2	5	7
Times	5	5	5
Real Numbers	10	25	35

And you get your answer: 10 ounces of mix was used.

On a harder problem, you may have to use a variable for the *Times* value:

> Ex) The ratio of pairs of pants to shirts in a closet was 3:5. If six more pairs of pants were added, the ratio of pairs of pants to shirts would be 1:1. How many shirts were in the closet?

Fill in what you know, but put in an x for the *Times* value and multiply down:

Ratio Chart	Pants	Shirts	Total
Ratio	3	5	8
Times	x	x	x
Real Numbers	3x	5x	8x

Remember that we know if there were 6 more pairs of pants, the ratio would be 1:1, so the real numbers would also be equal. So add 6 to $3x$ and set the sum equal to $5x$, then solve for x:

$$3x + 6 = 5x$$
$$6 = 2x$$
$$3 = x$$

Now plug 3 in for x:

Ratio Chart	Pants	Shirts	Total
Ratio	3	5	8
Times	3	3	3
Real Numbers	9	15	24

So there were 15 shirts in the closet.

The Ratio Chart is a great tool, even on much harder problems, but it might just be the starting point and you may have to do further calculations.

PROPORTIONS

Proportions are just two fractions that have equal value but different denominators and numerators. Lots of SAT problems can be solved using proportions. Percent problems, similar triangle problems and ratio problems are just a few.

Ex) If $\frac{1}{3}$ of the apples in a barrel are red, and there are 26 red apples, how many apples are in the barrel?

This is a fairly easy problem if you use proportions.

The fraction $\frac{1}{3}$ represents $\frac{1 \text{ red apple}}{3 \text{ total apples}}$, but we know there are actually 26 red apples. So set up a proportion:

$$\frac{1 \text{ red apple}}{3 \text{ total apples}} = \frac{26 \text{ red apples}}{? \text{ total apples}}$$

And solve by cross-multiplying:

$$\frac{1}{3} = \frac{26}{x}$$
$$x = (3)(26)$$
$$x = 78$$

Be aggressive setting up proportions. Proportions are often one of the easiest ways to solve a problem.

Try real examples ➜ PT3 S2 Q5

RATE

The simple rate formula, $\text{Rate} \times \text{Time} = \text{Distance}$ or $\text{Rate} \times \text{Time} = \text{Work}$, is duplicated in the Rate Chart:

Rate Chart	Rate $\times$	Time $=$	Distance or Work
Rate 1			
Rate 2			

There are several different ways rate problems appear. Some rate problems involve two people working together, others involve objects traveling in the same or different directions. Still other problems involve traveling the same distance at two rates in two different directions. Here's how to tackle each type of rate problem:

- **When two people are working together...**

  ... their individual rates can be added to determine how much work they can do together.

  > Ex) Bill packs 3 boxes per hour and Edna packs 4 boxes per hour. Working together, how long will it take them to pack 28 boxes?

  Just fill in the rate chart, and add Bill and Edna's rates:

Rate Chart	Rate $\times$	Time $=$	Work
Bill	3		
Edna	4		
Bill & Edna	7	t	28

  So it takes them $t = 4$ hours working together.

- **When two objects are moving toward each other or away from each other...**

  ... their individual rates can be added to determine how quickly they are separating or approaching.

Ex) At 1 pm, a train leaves town A and heads directly to town B at 50 mph. Also at 1 pm, a second train traveling along parallel tracks leaves town B for town A at 30 mph. If town A and town B are 240 miles apart, at what time will the trains pass each other?

(A) 3 pm
(B) 3:30 pm
(C) 4 pm
(D) 4:30 pm
(E) 5 pm

Just fill in the rate chart and add the trains' rates. At the time that they pass each other, they will have traveled a total of 240 miles between them:

Rate Chart	Rate ×	Time =	Work
Train 1	50		
Train 2	30		
Trains 1 & 2	80	t	240

So they pass after $t = 3$ hours, which makes it (C) 4 pm.

- **When two objects are moving in the same direction…**

    … but at different rates, their individual rates can be subtracted to determine how quickly they are separating from each other. Also note that these objects never travel the same distance in the same amount of time… one will always be ahead of the other.

    Ex) Sarah and George decide to race each other between lifeguard towers on the beach. Sarah runs 10 meters per second, and George runs 8 meters per second. If the lifeguard towers are 200 meters apart, by how much does Sarah win the race?

    You could solve this two ways using the chart. First, fill in what you know. Note that we do know how far Sarah travels since she won the race, but we don't know how far George traveled in the same time since he is slower. However, they both ran for the same amount of time:

Rate Chart	Rate ×	Time =	Distance
Sarah	10	t	200
George	8	t	
Sarah-George			

Now simply compute Sarah's (and therefore George's) time.
$10t = 200$, so $t = 20$.

Now you can either use 20 seconds to figure out how far George traveled and subtract that from Sarah's distance, or use the Sarah – George rate to determine how far apart they were when Sarah won the race:

Rate Chart	Rate ×	Time =	Distance
Sarah	10	20	200
George	8	20	160
Sarah-George	2	20	40

So the answer is 40 meters. Way to go, Sarah!

- **When there is no specific number for Work or Distance...**

  ... Make Up Numbers that make the problem easy to figure out. Use common multiples of the rates.

  > Ex) Edie can do a job in 6 hours. Gina can do the same job in 8 hours. How long will it take them to do the job if they work together?

  You could use the number 1 to represent the "job" but you would have to work with fractions, so why not *Make Up Numbers* instead. Choose something that is evenly divisible by both rates. In this case, I'm going to say that one job is the same as building 24 widgets:

Rate Chart	Rate ×	Time =	Distance
Edie	4	6	24
Gina	3	8	24
Edie & Gina	7	t	24

  It's easy to figure that Edie's rate is 4 widgets per hour and Gina's is 3. Add the rates, and you get $7t = 24$ so $t = \frac{27}{7}$ or $3\frac{3}{7}$ hours.

- **Using a variable on a hard rate problem.**

  Sometimes, for example, a total time for a round trip with two different rates is given, but the problem doesn't give a distance. Use the variable t to represent the time for one direction and *total time –
  t* for the other direction. Calculate the distance in terms of t, then set the two distances equal to each other and solve for t.

Ex) Eileen climbed from the ground to the top of a tower at the rate of 15 meters per minute. She returned by the same route at 30 meters per minute. If the entire round trip took 6 minutes, how tall is the tower?

Put the information you know into the rate chart, including the variable t for time up the tower. Since total time is 6 minutes, make the time down the tower $6 - t$:

Rate Chart	Rate ×	Time =	Distance
Up the Tower	15	t	$15t$
Down the Tower	30	$6 - t$	$30(6 - t)$

Now make the distances equal, since she traveled by the same route:

$15t = 30(6 - t)$

$15t = 180 - 30t$

$45t = 180$

Since $t = 4$, the distance equals $15(4)$, or 60 meters.

| Try real examples ➜   PT1 S6 Q18 |

Review the chapter before trying these Math problems.

Remember to look for the **EASY WAY** to solve these problems.

Practice with these problems from *The Official SAT Study Guide:*

Practice Test	Section	Question
1	3	5, 19
	6	6, 9, 18
	9	2, 13
2	3	1, 13
	6	5, 6
3	2	5
	4	7, 10, 12

All test, section, question and page numbers refer to *The Official SAT Study Guide* (2004)

Be sure to carefully score the sections from *The Official SAT Study Guide* and review the questions you miss. Figure out why you missed each question and how you can get it right the next time!

Additional Practice:

Math Homework Drill 4

Note: Each question is numbered to indicate where the question would most likely appear in a math section, and therefore shows relative level of difficulty. Questions with no answer choices are Fill-Ins.

Solve each of the following problems and choose the best of the choices given. Use any available space for scratch work, if necessary.

10. If the average of 2 and a certain number is half the average of that number and 6, what is the number?

   (A) 2
   (B) 4
   (C) 5
   (D) 10
   (E) 12

19. A certain photocopier can make $3x + 1$ copies per minute for single-sided copies. When the copier is making double-sided copies, it can make $2y + 3$ copies per minute. If the copier is slower at making double-sided copies than it is at making single-sided copies, which of the following statements must be true?

   I. $x > y$

   II. $3x > 2y$

   III. x is an integer

   (A) I only
   (B) I and II only
   (C) II only
   (D) II and III only
   (E) I, II, and III

6. The Hardy Box Company makes cardboard boxes of various sizes, but all of their boxes adhere to the following rules:

1. The height and width are in the proportion of 1 to 3.

2. The length is always double the width.

3. The height is at least 6 inches.

Which of the following describes the dimensions of a Hardy Box Company box?

(A) length = 30in., width = 15in., height = 45in.
(B) length = 48in., width = 24in., height = 8in.
(C) length = 48in., width = 16in., height = 8in.
(D) length = 60in., width = 30in., height = 15in.
(E) length = 60in., width = 20in., height = 8in.

2. Maggie uses a recipe that calls for 6 apples to make 3 apple pies. If she used the same recipe, how many apples would it take to make 5 pies?

(A) $6\frac{1}{5}$
(B) 9
(C) 10
(D) $11\frac{3}{5}$
(E) 12

6. If b is the average of four integers and three of the integers are $b+3$, $2b-4$, and $1-3b$, which of the following is the fourth integer?

(A) $2-b$
(B) $\dfrac{b+2}{4}$
(C) $\dfrac{2b}{4}$
(D) $2b+4$
(E) $4b$

Answers:

MATH LESSON 5

GEOMETRY PART I

Fear not, the Geometry on the SAT is pretty basic. Tricky, yes, but not too difficult if you know a few of the basic rules and you know what to look out for.

GEOMETRY MAKING UP NUMBERS

Making Up Numbers is often a great way to figure out tough Geometry problems. Just because it's Geometry doesn't mean the variables are always fixed. You should think about *Making Up Numbers*:

- If you can't figure out the variables for angles or side lengths.

- If it might help to apply easy concepts to a hard problem.

- If *Making Up Numbers* won't contradict the basic things you know about Geometry. (For example, the sum of the angles of a triangle is 180°. You have to stay within that boundary.)

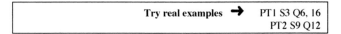

Try real examples ➜ PT1 S3 Q6, 16
PT2 S9 Q12

DRAW OR REDRAW THE FIGURE

Lots of the Geometry on the SAT is based on visual figures. Sometimes the test gives you a figure, sometimes just a description. When they do give you a figure, test writers sometimes warn: "Figure not drawn to scale." Even if they don't tell you this, ***don't trust their picture*** (especially on a medium or hard problem). You should always consider drawing or redrawing the figure. Redraw the figure in several different ways if possible. Don't be afraid to turn your test booklet around to get a different perspective on a figure.

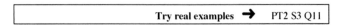

Try real examples ➜ PT2 S3 Q11

COORDINATE GEOMETRY

COORDINATE PLANE

The coordinate plane is the familiar x-y axis.

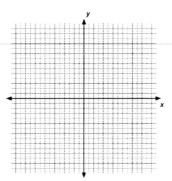

The **origin** is the place the x and y axes cross. Any point in the plane can be indicated by two coordinates:

- **x-coordinate.**

  A horizontal coordinate, which tells you how far right (positive x value) or left (negative x value) from the origin you move along the x-axis.

- **y-coordinate.**

  A vertical coordinate, which tells you how far up (positive y value) or down (negative y value) from the origin you move along the y-axis.

A two-coordinate position is always indicated as (x, y). The x is always before the y. Think alphabetically.

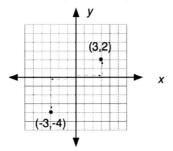

The coordinate plane is divided into 4 quadrants, labeled I, II, III, and IV. They start in the upper right and go *counterclockwise*:

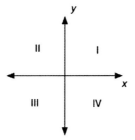

COORDINATE PROBLEMS ARE OFTEN POLYGON PROBLEMS

Many coordinate plane problems are really simple polygon problems in disguise, dealing with rectangles or right triangles. Carefully draw figures to scale, and try to spot the triangles, rectangles or other simple geometric figures within the coordinate plane:

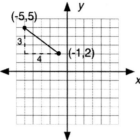

In the diagram above, for example, the points (-5, 5) and (-1, 2) could be two corners of a right triangle.

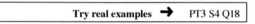

LINES AND SLOPE FORMULA

The slope of a line basically tells you the angle at which the line is drawn in the coordinate plane.

- A *positive slope* means the line goes up to the right.

- A *negative slope* means the line goes down to the right.

- A *zero slope* means the line is horizontal.

- An *undefined slope* means the line is vertical.

The letter m represents slope. The slope formula is:

$$m = \text{slope} = \frac{\text{rise}}{\text{run}} = \frac{y_1 - y_2}{x_1 - x_2}$$

... where two points on the line are (x_1, y_1) and (x_2, y_2).

The equation for a line (in slope-intercept form) is:

$$y = mx + b$$

... where m is the slope and b is the y-intercept.

The **y-intercept** is the place at which the line crosses the y-axis.

The **x-intercept** is the place at which the line crosses the x-axis.

> Note on x- and y-intercepts: You can always find the y-intercept by setting $x = 0$ in the equation, because the x value is 0 when the line crosses the y-axis. Likewise, you can always find the x-intercept by setting $y = 0$ in the equation, because the y value is 0 when the line crosses the x-axis.

A line may also be written in standard form:

$$Ax + By = C$$

… where $A > 0$ and A, B and C are all integers.

You will probably find the slope-intercept form the easiest to work with, so be prepared to solve a linear equation for y if necessary.

To draw a line from a formula:

❶ Solve the equation for y to get the line into slope-intercept form, if necessary.

❷ Place a point at the y-intercept.

❸ Count spaces from the y-intercept corresponding to the slope (rise over run) and place another point. Connect the points to draw a line.

Some other useful line and slope facts:

• **Parallel Lines.**

Parallel lines have the same slope.

• **Perpendicular Lines.**

Perpendicular lines have negative reciprocal slopes.

• **Negative Slopes.**

When counting negative slopes, you have to choose whether the negative sign goes with the top (rise) or the bottom (run) of the slope. The negative sign only applies to one or the other, not both.

• **Whole Number Slopes.**

If the slope is a whole number, think of it as the whole number over 1: a slope of $3 = \dfrac{3}{1}$.

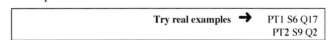

| **Try real examples** ➡ | PT1 S6 Q17 |
| | PT2 S9 Q2 |

DOMAIN, RANGE, AND GRAPHS

Domain and range for more complicated equations need some special attention. Often, domain and range are best determined on a graph.

- **Domain**

    As mentioned in the Math Vocabulary section, the Domain of a function includes all possible x values.

    In most cases, there are two math rules that determine the Domain of a function.

    ❶ You can't divide by 0. Any number that would make the denominator of a fraction 0 is eliminated from the Domain.

    $$\text{Ex)} \quad y = \frac{4x}{(x+3)}$$

    Since you know the denominator can't equal 0:

    $$(x+3) \neq 0$$
    $$x \neq -3$$

    So the Domain is all real numbers except -3.

    ❷ You can't take an even root ($\sqrt{}, \sqrt[4]{}, \sqrt[6]{}$) of a negative number. Any value that makes an expression under an even root negative is eliminated from the Domain.

    $$\text{Ex)} \quad y = 3(\sqrt[4]{3x+12})$$

    Since you know the even root can't be negative:

    $$3x + 12 \geq 0$$
    $$3x \geq -12$$
    $$x \geq -4$$

    So the Domain is all values of $x \geq -4$.

    On a graph, this means looking for how far left and right a curve extends. Here's an example:

In this graph (of the line $y = \sqrt{x} + 2$), the curve starts at $x = 0$ and appears to extend indefinitely to the right. It does not extend left of the y-axis, so the Domain is all values of $x \geq 0$.

- **Range**

  The Range of a function includes all possible y values. The Range is slightly more difficult to determine simply from an equation, and you probably won't be asked to do so.

  On a graph, finding the Range means looking for how far up and down a curve extends. Here's the same graph from above:

  The curve starts at 2 above the y-axis and appears to extend up indefinitely. It does not extend below $y = 2$, so the Range is all values of $y \geq 2$.

  Here's another example, this time a graph of the curve $y = x^3$:

  In this graph, the curve appears to extend indefinitely right, left, up and down. Therefore:

  Domain is all real numbers.
  Range is all real numbers.

TRANSFORMATIONS ON GRAPHS

For more complicated graphing problems, you may need to know how to shift or transform graphs. Transformations are typically fairly simple on the SAT. Let's take a look at three basic equations ($y = x^2$, $y = \sqrt{x}$, and $y = x^3$) and how transformations work:

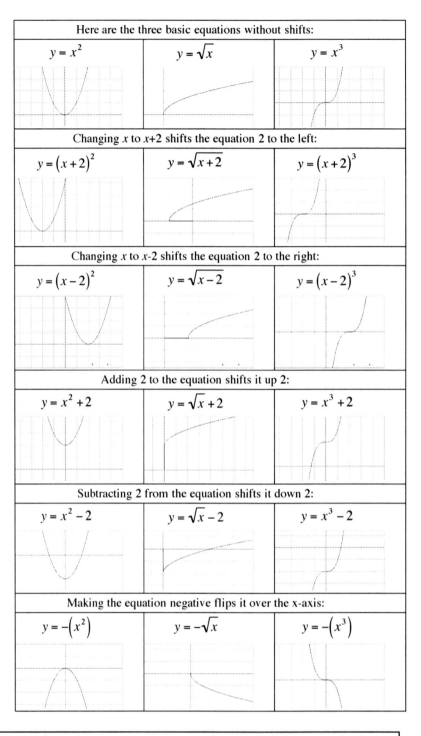

Here are the three basic equations without shifts:		
$y = x^2$	$y = \sqrt{x}$	$y = x^3$
Changing x to $x+2$ shifts the equation 2 to the left:		
$y = (x+2)^2$	$y = \sqrt{x+2}$	$y = (x+2)^3$
Changing x to $x-2$ shifts the equation 2 to the right:		
$y = (x-2)^2$	$y = \sqrt{x-2}$	$y = (x-2)^3$
Adding 2 to the equation shifts it up 2:		
$y = x^2 + 2$	$y = \sqrt{x} + 2$	$y = x^3 + 2$
Subtracting 2 from the equation shifts it down 2:		
$y = x^2 - 2$	$y = \sqrt{x} - 2$	$y = x^3 - 2$
Making the equation negative flips it over the x-axis:		
$y = -(x^2)$	$y = -\sqrt{x}$	$y = -(x^3)$

One of the easiest ways to solve a transformation problem is to look carefully at the graph and pick out an (x, y) point or two that you *know* lie on the graph. Then insert those x and y values into the equations in the answer choices to see if they work.

AXIS OF SYMMETRY

Quadratic functions in the form $ax^2 + bx + c$ are symmetrical about a vertical line called the axis of symmetry. The vertical line formula for the axis of symmetry is simply:

$$x = \frac{-b}{2a}$$

Ex) The graph of $y = 3x^2 + 12x - 7$ is symmetrical about the line $x = \dfrac{-12}{(2)(3)}$ or $x = -2$.

You can use the axis of symmetry to find the vertex of a graph by popping the x value of the axis of symmetry into the equation and solving for y.

REFLECTIONS ON GRAPHS

Some problems may ask you about Reflections. Reflections are often called "flips." On the SAT, a line is usually reflected or flipped across the x-axis or y-axis.

- **Reflecting across the x-axis**

  The x-coordinate of any point on the graph stays the same, but the y-coordinate is multiplied by –1. In the graph below, the dotted line triangle is a reflection across the x-axis of the solid line figure.

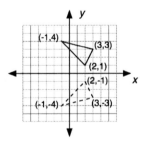

- **Reflecting across the y-axis**

  The y-coordinate of any point on the graph stays the same, but the x-coordinate is multiplied by –1. In the graph below, the dotted line triangle is a reflection across the y-axis of the solid line figure.

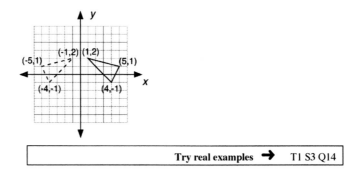

Try real examples ➡ T1 S3 Q14

FUNCTIONS

If you've taken algebra, then you're most likely familiar with the format $f(x) = x^2 + 2$. To solve a problem, for example $f(5)$, you simply replace every occurrence of x with 5:

$f(5) = 5^2 + 2 = 25 + 2 = 27$.

The first thing to remember about functions is that "$f(x) =$" is, for all practical purposes on the SAT, exactly the same as "$y =$." Functions just describe lines or curves in the coordinate plane. For every x value, there is a corresponding y or $f(x)$ value and the function can be used to generate a set of (x, y) coordinates, also written as $(x, f(x))$ coordinates. For example:

If $f(x) = x^3 - 4$ (or $y = x^3 - 4$) then:

x	$f(x)$ or y
-2	-12
-1	-5
0	-4
1	-3
2	4

Likewise, you can enter a function into your graphing calculator.

For many function problems on the SAT, points on the coordinate plane are important. Often you can tell which points on a curve correspond to integer values on the coordinate grid, and you can use these points to solve a problem or check answer choices. For example, in the figure below (a graph of the function $f(x) = -x^3$), the points (-1,1), (0,0) and (1,-1) are clearly on the graph.

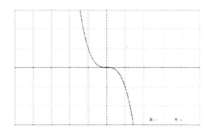

Achieve Tutorials *MAximum SAT*

Often, you need to know how to interpret behavior of a function on a graph. Usually, this just involves finding a *y*-value for a given *x*-value.

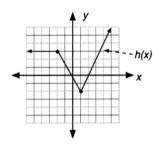

Ex) The diagram above shows the graph of the function *h(x)*. What is the value of *h(-3)*?

To solve this problem, simply find the point on the graph where $x = -3$. That's at point (-3, 3), so *h(-3)* = 3.

NESTED FUNCTIONS

The SAT also tests your understanding of Nested Functions, or functions within functions. These problems are really just complicated extensions of Order of Operations problems. Let's look at an example:

Ex) If $f(x) = 2x - 3$ and $g(x) = x^2 - 2$ then what is $f(g(x))$ when $x = 3$?

To solve it, do the function inside the parentheses first, in this case $g(x)$ when $x = 3$:

$$g(3) = 3^2 - 2 = 7$$

Now just pop the number 7 into $f(x)$:

$$f(7) = 2 \times 7 - 3 = 11$$

So the answer is 11.

WEIRD SYMBOL FUNCTIONS

The SAT may try to trick you by putting function problems in a different format, something you're not used to seeing. For example:

$$\llcorner a = a^2 + 2$$
So: $\llcorner 5 = 5^2 + 2 = 27$
...or...
$$\overline{\overline{a,b}} = a^2 - b^2 - 2$$
So: $\overline{\overline{5,4}} = 5^2 - 4^2 - 2 = 25 - 16 - 2 = 7$

Sometimes weird symbol functions deal with nested functions.

If $\nabla x = \dfrac{x}{2}$ then what does $\nabla(\nabla 12) = ?$

This is like an $f(f(x))$ function. Solve the inside first:

$\nabla 12 = \dfrac{12}{2} = 6$, then replace the inside functions with your answer.

The problem becomes:

$\nabla 6 = \dfrac{6}{2} = 3$

Try real examples ➡ PT1 S3 Q18; S6 Q13
PT2 S3 Q10
PT3 S4 Q8

AREA VS. PERIMETER (CIRCUMFERENCE)

Don't be an SAT chump! Never confuse area and perimeter! It's easy to do if you're rushing, and the SAT will punish you if you don't pay attention. On almost every perimeter problem, there is an incorrect answer choice that gives area. On almost all area problems, there is an incorrect answer choice that gives perimeter.

Perimeter is the sum of all the sides of a many-sided figure.

Perimeter is measured in units of distance.

Think: How far is it around the outside?

(**Circumference** is the name given to the perimeter of a circle.)

Area is a whole region.

Area is measured in square units like ft^2, m^2, in^2, etc.

Think: How many squares make up the whole figure? Or: How much ground does that figure cover?

(Formulas for area vary. The ones you need are listed later in this chapter.)

ANGLES, LINES, RAYS, AND SEGMENTS

ANGLES

Angles are formed by two lines, rays or segments, which intersect at a point.

- **Vertex.**

  The point of intersection is called the **vertex**.

- **Angle symbol ($\angle$).**

  Angles are described using the angle symbol ($\angle$) followed by three points: One that lies on one side of the angle, the vertex, then a point that lies on the other side of the angle. The vertex is always written in the middle:

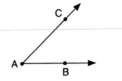

∠CAB or ∠BAC

Note that you could just call this ∠A because only one angle in the picture has a vertex of A. However, in a more complicated picture, you need to use the three-letter method of naming angles:

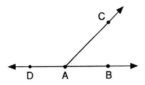

Which angle is ∠A? You can't tell, so use three letters.

Sometimes angles are represented by numbers or letter in a diagram:

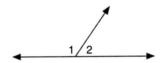

Here are some things you need to know about angles:

- **Angles are measured in degrees (°) on the SAT.**

- **An *acute angle* is less than 90°.**

- **A *right angle* equals 90° (⌐).**

- **An *obtuse angle* is greater than 90°.**

LINES

A **line** continues forever in both directions and may be referred to by a lowercase script letter, for example, line *ℓ*...

... or by two points on the line with a double arrow over the letters, for example, $\overleftrightarrow{AB}$:

RAYS

A **ray** has one endpoint and continues forever in one direction and may be referred to by two points on the line with one arrow over the letters, for example, $\overrightarrow{CD}$:

SEGMENTS

A **segment** has two endpoints and may be referred to by two points on the line with one bar over the letters, for example $\overline{EF}$:

STRAIGHT ANGLES

Straight angles are just lines. There are 180° around any point on *one side* of a straight line, or straight angle, and the sum of two or more angles that form a straight line is 180°.

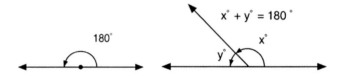

There are 360° around any point *if* you include both sides of the line.

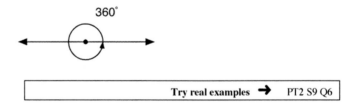

Try real examples ➡ PT2 S9 Q6

INTERSECTING LINES

Whenever two lines intersect, angles opposite each other, called **vertical angles**, are equal in measure.

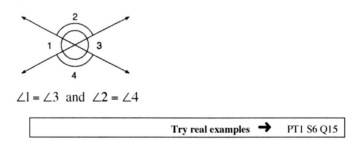

$\angle 1 = \angle 3$ and $\angle 2 = \angle 4$

Try real examples ➡ PT1 S6 Q15

PERPENDICULAR LINES

Perpendicular lines ($\perp$) form right angles.

Two lines that are perpendicular have negative reciprocal slopes.

PARALLEL LINES

Parallel lines are lines in the same plane that never intersect. They are always exactly the same distance apart. The symbol // is used to indicate lines are parallel. On a diagram, ▶▶ or a similar symbol is used. For example, line *ℓ* // *m*:

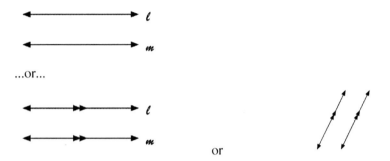

...or...

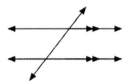   or

A line in the same plane that crosses parallel lines is called a transversal:

Parallel line problems usually deal with angles. The rule for parallel lines and transversals is fairly simple:

When a transversal intersects two or more parallel lines (and the transversal is not perpendicular to them), only two sizes of angles are formed:

> Angles bigger than 90° (obtuse angles)
> and
> Angles smaller than 90° (acute angles)

> All the small angles are equal.
>
> All the big angles are equal.
>
> Any small angle plus any big angle equals 180°.

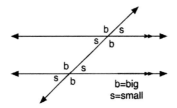

You have to be careful, though. On more complex diagrams, the test writers may be trying to trick you into thinking that an angle formed by one transversal equals an angle formed by a *second* transversal, but they aren't necessarily the same. Stick to one transversal at a time!

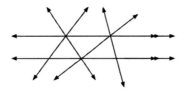

Try covering an unrelated transversal with your pencil so you can focus on the one transversal you're dealing with.

Try real examples ➡	PT3 S2 Q9

TICK MARKS

Tick marks on a geometric figure indicate that segments are the same length or that angles have the same measure. They rarely appear on the SAT, but you should use them to keep sides and angles organized.

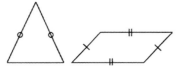

Sides and angles with the same tick marks have equal measure.

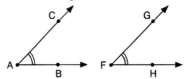

The measure of $\angle$GFH = the measure of $\angle$CAB or
$m\angle$GFH $= m\angle$CAB.

QUADRILATERALS

Quadrilaterals are simply 4-sided figures:

 are all quadrilaterals.

- **Square.**

    A square has four equal sides and 4 right angles:

- **Rectangle.**

    A rectangle has 4 right angles. Opposite sides are equal:

- **Parallelogram.**

    A parallelogram has both pairs of opposite sides parallel. Opposite sides are equal:

- **Trapezoid.**

    A trapezoid has one pair of opposite sides (called bases) parallel:

    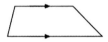

AREA AND PERIMETER

- **Square.**

    Area = $s \times s = s^2$

    Perimeter = $4s$

- **Rectangle.**

    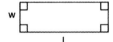

    Area = $l \times w$

    Perimeter = $2(l + w)$

- **Parallelogram.**

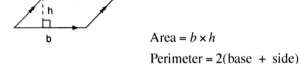

Area = $b \times h$

Perimeter = $2(\text{base} + \text{side})$

Note: The h (height) is the perpendicular distance between the top and bottom bases. Don't use the diagonal side for height!

- **Trapezoid.**

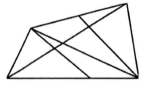

Note: You can always break a trapezoid into rectangles and right triangles! No need to learn special formulas.

TRIANGLES

There are a lot of triangle problems on the SAT. Here's what you need to know.

ANGLES

> The three angles of a triangle add up to $180°$.

Pretty basic stuff, right? Well, it is, but that doesn't mean the geometric figures are always easy. Take a look at the following. How many distinct triangles are in this figure?

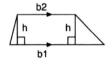

Can you spot 20 different triangles here? Keeping the angles straight can be tricky. It is often helpful to redraw a small portion of a confusing diagram, or to use your pencil to trace the outline of the one triangle you're dealing with.

> Here's another thing to watch: In any triangle, the longest side is opposite the largest angle; the smallest side is opposite the smallest angle.

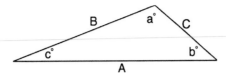

In this triangle, if $a° > b° > c°$, then $A > B > C$.

If two angles look the same, but the problem tells you that they are not the same, exaggerate the differences to see what's going on. For example, if the problem tells you that $\angle 1 > \angle 2$, but the diagram looks like this:

Redraw the triangle so that $\angle 1$ looks greater than $\angle 2$, like this:

You can often *Make Up Numbers* for angles, as long as you don't violate the $180°$ in a triangle rule.

Try real examples ➜	PT3 S8 Q4

AREA AND PERIMETER

The formula for finding the area of a triangle is:

$$\text{Area} = \frac{1}{2}\left(\text{base} \times \text{height}\right)$$

The only really tricky thing here is using the correct height. The height is the perpendicular distance from one vertex to the opposite side (the base). For right triangles, it's not too bad:

For acute triangles (where no angle is greater than $90°$) it's still pretty easy:

Sometimes the height is outside the triangle, which can be trickier. This can happen when the triangle is obtuse (has one angle larger than 90°). If you can't draw a perpendicular line from the vertex to the base inside the triangle, then extend the base and drop a perpendicular line to the extension:

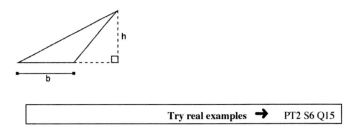

| | Try real examples ➡ PT2 S6 Q15 |

ISOSCELES TRIANGLES

An isosceles triangle has two equal sides and two equal angles, called base angles. The equal sides are opposite the equal angles:

Surprisingly, one of the most common places to find isosceles triangles is inside circles. Since all radii in a circle are the same length, any triangle with two radii as sides is isosceles:

For more on circles, see the Circles section.

| | Try real examples ➡ PT S6 Q11 |

EQUILATERAL TRIANGLES

Equilateral triangles have three equal sides and three equal angles that all measure 60°:

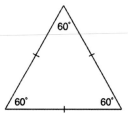

Look for equilateral triangles inside circles, and remember that a regular hexagon (six-sided figure) can be divided up into six equilateral triangles of the same size.

For more on equilateral triangles, see the 30-60-90 Triangle sections below.

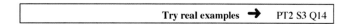

Try real examples ➡ PT2 S3 Q14

RIGHT TRIANGLES

Right triangles are simply triangles that contain one right angle. Since a right angle measures 90°, and all the interior angles of a triangle add up to 180°, the two non-right angles must add up to 90°.

The side opposite the right triangle has a special name: the **hypotenuse**. The hypotenuse is almost always represented by the letter c. The other sides are often referred to as a, b, or s, but any variable may be used to represent them.

• **Pythagorean Theorem.**

Good old Pythagoras. He was this guy, see, who did a lot of careful measuring, see, and came up with a theorem, see... He figured out there was a pretty simple way to relate the three sides of a right triangle (and **only** a right triangle). You should know it pretty well:

$$a^2 + b^2 = c^2$$

... where c is the hypotenuse and a and b are the sides (or *legs*, as they are sometimes called in a right triangle). You may have to use this occasionally, but the good news is that you normally only see a few types of right triangles on the SAT, and if you memorize them, you can get the right answers a lot faster and won't have to use the Pythagorean Theorem:

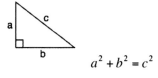

$$a^2 + b^2 = c^2$$

- **3-4-5 / 6-8-10 Triangles.**

   These triangles appear all the time on the SAT. They like to use them simply because the sides of the triangle just happen to work out evenly ($3^2 + 4^2 = 5^2$). They can also be multiples of the 3-4-5 triangle, like 6-8-10 triangles or 30-40-50 triangles. Keep your eye out for these, but remember, *this only applies to right triangles*:

- **5-12-13 Triangles.**

   Again no rocket science here, just another kind of right triangle that happens to work out evenly ($5^2 + 12^2 = 13^2$). Look for 10-24-26 versions of the triangle as well:

- **Right Isosceles Triangles (45-45-90).**

   You could use the Pythagorean Theorem to figure out 45-45-90 triangles, but you'll solve problems a lot faster if you just memorize them.

   Like all isosceles triangles, these have two equal sides and two equal angles. In this case, the two angles measure $45°$ each. Hence the name 45-45-90 triangle. (See how clever that is. Those Geometry dudes & dudettes are sharp!)

   Just remember that the hypotenuse is $\sqrt{2}$ times bigger than the sides:

   It's pretty easy when the two legs of a 45-45-90 triangle are integers. It gets trickier if the hypotenuse is an integer.

For example, if the hypotenuse = 8:

You expect to see the square root with the hypotenuse, but it's not there. So what do you do?

There are two approaches that might help:

The first is to remember that the hypotenuse equals $a\sqrt{2}$. So:

$$a\sqrt{2} = 8$$
$$a = \frac{8}{\sqrt{2}}$$

Don't forget to rationalize the denominator:

$$a = \frac{8}{\sqrt{2}} \times \frac{\sqrt{2}}{\sqrt{2}}$$
$$a = \frac{8\sqrt{2}}{\sqrt{2}\sqrt{2}}$$
$$a = \frac{8\sqrt{2}}{2} = 4\sqrt{2}$$

The second method is to remember the following: To go from the side to the hypotenuse, multiply by $\sqrt{2}$, so to go from the hypotenuse to the side, simply divide by $\sqrt{2}$. (The math is very similar to the problem above.)

To remember that the $\sqrt{2}$ is part of a 45-45-90 triangle, remember there are **2** equal sides and **2** equal angles, so you use $\sqrt{2}$.

Note: 45-45-90 triangles are exactly one half of a square!

- **30-60-90 Triangles.**

   These are similar to 45-45-90 triangles in that the sides don't work out evenly and there is a square root involved. That's pretty much where the similarity ends:

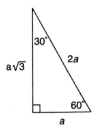

One common mistake is to think that the $\sqrt{}$ always goes on the hypotenuse of a right triangle. Please remember that the $a\sqrt{3}$ does NOT go on the hypotenuse. If you remember that $\sqrt{3} \approx 1.7$, you can figure out that the $a\sqrt{3}$ is actually the middle length side of the triangle, or the longer of the two legs:

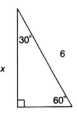

Ex) In the triangle above, what is the value of x?

To keep this straight, make a chart and fill in what you know:

a	
$a\sqrt{3}$	
$2a$	6

So, if $2a = 6$, $a = 3$ and therefore $a\sqrt{3} = 3\sqrt{3}$.

Note: 30-60-90 Triangles are exactly 1/2 of an equilateral triangle! So, if you know the sides of an equilateral triangle, you can figure out the height and therefore the area of the triangle!

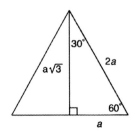

| **Try real examples** ➡ | PT1 S9 Q9 |
| | PT2 S9 Q15 |

SIMILAR TRIANGLES

Triangles are similar if all three angles of one triangle have the same measure as the three corresponding angles of the other triangle. The sides of similar triangles may not be the same length, but they are proportional (in the same ratio)! Here are two simple similar triangles:

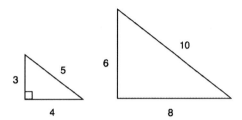

Note the ratio of *all* of the corresponding sides, and therefore the ratio of the two triangles, is the same, in this case 1:2.

Often, similar triangles on the SAT will be in overlapping figures. For example:

You have to be somewhat careful with overlapping similar triangles. Make sure you are comparing the correct sides. For example:

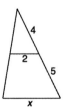

You might be tempted to say that the ratio of the two triangles above is 4:5, but it's not. Think of comparing one side of the small triangle to the *whole* corresponding side of the other triangle. The ratio here is 4:9. So to solve for *x*, set up a simple proportion:

$$\frac{4}{9} = \frac{x}{2} \quad \Leftarrow \text{ cross multiply}$$

$$4x = (2)(9)$$

$$x = \frac{18}{4} = \frac{9}{2} = 4.5$$

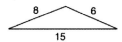

Try real examples ➡	PT1 S6 Q11

MISSION IMPOSSIBLE TRIANGLES

Oh, those nasty SAT chumps. They've decided to create hard problems using a relatively obscure Geometry rule. The rule deals with some triangles that just can't exist. Take a look at the triangle below and see if you can spot what's wrong:

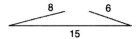

Spot it?

The problem here is that the sides of length 8 and 6 aren't long enough to form a triangle with a third side of length 15. Here's what this figure would really look like drawn to scale:

See how the two sides could never really form a triangle?

The rule they're testing is: "The sum of any two sides of a triangle must be larger than the third side." Makes sense when you think about it.

On some harder problems, they're likely to disguise this rule. A problem might be worded something like this:

> Ex) City X is 7 miles from city Y and city Y is 4 miles from city Z. If cities X, Y and Z do **NOT** lie on the same line, which of the following can be the distance, in miles, between city X and city Z?
>
> (A) 2
> (B) 3
> (C) 10
> (D) 11
> (E) 15

This is really just the same kind of question, but disguised. There is a clever way to think about all of these problems, and that is to draw one line segment representing one distance (or side of the triangle) and one circle, representing all the possibilities for the endpoint of the other distance. It's easier to show than describe:

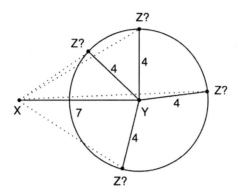

The distance from X to Y is fixed at 7. The distance from Y to Z is fixed at 4, but the problem doesn't tell us where Z is in relation to X or Y. The circle (with radius 4) represents all the different places Z could be. It could be very close to X (almost in between X and Y) or it could be very far from X (on the other side of Y). Since it can't be on a straight line, the distance from X to Z (represented by the dotted lines) could be anywhere between (but not including) 3 and 11. Therefore:

$3 <$ (distance from X to Z) < 11, so the answer is (C) 10.

Be careful because some problems allow the points to be on the same line, and some don't. Read the questions carefully!

TRIGONOMETRY (AS AN ALTERNATIVE SOLUTION)

You don't actually need to know any Trigonometry on the SAT, though you can use trigonometry to solve some problems that you could also solve using other methods (for example, working with 30-60-90 and 45-45-90 Triangles).

If you are extremely comfortable with using Trigonometric functions such as sine, cosine and tangent, feel free to use them, but remember there is almost always an easier way to solve a problem. Because of this, we're not going to go into trig functions. If you know them, good for you. If not, don't waste your time for the SAT I. (FYI, The SAT II Math Ic and Math IIc both test your understanding of Trigonometry.)

Review the chapter before trying these Math problems.

Remember to look for the **EASY WAY** to solve these problems.

Practice with these problems from *The Official SAT Study Guide:*

Practice Test	Section	Question
1	3	3, 6, 14, 16, 18
	6	2, 11, 13, 15, 16, 17
	9	4, 7, 9, 11, 15
2	3	10, 11, 12, 14, 16, 17
	6	2, 4, 8, 11, 15, 16
	9	2, 5, 6, 11, 12, 15, 17
3	2	4, 9, 13, 15
	4	5, 7, 8, 11, 13, 14, 18
	8	4, 6, 11, 16

All test, section, question and page numbers refer to *The Official SAT Study Guide* (2004)

Be sure to carefully score the sections from *The Official SAT Study Guide* and review the questions you miss. Figure out why you missed each question and how you can get it right the next time!

Additional Practice:

Math Homework Drill 5

Note: Each question is numbered to indicate where the question would most likely appear in a math section, and therefore shows relative level of difficulty. Questions with no answer choices are Fill-Ins.

> Solve each of the following problems and choose the best of the choices given. Use any available space for scratch work, if necessary.

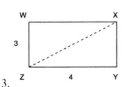

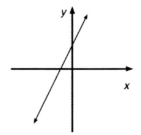

3.

Note: Figures not drawn to scale

If the figures above are both rectangles, which of the following is the longest line segment?

(A) *AB*
(B) *BD*
(C) *WX*
(D) *AD*
(E) *WZ*

2.

If the line above can be described by the function $f(x) = 2x + 3$, what is the ratio of *x* to *y* for any point (*x*, *y*) that falls on the line?

(A) 1 to 5
(B) 2 to 3
(C) 2 to 5
(D) 3 to 5
(E) It cannot be determined from the information given

14. If a line can be described by the equation $y = \frac{1}{3}x + 1$, which of the following equations describes a line that is perpendicular to this line?

(A) $y = \frac{1}{3}x - 1$

(B) $y = x + 3$

(C) $y = 3x - 1$

(D) $y = -3x + 2$

(E) $y = \frac{1}{9}x + \frac{1}{3}$

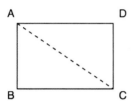

2.

In the rectangle above, if $AB = 4$ and $AD = 6$, what is the distance from A to C?

(A) $\sqrt{10}$

(B) $\sqrt{40}$

(C) 6

(D) $\sqrt{52}$

(E) 10

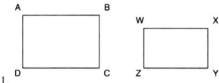

Note: Figures not drawn to scale.

11.

Rectangles $ABCD$ and $WXYZ$ have the same proportion between each rectangle's length and width. If $AB = 12$, $BC = 4$, and $WZ = 3$, what is the area of rectangle $WXYZ$?

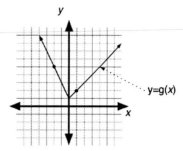

13.

The xy-coordinate plane above shows the graph of the function $y = g(x)$. If $y = f(x)$, where $f(x) = x^2 + 1$, was graphed on the same xy-coordinate plane, how many points of intersection would there be between $f(x)$ and $g(x)$?

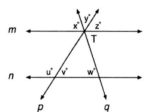

15.

Note: Figure not drawn to scale.

In the figure above, lines m and n are parallel and lines p and q intersect at point T. If $u = 140$, what is the value of z?

16. If $f(x) = 3x + 4$ and $g(x) = 4x + 3$, what is the value of x when $f(g(x)) = 33$?

18. Two rectangles with equal areas have widths of 4 and 6 respectively. If the total of their lengths is 10, what is the total of their areas?

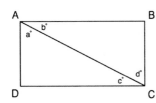

4.

Note: Figure <u>not</u> drawn to scale.

In rectangle ABCD shown above, if $d = 55$, what is the value of $b + c$?

(A) 35
(B) 45
(C) 55
(D) 70
(E) 90

8.   The area of a square of side length s is 144. A rectangle with an area of 84 has a length l equal to s and a width w. What is the value of $(l + w)^2$?

(A) 38
(B) 144
(C) 228
(D) 289
(E) 361

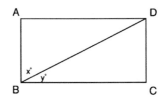

9.

In rectangle ABCD above, if $x = 60$ and $BD = 4$, what is the area of the rectangle?

(A) $2\sqrt{3}$
(B) $4\sqrt{3}$
(C) 6
(D) 8
(E) $8\sqrt{3}$

15.1. In the xy-coordinate plane, line m is described by the equation $y = 2x + 3$. If the graph of the equation $y = x^2 - b$ intersects line m at the point where line m crosses the x-axis, what is the value of b?

(A) $-\sqrt{3}$
(B) $2\sqrt{3}$
(C) $\dfrac{3}{2}$
(D) $\dfrac{9}{4}$
(E) 3

Answers:

CIRCLES

Do you hate circles? Well, stop it! At least for the SAT. Circle problems are not nearly as hard as people fear. Here's everything you need to know about circles.

ANGLES

There are 360° around the center of a circle.

You should be able to quickly recognize that 90° makes up 1/4 of the circle and 180° makes up half the circle. Half of a circle is called a *semicircle*.

Since triangles often appear inside circles, look for angles formed by sides of a triangle with one vertex on the center of the circle.

Consider drawing circles around regular polygons or around a point on a line and looking at the angles formed.

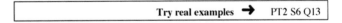

Try real examples ➡ PT2 S6 Q13

RADIUS AND DIAMETER

The radius (*r*) is a line from the center of a circle to the edge of the circle. All radii in a circle are the same length.

The diameter (*d*) is a line segment drawn from one side of a circle to the other, though the center. A diameter is the longest segment that can be drawn in a circle. The diameter is twice as long as the radius: $d = 2r$.

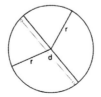

AREA

You should definitely memorize the formula for the area of a circle:

$$A = \pi r^2$$

Where A is the area, r is the radius and π (pi) is approximately 3.14.

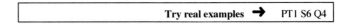

Try real examples ➡	PT1 S6 Q4

CIRCUMFERENCE

The circumference (C) is the distance around the edge of a circle. It's the special name given to the perimeter of a circle. You should memorize both forms of this equation:

$$C = 2\pi r \quad \text{or} \quad C = \pi d$$

Note that $2r$ and d are interchangeable.

Note: People mix up area and circumference all the time. Pay close attention to the problem, and don't rush or you're likely to make the same mistake.

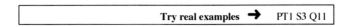

Try real examples ➡	PT1 S3 Q11

CHORDS

Chords don't appear too often on the SAT. A chord is just a line segment with its endpoints on the edge of a circle. The diameter is the longest chord, but chords can also be very short:

ARCS

An arc is a portion or segment of a circle. Arcs have a degree measure of 0° to 360° and are labeled by their endpoints. A *minor arc* is less than 180°. Assume that the SAT is asking about minor arcs unless the problem tells you otherwise.

Arcs also have an arc length, measured along the curve of the arc. An Arc length is a portion of the circumference of a circle:

Achieve Tutorials MAximum SAT

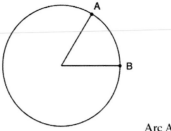

Arc AB or $\overset{\frown}{AB}$

PROPORTIONALITY IN CIRCLES

Circles are beautiful simple things. Just about everything in a circle is proportional: angles to arcs to shaded regions. Take a look at the following diagram:

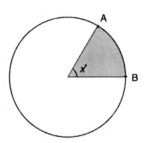

In the diagram, [the angle $x°$ compared to $360°$] is proportional to [the length of arc AB compared to the whole circumference] is proportional to [the shaded region compared to the area of the whole circle]:

$$\frac{x°}{360°} = \frac{\text{length of arc AB}}{\text{circumference}} = \frac{\text{area of shaded region}}{\text{area of circle}}$$

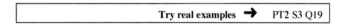

Try real examples ➡	PT2 S3 Q19

CIRCLES AND OTHER FIGURES

When circles appear in overlapping figure problems, there are only two parts of a circle that might correspond to the parts of a triangle or rectangle: the radius or the diameter. Look for the corresponding parts:

In this case, the height of the rectangle is the same as the diameter of the circle.

TANGENTS

A tangent is a line that touches another line or curve at one and only one point. On the SAT, tangents are usually confined to circles:

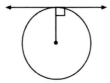

Tangents to circles are always perpendicular to the radius that is drawn to the point where the tangent touches the circle (the point of tangency). This is handy, since tangent lines often form right triangles.

CIRCLES ON THE COORDINATE PLANE

Sometimes the SAT throws in problems that deal with a circle on the *xy*-axes. Usually, they just want you to understand a few things about horizontal or vertical segments in the circle (often simply diameters).

If you know the radius of a circle and the center of a circle, it's easy to find 4 points on the circle: The points that are directly above, below, left and right of the circle. Just count the length of the radius up, down, left or right from the center. In the example below, the center of the circle is at (2, -2) and the radius is 3:

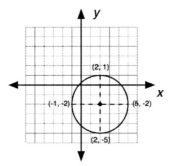

Note that any vertical or horizontal line that passes through the circle (and is not tangent to the circle) intersects the circle at two points. If the segment is vertical, the *x*-coordinates of the points of intersection are the same, and if the segment is horizontal, the *y*-coordinates of the points of intersection are the same.

Try real examples ➡ PT2 S9 Q8

ODD SHAPES

BREAKING UP INTO FAMILIAR SHAPES

The SAT will really only ask you to deal with a few basic shapes. If you see something weird, try to break it up into those familiar shapes that you know how to deal with. Here's a really tough example:

Might be broken up into…

… a semicircle, a right triangle and an equilateral triangle. This one is a little far-fetched, but you get the idea.

OVERLAPPING FIGURES AND SHADED REGIONS

Almost all shaded region problems boil down to the same basic principle:

To find the area of a shaded region, get the area of the whole figure, then subtract the area of the unshaded part.

You should also look out for shaded region problems in which the whole figure can be divided into equal shapes. A rectangle, for example, might be divided into 2 or 4 or 8 or more congruent triangles. For example:

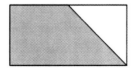

This figure might be broken up into 4 equal triangles like this:

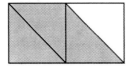

So now it's pretty easy to see that the shaded region is 3/4 of the whole figure.

Try real examples ➔ PT1 S3 Q6; S9 Q11

THREE-DIMENSIONAL FIGURES

Don't fear the three-dimensional figures on the test. If you need a formula for volume or surface area of a difficult figure, they'll give it to you. And much of the time, it's not even a 3-D problem…

NOT REALLY 3-D

Most problems on the SAT that look like they're about 3-D figures are really about two-dimensional figures hidden in the 3-D picture. And most often they are about triangles. So keep an eye out for triangle problems within the 3-D image.

SURFACE AREA

The surface area of a figure is simply the sum of the areas of all the faces of the figure.

For rectangular solids, remember to count all six sides. Or you can just count the three faces you can see and multiply the sum by 2:

In a rectangular solid, the front face is the same as the back face, the left is the same as the right, and the top is the same as the bottom.

VOLUME

Volumes are always in cubic units and should never be confused with area. In general, the SAT deals with *right* figures whose edges are perpendicular to the base. In *right* figures:

$$\text{Volume} = \text{area of base} \times \text{height}$$

There are only a couple of specific volume formulas you should know. The first is pretty easy: It deals with rectangular solids:

- **Rectangular solids.**

    Volume = $l \times w \times h$

- **Cylinders.**

    The volume of a cylinder deals with the circular base and the height:

    Volume = $\pi r^2 h$

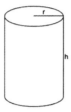

For figures like cones or pyramids formulas will be given on the test.

Try real examples ➜	PT1 S3 Q16

VISUALS

Sometimes one of the hardest things to do is to "see" the problem correctly. Lots of SAT problems rely on careful perception of the figure. Redraw the figure, break it down into manageable pieces, turn the page around to get a different perspective, etc.

Try real examples ➜	PT2 S3 Q4

Review the chapter before trying these Math problems.

Remember to look for the **EASY WAY** to solve these problems.

Practice with these problems from *The Official SAT Study Guide:*

Practice Test	Section	Question
1	3	6, 11, 16
	6	4
	9	11
2	3	4, 19
	6	13
	9	8
3	2	11, 19
	4	2
	8	8, 10

All test, section, question and page numbers refer to *The Official SAT Study Guide* (2004)

Be sure to carefully score the sections from *The Official SAT Study Guide* and review the questions you miss. Figure out why you missed each question and how you can get it right the next time!

Additional Practice:

Math Homework Drill 6

Note: Each question is numbered to indicate where the question would most likely appear in a math section, and therefore shows relative level of difficulty. Questions with no answer choices are Fill-Ins.

Solve each of the following problems and choose the best of the choices given. Use any available space for scratch work, if necessary.

6. Points *A*, *B*, and *C* lie on a circle of radius 4. If *d* is the distance along the circle from point *A* to point *C* NOT through point *B*, what is the distance from point *A* to point *C* through point *B*, in terms of *d*?

    (A) $4 - d$
    (B) $d - 16\pi$
    (C) $16\pi - 2d$
    (D) $2d^2 - 4$
    (E) $8\pi - d$

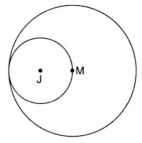

11.

In the figure above, *M* is the center of the larger circle and *J* is the center of the smaller circle. If the area of the smaller circles is 25π, what is the diameter of the larger circle?

(A) 5
(B) 10
(C) 5π
(D) 20
(E) 25

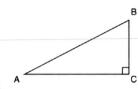

16.

A square with a perimeter of y has the same area as the right triangle shown above. If AC is twice the length of BC, what is the length of BC in terms of y?

(A) $2\sqrt{y}$

(B) $\dfrac{y}{4}$

(C) $\dfrac{y}{2}$

(D) $\dfrac{y^2}{4}$

(E) $\dfrac{y^2}{16}$

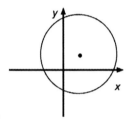

18.

Note: Figure not drawn to scale.

The circle shown above has a radius of 5. If the center of the circle is the point $(x, f(x))$, where $f(x) = 2x + 1$, which of the following describes a point that is NOT located along the circumference of the circle?

(A) $(x + 5, 2x + 1)$
(B) $(x + 5, 2x + 6)$
(C) $(x, 2x - 4)$
(D) $(x - 5, 2x + 1)$
(E) $(x, 2x + 6)$

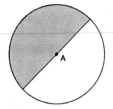

4.

If the circle above with center A has a circumference of 40π, what is the area of the shaded region?

(A) 20π
(B) 80π
(C) 160π
(D) 200π
(E) 400π

17. In the xy-coordinate plane, a circle with its center at $(5,3)$ is tangent to the y-axis at $y = 3$. If line m intersects this circle at this tangent point and a point where the circle intersects the x-axis, what is the greatest possible slope of line m?

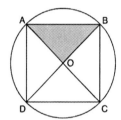

11.1.

If square ABCD is inscribed inside circle O as shown above, the shaded region is what fraction of the area of circle O?

(A) $\dfrac{1}{4\pi}$

(B) $\dfrac{1}{2\pi}$

(C) $\dfrac{1}{4}$

(D) $\dfrac{1}{\sqrt{2}}$

(E) $\dfrac{\pi}{4}$

Answers:

MATH LESSON 7

THE WEIRD STUFF PART I

REMAINDER

The trick on SAT remainder problems is that the test writers usually don't give you the number you're dividing into. For example:

> Ex) When x is divided by 7, the remainder is 2. What is the remainder when $6x$ is divided by 7?

We could rewrite this as: $7\overset{R2}{\overline{\smash{\big)}x}}$

You simply have to pick a number that satisfies the original question. It is often easiest to simply add the divisor and the remainder (in the example above, add 7 + 2) and use that number:

$$
\begin{array}{r}
1R2 \\
7\overline{\smash{\big)}9} \\
-7 \\
\hline
2
\end{array}
$$

Then just multiply 6 x 9 and find the new remainder.

$$
\begin{array}{r}
7R5 \\
7\overline{\smash{\big)}54} \\
-49 \\
\hline
5
\end{array}
$$

So the remainder is 5.

One tricky remainder problem involves a division problem in which the divisor is bigger than the number being divided. In that case, the number being divided is the remainder. For example:

$$
\begin{array}{r}
0R5 \\
7\overline{\smash{\big)}5} \\
-0 \\
\hline
5
\end{array}
$$

Try real examples ➡ PT2 S9 Q9

SEQUENCES AND SERIES

New on the SAT are questions involving arithmetic or geometric sequences. You'll often see these problems dealing with real life situations like population growth or even radioactive decay. Don't worry, though, these problems are not that tough. You just need to know how to deal with them.

A sequence is just a series of numbers that follows some sort of pattern.

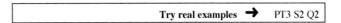
Try real examples ➡ PT3 S2 Q2

ARITHMETIC SEQUENCES

An arithmetic sequence is a series of numbers in which there is a constant number added to each proceeding term. For example:

2, 12, 22, 32, 42, 52...

is an arithmetic sequence in which 10 is added to one term to get the next term in the sequence.

Usually you won't need to do more than simply recognize the sequence and write it down. However, in case you need to figure out something more complicated, for example, what the 505th term in the sequence is, you can use the formula for arithmetic sequence:

$$a_n = a_1 + k(n-1)$$

... in which a_n is the "nth term" of the sequence, a_1 is the first term of the sequence, k is the number added to each successive term, and n is the number of the term you're trying to find.

> Ex) In the sequence 5, 7, 9, 11, 13, ... what is the value of the 343th term in the sequence?
>
> (A) 686
> (B) 687
> (C) 688
> (D) 689
> (E) 670

To solve it, figure out the arithmetic sequence formula for this sequence. Each term is just the preceding term plus 2, so a_1 is 5, k is 2 and n is, of course, 343:

$$a_{343} = 5 + 2(343 - 1)$$
$$a_{343} = 5 + 2(342)$$
$$a_{343} = 5 + 684$$
$$a_{343} = 689$$

So the answer is (D).

There is an alternative way to solve this question using patterns. If you were to write out a few more terms in the sequence, you would see that the last digit starts to repeat after the 5th term:

5, 7, 9, 11, 13, 15, 17, 19, 21, 23, 25, ...

So every 5th term must end in 3! Look for a term near the 343rd term that is a multiple of 5. How about the 340th? Well, that term must end in 3, so the 341st term must end in 5, the 342nd term must end in 7, and, voila!, the 343rd term must end in 9. Only one answer choice ends in 9, so the answer is (D).

GEOMETRIC SEQUENCES

A geometric sequence is a series of numbers in which there is a constant multiplier between each term. For example:

2, 12, 72, 432, 2592, 15552...

...is a geometric sequence in which one term is multiplied by 6 to get the next term in the sequence.

Geometric sequences are examples of *exponential growth.*

Usually you won't need to do more than simply recognize the sequence and write it down. However, in case you need to figure out something more complicated, for example, what the 234th term in the sequence is, you can use the formula for arithmetic sequence:

$$a_n = a_1 \times m^{(n-1)}$$

...in which a_n is the "nth term" of the sequence, a_1 is the first term of the sequence, m is the multiplier, and n is the number of the term you're trying to find.

Ex) In the sequence 1, 3, 9, 27, 81... what is the value of the 11th term?

(A) 63
(B) 243
(C) 6561
(D) 19683
(E) 59049

To solve it, figure out the geometric sequence formula for this sequence. Each term is just the preceding term times 3, so a_1 is 1, m is 3 and n is, of course, 11:

$$a_{11} = 1 \times 3^{(11-1)}$$
$$a_{11} = 3^{(10)}$$
$$a_{11} = 59049$$

So the answer is (E).

There are two alternative ways to solve this question. First, you could carefully use your calculator. It wouldn't be too hard to get to the 11th term. Or second, you could use patterns again. If you were to write out a few more terms in the sequence, you would see that the last digit starts to repeat after the 4th term:

1, 3, 9, 27, 81, 243...

So every 4th term must end in 7! Look for a term near the 11th term that is a multiple of 4. How about the 12th? Well, the 12th term must end in 7, so the 11th term must end in 9. Only one answer choice ends in 9, so the answer is (E).

| | Try real examples ➜ PT2 S6 Q14 |

CHARTS AND GRAPHS

Charts and graphs can be deceptive. Always read graphs and charts carefully. Information is often hidden in titles and footnotes. Here's a real world example of a deceptive chart from a credit card offering 5% cash back on purchases:

Get 5% CASH BACK through November 30, 2005 on your everyday purchases.

	Sample monthly spending	Sample cash back earned during total promotion period
Supermarkets	$120.00	$18.00
Discount Stores	$65.00	$9.75
Drug Stores	$35.00	$5.25
Gas Station	$75.00	$11.25
Total	$295.00	**$44.25**

Actual amounts may vary depending on card usage. Cash back is not earned on returned purchases, cash advances, convenience checks fees and finance charges. Promotional period begins Sept. 1, 2005.

What's wrong with this chart? The chart leads readers to believe that if they spend $295, they'll get $44.25 back. But that's not 5%! Let's take a closer look at all the "Sample cash back" numbers in the gray column. None of them are 5% of the amounts to the left! They're all 15%! How can they get away with this?

It's all in the headings. The left column is "Sample monthly spending," the right column is "Sample cash back earned during total promotion period," which lasts **three** months!

The lesson is pretty simple: read charts and graphs carefully. Check headings, titles, footnote and units.

A note on graphs: If you have to approximate information on charts, try using the edge of your answer sheet to line up, for example, the top of a bar graph with the scale on the left axis.

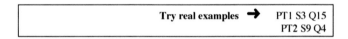

Try real examples ➜ PT1 S3 Q15
PT2 S9 Q4

PROBABILITY

Probabilities indicate the likelihood that some event will happen. **Probabilities are on a scale of 0 to 1.** If there is no chance something will happen, the probability is 0. If an occurrence is assured, the probability is 1.

You could take a yearlong course on computing complex probabilities, but fortunately you don't need all of that to ace probability questions on the SAT.

SINGLE EVENTS

A simple probability of one event occurring follows the formula:

$$\frac{\text{the number of desired outcomes}}{\text{the total number of possible outcomes}}$$

Ex) What is the probability that when a standard six-sided die is rolled, the number on the top will be a 2 or a 4?

The solution is:

$$\frac{\text{the number of desired outcomes}}{\text{the total number of possible outcomes}} = \frac{2}{6} = \frac{1}{3}$$

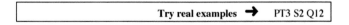

Try real examples ➜ PT3 S2 Q12

MULTIPLE EVENTS: NO CHANGE IN FUTURE OUTCOMES

Often multiple events involve things that don't change the total possible outcomes from event to event, for example flipping a coin or rolling a die. Flipping a coin once doesn't change what will happen when you flip it a second time.

When dealing with these types of multiple events, compute the possibility that each individual event will occur, then multiply the resulting probabilities:

> Ex) What is the probability that flipping a coin three times will result in three heads? Ignore the possibility that the coin will land on its side.

The probability that the first flip will be heads is 1/2, the probability of getting heads on the second flip is 1/2 and, surprise, surprise, the probability of getting heads on the third flip is 1/2. So:

$$\frac{1}{2} \times \frac{1}{2} \times \frac{1}{2} = \frac{1}{8}$$

MULTIPLE EVENTS: WITH CHANGE IN FUTURE OUTCOMES

Sometimes multiple events involve a change in the possible outcomes for future events. For example, if you have a bag with two red marbles and two black marbles, and you pull out one red marble and don't put it back, you change the number of marbles in the bag.

To compute probability for this type of problem, you need to treat each event separately, and *assume that you got what you wanted* in order to compute the probability of the next event!

> Ex) Enrique has a bag of candy that contains 6 peanut butter bars and 8 chocolate bars. If he reaches into the bag and pulls out two bars at random, what is the probability that they will both be peanut butter bars?

First, treat this as two successive events. The chance that Enrique will pull out a peanut butter bar on the first grab is:

$$\frac{\text{the number of peanut butter bars}}{\text{the total number of candy bars}} = \frac{6}{14} = \frac{3}{7}$$

For the second grab, we must assume that he pulled out a peanut butter bar the first time, so the probability of grabbing a peanut butter bar the second times is:

$$\frac{\text{the number of peanut butter bars left}}{\text{the total number of candy bars left}} = \frac{5}{13}$$

So the probability that he will pull out two peanut butter bars in a row is the product of the two individual probabilities:

$$\frac{3}{7} \times \frac{5}{13} = \frac{15}{91}$$

THE PROBABILITY TREE: MULTIPLE ORDERS OF EVENTS

There are times when probability computations become more difficult, but there will usually be a simple way to solve the problem. You can use a probability tree to see all the possible outcomes. These work particularly well on problems with fairly few possible outcomes, like flipping coins. Here's the probability tree for flipping a coin four times:

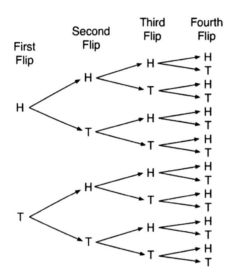

Following the paths of arrows from left to right shows you all 16 possible orders of the four flips. For example, if you get heads on the first flip, you have eight more possible orders. If you get heads on the first flip and tails on the second flip, you have four more possible orders.

Using the tree above, what is the probability that you will get heads three times and tails once? The right hand column indicates the total number of possible arrangements of flips, in this case 16. Follow through from left to right and track all the orders that result in 3 heads and 1 tails:

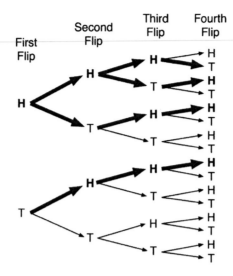

So there are 4 desired results out of 16 possible results, or 1 out of 4 when reduced.

This problem was more difficult to do without the probability tree because there are multiple orders of the desired result possible. It would be fairly easy to compute the probability of getting H–H–H–T $(\frac{1}{2} \times \frac{1}{2} \times \frac{1}{2} \times \frac{1}{2} = \frac{1}{16})$ but what about H–H–T–H, H–T–H–H or T–H–H–H? Without the probability tree, you would have to figure out how many orders were possible (4 in this case), compute the probability of each individual order happening (they'll all be the same). Then add the probabilities of the individual orders:

$$\text{HHHT} \quad \frac{1}{2} \times \frac{1}{2} \times \frac{1}{2} \times \frac{1}{2} = \frac{1}{16}$$

$$\text{HHTH} \quad \frac{1}{2} \times \frac{1}{2} \times \frac{1}{2} \times \frac{1}{2} = \frac{1}{16}$$

$$\text{HTHH} \quad \frac{1}{2} \times \frac{1}{2} \times \frac{1}{2} \times \frac{1}{2} = \frac{1}{16}$$

$$\text{THHH} \quad \frac{1}{2} \times \frac{1}{2} \times \frac{1}{2} \times \frac{1}{2} = \frac{1}{16}$$

$$\frac{4}{16} = \frac{1}{4}$$

GEOMETRIC PROBABILITY

This is just a fancy name for a simple idea. Geometric probabilities simply ask you to find a ratio of a small portion of a figure to an entire figure. Here's an example:

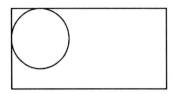

Ex) In the figure above, if the radius of the circle is 3 and the area of the rectangle is 128, what is the probability that a point chosen at random in the rectangle will fall within the circle?

To solve it, simply solve for the ratio of the area of the circle to the area of the entire figure, the rectangle:

Area of the circle = $\pi \times r^2 = \pi \times 3^2 = 9\pi$

So the probability is: $\dfrac{9\pi}{128}$

Try real examples ➡ PT2 S3 Q7

COMBINATIONS / PERMUTATIONS

Combinations and permutations (you don't need to know the names) deal with how many different groups of things are possible or how many different arrangements of things are possible. You could learn complicated formulas, the "real" way to do these problems, or you could learn the basic, easy way!

Many of these problems can be solved by simply writing out all of the possible arrangements or groups. If it looks like it won't take too long, try to write them all out. If it looks like the numbers are going to be pretty big, it's time to do some math.

If you have to do the math, the most important question to ask is: *Does order matter?*

Here's a simple breakdown of the different types of problems:

Combinations	Permutations
Groups	Arrangements, orders
For example, if you have 3 items, A, B and C, how many different groups of three can they form? Only one, because *order doesn't matter.*	For example, if you have 3 items, A, B and C, how many different arrangements of three can they form? Six, because *order matters.*
A B C	A B C A C B B A C B C A C A B C B A
You typically get a reasonably small number of possible groups, but they can be slightly harder to compute.	You typically get more orders than you think are possible, but these are actually the easier to compute.
Remember this: If order **D**oesn't **M**atter, **D**ivide and **M**ultiply. (D-M-D-M)	Remember this: If **O**rder **M**atters, **O**nly **M**ultiply (O-M-O-M)

Let's take a look at what that means:

ORDER MATTERS: ARRANGEMENTS AND PERMUTATIONS

Think of the items you are going to arrange as "game pieces," and the slots they will fill as "spaces."

- **Draw out the spaces.**

    The first step of solving one of these problems is to determine how many spaces you're looking to fill. You may not use all of the game pieces, so be cautious. Draw an underline for each of the spaces.

- **Fill in the first space.**

    The next step is to determine how many different game pieces could fit in the first space. Write the number above the first underline.

- **Fill in the remaining spaces.**

    Then, determine how many different game pieces are *left* to fit in the second space. If you're "using up" game pieces, it is usually one less than the previous space. Remember, you have to assume that one of the game pieces went into the first space. Write the number above the second underline.

Proceed to fill in all the spaces as above.

- **Multiply.**

    Finally, remember, if *Order Matters, Only Multiply*. So, multiply the numbers together. That's it!

Let's start with a simple example:

> Ex) There are five runners in a race. If the first place runner is awarded a gold medal, the second place runner a silver medal and the third place runner a bronze medal, how many different arrangements of medal winners are possible?

Here's the solution:

We're really dealing with only three spaces: gold, silver and bronze. Draw the spaces:

— — —

There are 5 different runners in the race; so 5 different people could finish first. Write that in the first space:

<u>5</u> — —

After one runner finishes first, there are only 4 runners left who could come in second:

<u>5</u> <u>4</u> —

And after the first and second places are filled, there are only 3 runners left competing for third:

<u>5</u> <u>4</u> <u>3</u>

Now just multiply:

$5 \times 4 \times 3 = 60$

So there are 60 possible arrangements of medal winners.

Try real examples ➡	PT1 S6 Q14

ORDER DOESN'T MATTER: GROUPS AND COMBINATIONS

Again, think of the items you are going to arrange as "game pieces," and the slots they will fill as "spaces."

- **Draw out the spaces.**

  The first step of solving one of these problems is the same as when order matters: Determine how many spaces you're looking to fill. You may not use all of the game pieces, so be cautious. Draw an underline for each of the spaces.

- **Number the spaces.**

  The second step is different from the process above. Simply number the spaces, starting with 1, and write the number under each space. If you have 4 spaces, you will number 1 through 4 below the spaces.

- **Fill in the first space.**

  The next step is to determine how many different game pieces could fit in the first space. Write the number above the first underline.

- **Fill in the remaining spaces.**

  Then, determine how many different game pieces are *left* to fit in the second space. If you're "using up" game pieces, it is usually one less than the previous space. Remember, you have to assume that one of the game pieces went into the first space. Write the number above the second underline.

  Proceed to fill in all the spaces as above.

- **Divide and Multiply.**

  Finally, remember, if Order Doesn't Matter, Divide and Multiply. So, multiply the numbers across the top and divide by the numbers on the bottom. That's it!

Let's start with a simple example from a politically correct track meet:

> Ex) There are five runners in a race. In order to make the top three runners all feel good about themselves, the first three runners are each awarded an identical gold star. How many different groups of gold star winners are possible?

Note the difference here: We're talking about groups, not arrangements.

Here's the solution:

We're dealing with only three spaces, for the first three runners to finish. Draw the spaces:

— — —

Next, number the spaces on the bottom:

$$\frac{\quad}{1} \ \frac{\quad}{2} \ \frac{\quad}{3}$$

There are 5 different runners in the race, so 5 different people could finish first. Write that in the first space:

$$\frac{5}{1} \ \frac{\quad}{2} \ \frac{\quad}{3}$$

After one runner finishes first, there are only 4 runners left who could finish second:

$$\frac{5}{1} \ \frac{4}{2} \ \frac{\quad}{3}$$

And after the first and second places are filled, there are only 3 runners left competing for third:

$$\frac{5}{1} \ \frac{4}{2} \ \frac{3}{3}$$

Now just multiply and divide:

$$\frac{5}{1} \times \frac{4}{2} \times \frac{3}{3} = 10$$

So there are 10 possible politically correct groups of gold star winners.

Combination and permutation problems do get more complicated when dealing with game pieces from separate, unrelated groups. For example, if you were forming a four-person congressional committee with two Senators and two Representatives, you would have to deal with the Senators and Representatives separately:

> Ex)   A four-person congressional committee is to be composed of two members of the US Senate and two members of the US House of Representatives. If there are 100 Senators and 435 Representatives, how many different, unique committees could be formed?

Here's how you do it:

First, we have to deal with the Senators and Representatives as completely separate groups, then multiply the results together.

The first question to ask is, does order matter? The answer is no, Order **D**oesn't **M**atter so **D**ivide and **M**ultiply.

There are two spaces for Senators and two spaces for Representatives, so:

$$[\underline{\ \ } \ \underline{\ \ }] \times [\underline{\ \ } \ \underline{\ \ }]$$

We need to number the spaces *in each group*:

$$[\underset{1}{\underline{\ \ }} \ \underset{2}{\underline{\ \ }}] \times [\underset{1}{\underline{\ \ }} \ \underset{2}{\underline{\ \ }}]$$

Next write in the possible numbers of Senators and Representatives who could fill the positions and calculate your answer:

$$\overset{\text{Senators}}{\left[\frac{100}{1} \times \frac{99}{2} \right]} \times \overset{\text{Representatives}}{\left[\frac{435}{1} \times \frac{434}{2} \right]} = 467{,}255{,}250$$

Note that the number is huge! You probably won't get something quite this large on the SAT, even though the math is easy on your calculator.

Review the chapter before trying these Math problems.

Remember to look for the **EASY WAY** to solve these problems.

Practice with these problems from *The Official SAT Study Guide:*

Practice Test	Section	Question
1	3	4, 15
	6	5, 14
2	3	5, 7
	6	3, 14, 17, 18
	9	4, 9
3	2	2, 3, 20
	4	2
	8	5, 15

All test, section, question and page numbers refer to *The Official SAT Study Guide* (2004)

Be sure to carefully score the sections from *The Official SAT Study Guide* and review the questions you miss. Figure out why you missed each question and how you can get it right the next time!

Additional Practice:

Math Homework Drill 7

Note: Each question is numbered to indicate where the question would most likely appear in a math section, and therefore shows relative level of difficulty. Questions with no answer choices are Fill-Ins.

Solve each of the following problems and choose the best of the choices given. Use any available space for scratch work, if necessary.

3. RULE: In a series, each number is the sum of the previous number and that number minus 3.

If a series of numbers following the rule above begins with 4, which of the following numbers CANNOT be in the series?

(A) 5
(B) 7
(C) 9
(D) 11
(E) 19

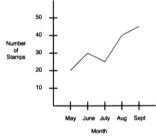

4.

The graph above shows how many stamps Ms. Caul had in her stamp collection at the beginning of each month from May to September. If Ms. Caul sold 5 of her stamps during August, how many stamps did she buy during August?

(A) 0
(B) 5
(C) 10
(D) 15
(E) 20

5. A six-sided die has a number from 1 to 6 written on each side with no number repeated. If Kari rolls the die twice, what is the probability that the first roll will be a lower number than the second roll?

(A) $\dfrac{1}{6}$

(B) $\dfrac{5}{12}$

(C) $\dfrac{1}{2}$

(D) $\dfrac{7}{12}$

(E) $\dfrac{19}{36}$

14. Karina has five different pictures she is going to arrange in a horizontal row on the wall of her bedroom. How many different arrangements could she make with these pictures if she always uses all five pictures?

Decimal	Letter
3.4 - 4.0	A
2.4 - 3.3	B
1.4 - 2.3	C
0.7 - 1.3	D
0.0 - 0.6	F

7.

The teacher of a math class uses the decimal conversion chart above to assign students their letter grades. If the teacher uses the function $G(p) = 0.1p - 5.5$ to determine the decimal grade, where p is the total number of points earned on all tests, what letter grade would a student with 79 total points get?

(A) A
(B) B
(C) C
(D) D
(E) F

Answers:

MATH LESSON 8

GROUPS

Group problems typically deal with overlapping subgroups and trying to figure out how many people are in the whole group. The best way to deal with these is usually using a Venn diagram, which is made up of two or more overlapping circles.

In a simple Venn diagram, two groups overlap:

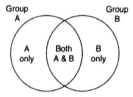

Occasionally there will be another group totally outside group A and group B.

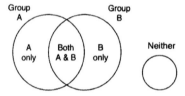

Sometimes three groups overlap:

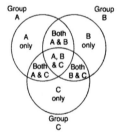

The labels on the outside for group A, B and C indicate how many are in that group as a whole, while the numbers inside the regions of the circle represent the number in only that region.

To determine how many people there are total, add up all the numbers INSIDE the circles.

Here are some examples:

Ex) 17 people in a sports club play tennis, 14 play basketball, and 7 play both basketball and tennis. If everyone in the club plays either tennis or basketball, how many people are in the club?

Here's the solution:

First, draw your Venn diagram:

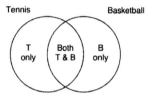

Next, fill in the information you know:

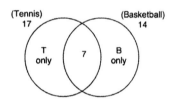

Now you can fill in the missing information. If 17 people play tennis, and 7 of those also play basketball, then 10 must play tennis only. If 14 people play basketball, and 7 also play tennis, that leaves 7 who just play basketball:

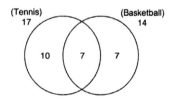

Now just add up the numbers *inside* the circles:
$10 + 7 + 7 = 24$, so 24 people are in the club.

Here's another:

Ex) In a class, 10 students take Spanish, 12 take French, 36 take Norwegian and 12 take no foreign language. If 5 students take Spanish and French, 3 students take French and Norwegian, 2 take Norwegian and Spanish, and 2 take all three (Norwegian, Spanish and French), how many students are in the class?

Here's the solution:

First, draw a 3-circle Venn diagram. Don't forget to add a separate circle for the people who study no language:

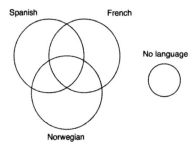

Now carefully fill in the numbers you know:

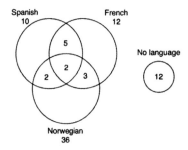

Now look at the circle for Spanish. Of the 10 Spanish students, 9 are in the overlap regions, leaving only one for the Spanish only region. Likewise, only 2 are left for the French only region and 29 are left for the Norwegian only region:

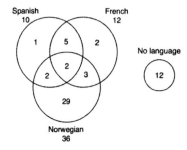

Now simply add all the numbers in the circles (including the number for the "no language" group):

1 + 5 + 2 + 2 + 2 + 3 + 29 + 12 = 56 total students.

Some group problems deal with logic problems involving one group completely within another group. For these problems, always draw a Venn diagram:

Ex) If all Fids are Fads, then which of the following must be true?

(A) No Fads are Fids
(B) All Fads are Fids
(C) No Fids are Fads
(D) Some Fads are Fids
(E) Some Fids are not Fads

To solve it, draw a Venn diagram showing how all Fids are Fads:

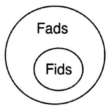

Note that the Fids group fits completely within the Fads group. A Fid must be a Fad. Some but not all Fads must be Fids. Answer choice (D) is correct.

DIGITS

A digit is simply any of the numerals 0 through 9. On the SAT, digits are often represented by capital letters.

DIGIT NAMES

You should know the digit names. You probably forgot is the Units digit (also known as the ones digit).

5,235.698

Thousands
Hundreds
Tens
Units (Ones)
Tenths
Hundredths
Thousandths

MISSING DIGITS

Missing digit problems typically involve addition, subtraction, multiplication and division. Your job is to figure out what the missing digits are.

These problems usually deal with carrying over. Pay attention to the left side of the result first, then the right side. One might look something like this:

Ex) In the addition problem below, each letter represents a distinct digit. What digit is represented by the letter A?

```
  AB
+ B4
 C0C
```

Here's how to solve it:

Let's start on the left side of the answer. Look at the leftmost digit C. It's in the hundreds place, which means that something had to carry over from the addition of the tens place. Since you can't ever carry over more than 1 in an addition problem, the value of C must be 1. Rewrite the problem putting a 1 wherever there is a C:

```
  AB
+ B4
 101
```

Okay, now let's switch our attention to the right side of the answer. B + 4 must equal 1, but how could that be? Only if B + 4 actually equals 11 and a 1 is carried, so B must be 7. Replace all the B's. Don't forget to carry the 1:

```
  ¹
  A7
+ 74
 101
```

All that's left is the A, but we know that the carried 1 + A + 7 = 10, so A must be 2.

On more difficult digit problems, you may have to try a couple of digits to figure out which one works for the problem.

Note! Most digit problems specify that the missing digits must be distinct, meaning all the digits (A, B and C in the example above) are different.

EXTREMES

On some problems it is necessary to think about the largest or smallest a variable or number could be. On these problems, you will need to force a number or variable to its largest or smallest extreme. Difficult average problems are often extremes problems.

- **Largest value.**

  To figure out the largest *one* number could be, you often need to make all the *other* numbers as small as possible.

- **Smallest value.**

  To figure out how small *one* number could be, you often need to make all the *other* numbers as large as possible.

- **Watch out for 0.**

  If the range of values possible for a variable crosses over 0, try using 0 as well as large or small values.

- **Trying the boundaries.**

  If a problems deals with inequalities, for example $x > 7$, try using the smallest or largest number that the variable can't be, in this case $x = 7$. Then think that since x can't actually be 7, the answer you get must be a little bit too big or too small (depending on the specifics of the problem).

Now let's take a look at an Extremes problem:

> Ex) The average of five distinct positive integers is 24. If the median is equal to the mean, what is the greatest possible value of one of the numbers?

Here's how you do it:

First, there's a lot of math jargon here, so let's keep everything straight. The five numbers are all distinct, so each is different. They're all positive. They're all integers.

Okay, so far so good. Now we know the median is the same as the mean. Therefore the middle number is the same as the average, so it must be 24. Write down what you know. We've used letters to represent the unknown values:

a b 24 d e

Now, in order to make *one* number as big as possible, we have to make all the *other* numbers as small as possible. So, a and b could be 1 and 2:

> 1   2   24   d   e

The value of d must be larger than the median, so it could be 25 at the least:

> 1   2   24   25   e

Now, remember the average T:

$$\frac{Total}{\text{\# of items}} \bigg| \ Average$$

So: $\dfrac{Total}{5} \bigg| \ 24$, and therefore the total = 5 x 24 = 120.

If the total = 120, then 1 + 2 + 24 + 25 + e = 120. e = 68, so the largest one of the numbers could be is 68!

Try real examples ➡ PT2 S6 Q13

PATTERNS

Pattern problems ask you to peer off into the distance or look into the future to find answers that seem like they would take a lot of time to compute. Here's a simple example:

> Ex) In the world's longest string of Christmas lights, the first light is Green, the second is Yellow, the third is Blue, the forth is Red, the fifth is Purple and the sixth is Orange. If the lights continue in this pattern, what color is the 2,456,215th light?

Pretty nasty, right? Well, not really, if you can spot the pattern.

Here's the solution:

In this case, since the colors repeat themselves every 6 lights, then every multiple of 6 lights will be Orange. So find a number very close to 2,456,215 that is a multiple of 6. You can use your calculator, or use the divisibility rules, to figure out that 2,456,214 is evenly divisible by 6. That means the 2,456,214th light is Orange, so the next one must be Green.

Pattern problems can be very different, but the general rule applies: Start writing out the sequence and see if you can find a repeating pattern. Extrapolate from there.

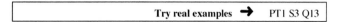

Try real examples ➜ PT1 S3 Q13

CONSECUTIVE INTEGER PATTERNS

Some pattern problems will ask about consecutive integers, and often the sums of consecutive integers. There are a couple of tricks that you can use to figure them out.

First, let's look at a problem that tells you how many consecutive integers are in a sum:

> Ex)   The sum of six consecutive integers is 735. What is the largest of these integers?

Here's how to solve it: Simply divide the sum by the number of integers (in essence, you're getting the average number).

$$735 \div 6 = 122.5$$

This number, 122.5, is either the center number, or very close to it. Since the numbers are integers, try 122 and 123:

… 122 + 123…

Now simply add two numbers on the left, two on the right, and check the sum.

$$120 + 121 + 122 + 123 + 124 + 125 = 735$$

So the largest of the integers is 125.

Another problem might deal with canceling out most of the integers in a sum:

> Ex)   The smallest integer in a set of consecutive even integers is −12. If the sum of the set of integers is 30, what is the largest integer in the set?

This type of problem deals with overlapping positive and negative numbers that cancel each other out. Line up the negative and positive numbers that add up to 0:

-12, -10, -8, -6, -4, -2, 0
 12, 10, 8, 6, 4, 2

Now look at the next numbers in the list that will add up to 30:

$$14 + 16 = 30$$

So the largest number in the set is 16.

Sometimes consecutive integer pattern problems ask how many *numbers* are in the set. In this case, don't forget to count the 0!

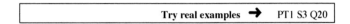

Try real examples ➡	PT1 S3 Q20

IMAGINARY NUMBERS (i)

As mentioned in the vocabulary section, the letter $i = \sqrt{-1}$. Now we've already told you that you can't take an even root of a negative number, so what gives? Well, that's why i is called the *imaginary number*! It doesn't really exist, but using it comes in handy in some math problems. All you really have to remember is what happens to i when you raise it to various powers. The results repeat every power of 4:

$i^1 = i = \sqrt{-1}$	$i^5 = i$
$i^2 = -1$	$i^6 = -1$
$i^3 = -i$	$i^7 = -i$
$i^4 = 1$	$i^8 = 1$

CALCULATORS AND IMAGINARY NUMBERS

Many calculators, including the TI-83, can do imaginary number calculations. However, some of them don't appear to work very well when raising i to higher powers. This is because the algorithm they use to compute imaginary numbers just *approximates* values.

For example, on the TI-83, if you try i^8 you'll get something that looks like this: $1 - 2E - 13i$. (This actually means $1 - (2 \times 10^{-13})(i)$.) Basically, without going into too much detail, just ignore the weird part of the number, the $-2E - 13i$. It's too small to worry about. The answer is 1. Likewise, if you enter i^7, you'll get something like $-3E - 13 - i$. In this case, ignore the $-3E - 13$ (which means -3×10^{-13}). The correct answer is $-i$.

Other calculators, like the TI-89, don't use the same algorithm and give you a more precise answer.

UNIQUE PROBLEMS

There will almost always be a couple of problems that don't quite fit into any of the categories described above. Don't panic! If you come across a problem type you don't recognize, just read the question carefully, write things down, try them out. And don't be afraid to skip it if you just can't get your head around it. You can always come back to it if you have time later.

ANSWER THE RIGHT QUESTION

The single biggest mistake people make on the SAT is reading the questions too quickly and trying to solve the question before really understanding what's going on. The SAT puts a lot of time pressure on you. Don't let that mess with your head. READ THE QUESTIONS CAREFULLY and always MAKE SURE YOU'RE ANSWERING THE RIGHT QUESTION. If a problem asks for the value of $3x$ and you solve for x and forget to multiply by 3, you're out of luck. There's no partial credit here. So take your time, and you'll find that you actually move through the test faster because you don't waste time solving the wrong question.

Review the chapter before trying these Math problems.

Remember to look for the **EASY WAY** to solve these problems.

Practice with these problems from *The Official SAT Study Guide:*

Practice Test	Section	Question
1	3	2, 13, 20
	6	12
2	3	9
	6	13
	9	10
3	8	9
4	2	1-20
	4	1-18
	8	1-16

All test, section, question and page numbers refer to *The Official SAT Study Guide* (2004)

Be sure to carefully score the sections from *The Official SAT Study Guide* and review the questions you miss. Figure out why you missed each question and how you can get it right the next time!

Additional Practice:

Math Homework Drill 8

Note: Each question is numbered to indicate where the question would most likely appear in a math section, and therefore shows relative level of difficulty. Questions with no answer choices are Fill-Ins.

Solve each of the following problems and choose the best of the choices given. Use any available space for scratch work, if necessary.

2. Rachel has estimated that her jar of coins has somewhere between 300 and 400 nickels. Which of these could be the total dollar value of the nickels in the jar?

  (A) $13.00
  (B) $16.50
  (C) $21.00
  (D) $23.40
  (E) $30.00

13. red, blue, teal, white, green, yellow, ...

  A necklace consists of a repeating pattern of colored beads as shown above. If the necklace has a total of 102 beads, what color is the final bead?

  (A) red
  (B) white
  (C) green
  (D) teal
  (E) yellow

20. The least number in a series of 17 consecutive integers is negative and the greatest number is positive. If n is the average of all the numbers in the series, what is the absolute value of the sum of the least and greatest numbers, in terms of n?

(A) $-2n$
(B) $n+8$
(C) $|2n-9|$
(D) $|n|$
(E) $|2n|$

12. If the average of 7 consecutive integers is 60, what is the sum of the least 4 of these integers?

5. On his 18th birthday, Vondeze was 6 feet 2 inches tall. Starting at his 13th birthday, he grew 3 inches every year from one birthday to another, except from his 16th birthday to his 17th birthday he grew only 2 inches, and from his 13th birthday to his 14th birthday he grew only 1 inch. How tall was Vondeze on his 13th birthday?

(A) 4 ft. 9 in.
(B) 4 ft. 11 in.
(C) 5 ft.
(D) 5 ft. 2 in.
(E) 5 ft. 3 in.

Answers:

CRITICAL READING

The term *Reading Comprehension* causes lots of people to squirm. And the *Critical Reading* section is basically a big Reading Comprehension test with some Sentence Completion questions thrown in for good measure. But don't fret. We'll show you how to do well.

First, a brief intro: Sentence Completion questions involve sentences with one or two blanks, and a list of five choices to fill the blank or blanks.

Reading Comprehension includes short passages with just a couple of questions and longer passages with several questions each. Two sets of questions will be based on two related passages and will require you to compare and contrast the passages.

Most people think that math is quite precise, and it's easy to see that there is a process involved in solving an algebra or arithmetic problem. But a system or process is just as important for solving Critical Reading problems. If you learn the process for each question type or each passage type, and practice so that the process becomes second nature, you'll be able to get a lot more answers correct. You'll even start to see patterns and get into the heads of the test writers.

CRITICAL READING LESSON 1

VOCABULARY

According to the Oxford Dictionaries, the English language contains as many as 750,000 words (if you include technical and regional vocabulary and distinct definitions of the same word). About 170,000 words are in relatively common use today.

That's all. Only 170,000 words.

Let's assume that you know around 5,000 words now (which is a little above average for a high school student). That leaves only 165,000 words to go! So with, say, 6 weeks left before the SAT, you only need to pick up about 55,000 words per week! Piece o' cake, right?

The good news is that the SAT doesn't test that many words. The words it does test are within a fairly small range, so don't go out and start memorizing the dictionary... unless you're into that sort of thing.

KNOW WHAT YOU KNOW

The most dangerous words on the SAT are the words you think you know, but actually don't. The SAT tries to trick you into choosing words that are commonly misunderstood. Don't fall into their trap!

- **Don't eliminate too fast.**

    If you aren't absolutely sure about a word, don't eliminate it or choose it until you've considered all the other answers first.

- **Consider secondary definitions...**

    ... especially if the first definition is totally out of scope, especially on the hard questions. Lots of words have more than one definition.

- **Think of a real world context...**

    ... in which you've heard the word, but keep in mind that you still may have misunderstood the word's meaning.

- **Beware of *sounds-like* or *looks-like* words.**

    Just because a word *looks like* or *sounds like* a word you know, that doesn't mean it's the same word. Check the spelling closely on these words.

USE THE LISTS!

There are many SAT-style words in the Vocabulary Lists at the end of this manual. The lists contain around 550 words that we think are likely to appear on the SAT. Some of the words have appeared multiple times in the past. Some of the words are within the narrow range that the SAT tests.

The list in this manual is a great place to start. If you're serious about improving your Critical Reading score, you should learn them all. You probably know many of them already, but make sure you understand the dictionary definition.

There is no guarantee that any of the words on the list will appear on any given SAT. However, it is likely that you'll see between 5 and 20 words from the list. Even if only three words from the list appear, that could significantly boost your score, so learn as many of the words as you can.

BEYOND THE LISTS

It's time to become a vocabulary hound. Any time you see or hear a word you don't know — on an SAT, in homework, in the newspaper, on HBO — look it up and add it to your list. Annoy your family and friends with your newfound vocabulary.

DICTIONARIES

Two of the best dictionaries to use for the SAT are the *Merriam-Webster's Collegiate Dictionary* and the *American Heritage Dictionary*. These are the dictionaries that the College Board uses when writing SAT questions. The *Oxford English Dictionary* is a fantastic dictionary, and probably the English language's most comprehensive dictionary, but you don't need to go that far for the SAT. If you don't have a recent copy of the Merriam-Webster's or the American Heritage, pick one up. You'll use it in college and beyond, so it's a great investment.

METHODS

There are many different ways to study and learn vocabulary. Since everybody is different, there is no single best way. Here are a few suggestions:

- **Flashcards.**

  Tried and true, but sometimes a little tedious. Make your own flashcards. By writing down the words and definitions yourself, you'll be getting the words into your head in a couple of different ways. Try to get the small flashcards on a ring that you can take wherever you go. Create two piles: One pile for the words you definitely know, another pile for those you don't. Try to move all the words from the second pile into the first. Work hardest on the pile you don't know, but periodically check the pile of words you definitely know to make sure you still know them.

- **Audio tape.**

  Make a tape, CD, or mp3 (for your iPod if you're lucky enough to have one!) of the vocabulary lists. On the recording, say the word, leave enough silence so that you can say the definition out loud when you listen to the tape later, and then record the definition. Listen in the car, during a workout, or while falling asleep.

- **Wacky associations.**

  Make crazy associations that will help you remember the words. The crazier the better. For example, if you're trying to remember that *maudlin* means overly sentimental, picture someone's Aunt Maude crying over a pair of slippers she lost in 1952.

- **Use the words.**

  Write sentences with the words you're learning. Confuse and amaze your family and friends with words like pulchritude and ascetic. Spice up text messages or instant messages to your friends, etc. Just use as much of your new vocabulary as you can as often as possible.

Sentence Completion problems give you a sentence with one or two blanks and ask you to pick the answer choice with the word or words that best fit the sentence. They're all about understanding the context of the sentence, with a side of vocabulary thrown in for good measure.

The first thing you need to know is that *the answer to a Sentence Completion question is in the sentence itself.* It's in there. You need to learn how to find it.

STAY WITHIN THE LINES

Remember coloring books? You were always told to stay within the lines. Some people remained caged by those pre-drawn lines, while others, those brave few, felt the creative urge to break the rules, to rebel against an unjust and restrictive society, to color wherever and whenever they wanted in a blaze of freedom and expression the likes of which spurred the very formation of this great nation!

I hate to break it to you, but the SAT is all about staying within the lines, *especially* on Sentence Completion problems.

Each sentence is like a self-contained little box. The question and the answer are both in there; you just have to dig around a little bit to find them. But stay within the lines:

- **DON'T use outside information.**

- **DON'T pick a word just because it sounds nice.**

- **DON'T try to fill in the blanks until you've read the *whole* sentence.**

Let's look at a simple example:

Fish are _____, living their lives in water.

We could come up with a lot of words to describe fish. Fish are slimy, fish are succulent, fish are pretty, and fish are tough to juggle. The problem with these answers is that there is nothing *in the sentence* about slimy, succulent, pretty or juggling, so those words can't be the right answer. *All* we know is that fish live their lives in water. So a word like "aquatic" would be perfect.

IGNORE THE ANSWERS

The answer choices may include nice words that sound good in the sentence but that are actually outside the lines. Don't be tricked by these detractor answers! With your answer sheet or your hand, *physically cover the answers* before you look at the sentence.

READ THE SENTENCE

Your next step is to read the sentence carefully. We recommend that you don't say the work "blank" as you read the sentence. Instead put in the word "something" or "some kind of" or "does something." This will already get your mind working on what that "something" may be. Also, ignore hard to pronounce names and just use initials instead.

For example, if the sentence looks like this:

> Ex)   Arty Fortonbloomenhaagen was a _____ editor, always letting typos and content errors slip past him.

You should read:

> Ex)   "A.F. was a 'some kind of' editor, always letting typos and content errors slip past him."

FIND THE HINT

You now know that the answer is in the sentence somewhere. The question is how to find it. Almost all of the sentences have hints buried somewhere that will help you. In fact, **many of the Sentence Completion sentences are extremely repetitive**, redundant, and repeat the same thing twice, once in the blank and once somewhere else in the sentence. To find the hint:

❶ Determine what role the blank plays in the sentence. Does it modify or describe someone or something? Is it an action? In our example above:

> Ex)   Arty Fortonbloomenhaagen was a _____ editor, always letting typos and content errors slip past him.

The blank describes A.F. and what kind of editor he was.

❷ Look for other information in the sentence that describes the same thing. Let's look at our example:

> Ex)   Arty Fortonbloomenhaagen was a _____ editor, always letting typos and content errors slip past him.

The ONLY other thing we know about A.F. as an editor is that he lets typos and content errors slip past. That must be the hint! So that blank must mean something like "lets typos and content errors slip by."

IN YOUR OWN WORDS

Now it's time to actually fill in the blanks with your own word or phrase based on the hint. *Write the word or phrase down* so you don't forget it. (After some practice, you may not need to write your word or phrase down for every problem, but you should always do it for hard questions.)

In our example above, we decided that the blank had to mean something like "lets typos and content errors slip by." So what is a good word or phrase to represent that? How about:

> "Careless"
> "Not careful"
> "Slipshod"
> … or even
> "likely to let errors slip through"

So now the sentence should read:

> Ex) "A.F. was a 'careless' editor, always letting typos and content errors slip past him."

LOOK FOR DEFINITIONS IN THE SENTENCE

Lots of Sentence Completion questions contain the definition of the word that fits in the blank right in the sentence! That's right, often the hint is really just the definition of the word. In fact, about one third of all Sentence Completion questions contain a clear definition of the blank. For example:

> Phillip ------- illness, only pretending to be sick.

In this example, the word in the blank has to mean the same thing as *pretending*. The word *feigned* would be a perfect answer.

Try real examples ➜	T1 S2:Q5, 7, 8; S5:Q2, 3; S8 Q5
	T2 S2 Q7, 8; S5:Q3; S8 Q1, 3, 4
	T3 S3 Q2; S7 Q1, 3, 6, 7; S9 Q2, 3

CROSS OFF THE WRONG ANSWERS

Now it's time to go to the answer choices. It is extremely important to use process of elimination here.

First, cross off the answers that are *definitely* not correct. Give the answers a little leeway. Though you may often come up with the exact word, you may have only come close to the right meaning, so leave in anything that's in the same ballpark.

- **Don't cross off words you don't know!**

- **Don't cross off anything that's reasonably close to your answer.**

Now, work with what's left. You need to start thinking like a dictionary.

- **Get more specific with your own words.**

- **Get more specific with the definitions of the answer choices.**

- **See which word actually relates back to the sentence.**

It's often easy to eliminate two or three answers. Sometimes the hardest work comes when choosing between two pretty good answers. Take the time to really analyze the last couple of answers.

DIRECTION WORDS

Some words change the direction of a sentence, while others send it merrily and consistently on its way. Some set up a contrast, others continuity. On the SAT, these "direction" words are used very literally. Here's a list of some common direction words.

Contrasting Words	Continuous Words
But	And
However	Therefore
Although	Thus
Now… then	Furthermore
Later	Along with
Nevertheless	Also
On the contrary	Moreover
Yet	In conclusion
Even so	Hence
Except	While
Save for	Since
From… to	Because
Not… until	By
Even more than	So… that
	" ; " *or* " : "

Whenever you see a direction word, circle it!

There are many other words or phrases that indicate whether the sentence will have a contrast or will be continuous, so keep your eye out for them.

On a very basic level:

- **Contrasting words...**

    ... usually indicate that the answer will be nearly opposite the hint.

- **Continuous words...**

    ... usually indicate the answer will be nearly the same as the hint.

There are exceptions, however, depending on the sentence structure. Contrasting words, for example, may set up a contrast that doesn't involve the blank directly, but still guides you toward the correct answer.

TWO-BLANK SENTENCES

Don't let two-blank sentences get you down. In fact, they're often easier than their one-blank cousins.

To tackle these, start with the easier of the two blanks. The second blank is often easier to fill in than the first. Once you've filled in the easier blank, tackle the other one.

| Try real examples ➡ | T1 S5:Q1 |

On a harder question, you might not be able to come up with a word or phrase for one of the blanks. That's O.K. You can work with the one blank you have filled in and eliminate two or three answer choices just from that one blank.

BLANK RELATIONSHIPS

No, we're not talking about your last boyfriend or girlfriend. On some hard two-blank Sentence Completion questions, there is no way for you to come up with the exact right words to fit in the sentence. In these cases, the sentence doesn't give you enough information to be specific, but it does give you enough to figure out *how the two blanks are related*. Are they basically the same thing, a different degree of the same thing, virtually opposite things, etc.? Once you've figured out the blank relationship, you can eliminate answers that don't fit the relationship.

Try real examples ➡	T1 S2 Q6; S8 Q3
	T2 S5 Q4; S8 Q3, 6
	T3 S7 Q7; S9 Q5

LAST RESORTS

Sometimes you won't be able to come up with an exact word because the sentence structure is confusing or some of the vocabulary in the sentence is difficult. This doesn't mean you can't get the right answer! Try to determine whether the blank represents a positive (+) or negative (-) word and write a "+" or "–" in the blank. Then cross off all the answer choices that don't agree with the blank.

- **Don't use this as a crutch!**

    This method should be considered a last resort only.

Try real examples ➜	T1 S8:Q2
	T2 S5 Q5; S8 Q2
	T3 S7 Q8

Another last resort technique when you can't come up with a word is to examine the answer choices. Ask yourself if the word in the answer choice has anything to do with the sentence. If it might, don't cross it off, but if it seems too far removed from the sentence, cross it off.

THE HARD QUESTIONS

Here's a final section on the most difficult Sentence Completion questions. Those vermin who write the SAT typically make the Sentence Completion questions difficult in two basic ways:

❶ They make the sentence structure complicated. That means that a fairly easy word *could* be the answer to a hard question. Often a close reading of the sentence is the key to getting these tough questions.

❷ They use tough vocabulary. But tough vocabulary comes in a lot of flavors.

- **Alternate definitions.**

    Sometimes they'll test fairly obscure second, third or fourth definitions of fairly easy words. Watch out for these alternative definitions.

- **Roots, prefixes and suffixes.**

    Sometimes they'll use words that have fairly common prefixes, suffixes and roots. You can often use your knowledge of these word building blocks to get the gist of a word. But give these words a lot of room; you never know how far they've strayed from the literal meaning of their roots.

- **Killer vocab.**

  And occasionally they use killer words that you just don't have a shot at figuring out no matter what you do. Don't sweat these words. Eliminate what you know to be wrong and guess between what's left.

Remember to guess if you can eliminate even one answer choice!

Glance over the chapter before trying these Sentence Completion problems. Also, any time you see a vocabulary word you don't know, add it to your list.

Practice with these problems from *The Official SAT Study Guide:*

Practice Test	Section	Questions
1	2	1-8
	5	1-5
	8	1-6
2	2	1-8
	5	1-5
	8	1-6

All test, section, question and page numbers refer to *The Official SAT Study Guide (2004)*

Be sure to carefully score the sections from *The Official SAT Study Guide* and review the questions you miss. Figure out why you missed each question and how you can get it right the next time!

Additional Practice:

Sentence Completion Homework Drill 1

Each of the following sentences has one or two blanks, which indicate that a word or group of words has been omitted. Answer choices A through E represent five words or groups of words that could fill the blank or blanks. Choose the word or group of words that best completes the meaning of the sentence as a whole.

1. The ------- of Michael's research paper — a study of changes in the Earth's atmosphere produced by increasing carbon dioxide levels — was relevant to both his Earth Science class and his Chemistry class.

   (A) tone
   (B) topic
   (C) message
   (D) amalgam
   (E) harangue

2. Although computers are becoming faster and more -------, prices continue to ------- as advances in technology make production easier.

   (A) efficient . . increase
   (B) powerful . . decline
   (C) cumbersome . . improve
   (D) inscrutable . . redouble
   (E) cerebral . . stagnate

3. The figures in Botticelli's *Garden of Earthly Delights* are strangely ------- despite being beautiful and apparently at peace.

   (A) calming
   (B) harmonious
   (C) euphonic
   (D) radical
   (E) disturbing

4. Taken out of context, the Chairman's comments on the company's ------- might seem -------, but overall he painted a fairly optimistic picture of the future.

   (A) horizon . . grim
   (B) profits . . convivial
   (C) success . . unremarkable
   (D) prospects . . disparaging
   (E) activities . . guarded

5. An overturned truck on the highway forced the state patrol to ------- traffic for several hours by establishing alternate routes to get motorists around the scene of the accident.

   (A) divert
   (B) impede
   (C) dissolve
   (D) augment
   (E) empower

6. Cheney's thorough and incisive critique of the latest work in cancer research has ------- the approach of the most ------- studies being done at major cancer research centers.

   (A) stimulated . . inscrutable
   (B) affected . . misconceived
   (C) questioned . . promising
   (D) dissolved . . recent
   (E) vexed . . experimental

7. After receiving a blue ribbon at the county fair, Seanitta was completely -------, the effort required to win overcoming her and sapping her last bit of energy.

   (A) elated
   (B) impugned
   (C) exhausted
   (D) disappointed
   (E) underwhelmed

8. Alfredo's teachers often pointed out that he was trying to sound ------- without having the knowledge or insight needed to support his assertions properly.

   (A) facile
   (B) lavish
   (C) profound
   (D) bombastic
   (E) sycophantic

Sentence Completion Homework Drill 2

1. While Marco had once considered many vegetables to be -------, after having learned of their nutritious qualities, he decided to try them anew and, to his happy surprise, found them to be -------.

   (A) disgusting . . reprehensible
   (B) inedible . . arable
   (C) wholesome . . scrumptious
   (D) unappetizing . . delicious
   (E) nourishing . . delightful

2. Though the professor could sometimes seem ------- to her colleagues, her students, who saw her as a highly effective instructor, considered her manner to be ------- rather than bossy and domineering.

   (A) distant . . affectionate
   (B) depreciatory . . histrionic
   (C) defiant . . enlightening
   (D) callous . . compendious
   (E) imperious . . authoritative

3. Certain critiques claimed that despite the obscurity of Jameson's language and references, his meaning was usually clear enough, but there were others who thought his metaphors ------- and unhelpful.

   (A) trite
   (B) lucid
   (C) insular
   (D) opaque
   (E) disastrous

4. The friction that is apparent at family holidays lays bare a deep level of ------- among the siblings.

   (A) amity
   (B) discord
   (C) facility
   (D) abrasion
   (E) disparagement

5. The charitable nature of Penn's actions demonstrates that despite her sometimes brusque words, she is really quite -------.

   (A) callous
   (B) onerous
   (C) mundane
   (D) ingenuous
   (E) magnanimous

Sentence Completion Homework Drill 3

1. What's surprising to many people is that the ------- of most advertising is not someone who needs the product being advertised but precisely the person who does not.

   (A) issue
   (B) factor
   (C) target
   (D) participant
   (E) constituent

2. The speed and ------- of international air travel has greatly ------- both tourism and global trade.

   (A) ease . . trumped
   (B) intricacy . . enhanced
   (C) simplicity . . augmented
   (D) actuality . . enlarged
   (E) efficiency . . hampered

3. Although many shoppers at the mega-store found that the diversity of items available ------- the difficulties of holiday shopping, some felt that this ------- was overwhelming and only made it more difficult to complete the task of finding suitable presents.

   (A) eased . . multiplicity
   (B) emboldened . . variety
   (C) palliated . . paucity
   (D) enhanced . . assortment
   (E) simplified . . uncertainty

4. Peter Falk's character Columbo often acted oblivious and forgetful, but it always turned out that his insight into the crime was both ------- and accurate.

   (A) harmonious
   (B) penetrating
   (C) unreliable
   (D) exacting
   (E) evident

5. The politician is generally considered to have a hostile public persona, but staff members find that this ------- disappears when the harsh gaze of the public eye is removed.

   (A) barbarity
   (B) moralism
   (C) redolence
   (D) obstinacy
   (E) antipathy

6. One effect of the allergy medicine is that it makes the user ------- even though it is intended to stop sneezing without inducing sleepiness.

   (A) ocular
   (B) sensitive
   (C) somnolent
   (D) aggressive
   (E) melancholy

Answers:

Sentence Completion Homework Drill 3		Sentence Completion Homework Drill 2		Sentence Completion Homework Drill 1
1) C		1) D		1) B
2) C		2) E		2) B
3) A		3) D		3) E
4) B		4) B		4) D
5) E		5) E		5) A
6) C				6) C
				7) C
				8) C

CRITICAL READING LESSON 2

READING COMPREHENSION

The Reading Comprehension section on the SAT isn't really about "comprehending" the reading passages. It's about getting the answers that the test writers think are the right answers.

It is important to understand the passages on a certain level. It is equally important to understand the questions. If you don't know what the question is asking, you can't get the correct answer, right? But here's the real secret: It's *most* important to clearly understand the answer choices. Let's say that again. *It is most important to understand the answer choices.* It is usually the wording of the answer choices that makes an answer "correct" or "incorrect."

So, we'll be looking very closely at the answer choices and what makes an answer right or wrong. But let's talk first about the passages themselves.

The first thing to note is that there is a short italicized contextual introduction to each longer passage (or pair of longer passages). These introductions are quite important and should be read carefully. They often help you to understand the passage as a whole, or at least the context of the passage.

Note: everyone reads differently. The techniques listed here work very well for most people. Give them a chance. If, however, you think you have a method that is better tailored to your reading style, talk to your SAT tutor or English teacher about it. She or he might be able to adjust your style a little to make you even more efficient.

READING THE PASSAGES

There are a couple of different styles of passages on the SAT, and you should tailor the way you read each passage to its particular style.

TEXTBOOK STYLE PASSAGES

The vast majority of passages are very similar to the writing you might find in one of your textbooks. They might deal with science, literature, history, sociology or any number of academically oriented subjects. The passage argues a specific point or introduces some ideas. There may be specific examples or contrasting ideas discussed. The hallmark of these passages is that they are almost always very well organized.

"So what?" you say? Well, you can use that organization to your advantage, because most well organized paragraphs put the main ideas in the first or last sentence of the paragraph. That's right, the main ideas of a textbook style passage can almost always be found in the first and last sentences of the paragraphs. Not every first or last sentence contains useful information, but many do. So here's how to read these passages:

- **First and last sentences**

   Don't read the whole passage. Really. Don't. It's okay. Only read the introduction and the first and last sentences of each paragraph.

   The fact is, you'll need to go back to the passage to look up details to answer specific questions. Why waste time reading that information twice, and reading a bunch of detail that you'll never need?

   You should be looking for specific things while you read these sentences.

   ❶ Figure out the paragraph-by-paragraph structure of the passage. Basically, what is happening in each paragraph? How do they fit together? This will help you quickly find the answers to specific questions that don't give a line reference.

   ❷ Look for repeated themes. Any time an idea or theme is repeated in two, three or more paragraphs, you know it is part of the main idea of the passage.

   ❸ Try to put together the overall gist of the passage. Does the author introduce an idea and then give an example? Does the author introduce two contrasting ideas and then decide which is better? Does the author describe a specific scientific theory?

   Once you have a grasp of the structure, the main themes and the overall gist, you're ready to tackle any questions they might throw at you.

   Note: Some passages aren't broken up into small, manageable paragraphs. If you are faced with extremely long paragraphs, you should pick out two or three sentences in the middle of the long paragraph and read those as well, so you don't miss the direction the passage is taking.

Another Note: This technique takes practice. You probably won't feel comfortable skipping over most of the passage at first, but by the time the test rolls around, this technique can make you more accurate and more efficient. You'll spend less time and get more answers right. So put in the time working on this technique.

VERY SHORT PASSAGES

Very short passages tend to be dense and packed with information. It is probably best to read these passages completely, but focus on the main theme and overall gist. Important information still tends to be in the first and last sentences, but there can be important themes and ideas in the middle of paragraphs here as well. Any theme that is repeated twice in a short passage is bound to be important.

NARRATIVE STYLE PASSAGES

Narrative style passages read like novels or short stories. They often include a decent amount of dialogue. Just like many narratives, these passages are often not well organized. The problem is that you can't use the First and Last Sentences technique very effectively on these passages. It is actually better to quickly read through the whole passage, paying special attention to the author's tone and the recurring themes. Don't sweat the details... yet.

TWO PASSAGES: COMPARE AND CONTRAST

Twice in Reading Comprehension sections, you will have two reading comp passages followed by a group of questions. Some of these questions will ask about both passages. The first few questions deal with the first passage. The next few questions deal with the second passage. The last few questions ask you to compare or contrast the two passages.

These passages are usually, but not always, Textbook Style. Assess the style as described above to choose an appropriate way to read the passage. You may want to read the individual passages differently.

Deal with the first passage first. Don't worry about the second passage. Answer the questions based on passage 1 only.

After you've finished all the passage 1 questions you can answer, move on to passage 2. Forget about passage 1. Just focus on the questions dealing only with passage 2.

After you've done all the individual questions for passages 1 and 2, quickly skim passage 1 again to refresh your memory, then tackle the questions based on both passages.

An alternate technique:

This is a technique only a few students have found useful: Read passage 1 first. After you've answered questions for passage 1, go ahead and read the questions that are based on *both* passages. Cross off any answer choices that contradict information you learned from passage 1. Realize that you'll probably leave in several answer choices since you won't yet be able to eliminate anything based on passage 2.

Next, read passage 2 and answer all of the passage 2 questions. Then go to the questions based on both passages, and eliminate anything you can from your reading of passage 2. Work with the answer choices you have left and don't hesitate to go back to passage 1 and passage 2 to eliminate answers.

ANSWERING THE QUESTIONS

There are, in very general terms, three types of Reading Comprehension questions on the SAT: General questions, specific questions, and contextual vocabulary questions. General questions might query you about the best title for the passage, the author's tone, the main idea of the passage, etc. Specific questions deal with the details. Contextual vocabulary questions ask you to figure out the specific meaning of a word based on its use in the passage. It is usually pretty easy to tell whether the question is general, specific or vocabulary, but occasionally what seems like a general question will turn out to be very specific or visa versa.

GENERAL QUESTIONS

You'll usually be able to answer most general questions after reading the first and last sentences of a passage (or the whole thing if it's very short or narrative as described above). You should have a good idea of the main point, the author's tone, and the structure of the passage. General questions rarely have a specific line reference.

Use process of elimination. Don't look for the right answer. Cross off the wrong answers.

Be very wary of answer choices that are too broad or too narrow. Answers to questions that ask for the main idea, for example, take the whole passage into consideration, not just one or two paragraphs.

SPECIFIC QUESTIONS

Specific questions are a different animal. *You need to go back to the passage to find the right and wrong answers.* Don't rely on your memory. These questions are often intentionally tricky.

Specific questions often have a line reference. Here's how to handle them:

- **Understand the question.**

  Read the question carefully. If you don't understand exactly what the question is asking, you will have a hard time getting the right answer.

- **Go back to the passage.**

  You must go back to the passage for these answers. Most specific questions on the SAT are line reference questions, which makes your job a lot easier. You just need to go to the line mentioned. Underline or box the word or phrase the question is asking about and move on to the next step.

  For specific questions without a line reference, you need to use your knowledge of the structure of the passage to find the information that will answer the questions. Decide which paragraph is most likely to contain the information and skim.

  Note that specific questions are usually in approximately chronological order. In other words, the answers to early questions are likely to be found near the beginning of the passage and answers to the later questions are likely to be found near the end of the passage.

  Once you've located the general area in which you expect to find the answer, go on to the next step.

- **Read 5 lines above, 5 lines below.**

  Quite often, the answer to a specific question will not come from the sentence that the question references, it will come from the sentences above or below. You must read to understand the context of the sentence.

Read approximately 5 lines above the reference to 5 lines below the reference. Start at the beginning of each sentence, not in the middle of one. Adjust your reading if the reference is at the beginning or end of a paragraph.

Occasionally, the last line of the preceding paragraph or the first line of the following paragraph will contain important information, so don't be afraid to read beyond a single paragraph.

You will almost always find the answer in the 5 lines above or 5 lines below. If you don't, read the paragraphs above and below.

If you're really stumped, don't be afraid to leave the question and come back to it later. You may come across the information to answer a tough question while answering another question.

CONTEXTUAL VOCABULARY QUESTIONS

Contextual vocabulary questions often test obscure second, third or fourth meanings of fairly common words. Your job is to figure out which meaning was intended in the passage.

Contextual vocabulary questions can be quite easy or extremely difficult, but you've already learned how to answer them. All you need to do is treat these questions like Sentence Completion questions, with one small change: Context from surrounding sentences matters.

- **Go back to the passage.**

  You need to go back to the passage to understand the context.

- **Leave out the word.**

  Ignore the word in question. Treat it like a blank in a Sentence Completion question.

- **Read 5 lines above, 5 lines below.**

  Unlike Sentence Completions, the information you need to answer the questions might not be in the sentence that contains the word, but in nearby sentences instead.

- **Make up your own word.**

  Just like Sentence Completion questions, make up a word or phrase based on the hints in the surrounding sentences.

- **Go to the answer choices.**

  Pick the answer that is closest in meaning to the word or phrase you chose.

HANDLING THE ANSWER CHOICES

This is it. The single most important step in getting the "correct" answer is dealing with the answer choices carefully.

- **Cross off what you know is wrong.**

  The first step is to read through each of the answer choices and cross off the two or three answers that are obviously wrong. Don't look for the right answer yet; just get rid of the garbage so it won't distract you. Give the answer choices a little breathing room and leave in anything that's in the ballpark.

- **The devil's in the details.**

  Quite often, answer choices are wrong because of *one single word*, or one short phrase. An answer that is only 90% right is not a good answer! Go to each of the remaining answer choices and read extremely carefully, looking for the one word or phrase that makes the answer choice wrong. Make a decision to either eliminate or leave in each answer choice.

- **General statements apply to the specifics in the passage.**

  Many correct answer choices use broad terms to describe the specific information that answers the question at hand. The answer choice itself may contain no specific information that relates to the passage. Don't be afraid to choose one of these answer choices! The key is to make sure the general terms apply to the specifics of the passage.

- **Paraphrases are GOOD.**

  Correct answer choices rarely quote *directly* from the passage. Most often, they say basically the same thing using different words. Paraphrasing like this is one of the ways the test writers make the questions harder. Don't eliminate an answer choice just because the language is different from the passage. Look into the meaning behind the language.

- **Wishy-washy words are *usually* GOOD.**

  Answers that contain easy to defend words like "some" or "often" or "sometimes" are often very good choices because it is difficult to prove them wrong. Here are sections of good answer choices:

  > GOOD: qualified agreement
  > GOOD: this group shared some common bonds
  > GOOD: subtlety is lost on many
  > GOOD: ambivalent
  > GOOD: values freedom, but to a different degree

- **Extreme words are *usually* BAD.**

  More often than not, extreme answer choices are bad answer choices. Of course, this depends on the wording of the question. Some questions call for extreme answer choices, but they are few and far between. Extreme answers often include words like "all" or "every" or "only" or "never" or "always."

  > BAD: absolute revulsion
  > BAD: only those people in the room felt the same way
  > BAD: modern man does not appreciate subtlety
  > BAD: indifferent
  > BAD: never values freedom

Review the chapter and focus on reading techniques before trying these Reading Comprehension problems. Also, any time you see a vocabulary word you don't know, add it to your list.

Pay special attention to the wording of the questions and answer choices!

Practice with these problems from *The Official SAT Study Guide:*

Practice Test	Section	Questions
1	2	9-24
	5	6-24
	8	7-19
2	2	9-24
	5	6-24
	8	7-19

All test, section, question and page numbers refer to *The Official SAT Study Guide (2004)*

Be sure to carefully score the sections from *The Official SAT Study Guide* and review the questions you miss. Figure out why you missed each question and how you can get it right the next time!

Additional Practice:

Reading Comprehension Homework Drill 1

The following passages are the basis for the questions below; if there are two passages, questions may ask about the relationship between the related passages. Answer the questions based on what is directly stated or what can be inferred from the passages and the italicized introduction, if provided.

Questions 9-12 are based on the following passages.

Passage 1
In every system of morality, the author proceeds for some time in the ordinary ways of reasoning, and establishes the being of a God, or makes observations concerning human
Line affairs; when of a sudden I am surprised to
5 find, that instead of the usual copulations of propositions, is, and is not, I meet with no proposition that is not connected with an ought, or an ought not. This change is imperceptible;
10 but is however, of the last consequence. (For source reference, see endnote [1])

Passage 2
Thinking is an active process and the static conception of a thought is its opposite. Where thinking is the vitality of psychological being, a thought is opposed to that vitality. No sense or
15 imagining of something beyond or external to the act of thinking in itself for the thinker can

be real, and therefore cannot be said to exist, even if, to continue the act of thinking it must be said that it does exist as a creation of the act
20 of thinking if even then it remains unreal. (For source reference, see endnote [2])

9. In lines 5-10, the author of Passage 1 mentions a process that suggests that

(A) we ought not build morality upon facts
(B) humans are incapable of moral reasoning
(C) morals are built on factual propositions
(D) surprises are the foundation of morality
(E) connecting is and is not is important

10. The author of Passage 2 would most likely respond to the main point of Passage 1 by

(A) arguing that morality is always built on static conceptions
(B) observing that propositions about God are necessary to the vitality of psychological being
(C) stating that the act of thinking about human affairs can never be real
(D) pointing out that moral reasoning must, like all thought processes, actively introduce new ideas
(E) claiming that there are no ordinary ways of reasoning that are not consequential

11. The two passages differ in their views about the nature of thinking because the author of Passage 1 is

(A) surprised by the necessity of a shift during the thought process
(B) unable to figure out how the process of moral reasoning takes place
(C) too shocked by the flaws of moral reasoning to draw the proper consequences
(D) dismayed by the need to talk about God and human affairs in the same sentence
(E) unconvinced that thinking in itself for the thinker can be real

12. Which of the following statements might both authors be likely to agree is true?

(A) Nothing that humans think up is ever true.
(B) The human mind plays an active role in all forms of reasoning.
(C) Human psychological being is vital yet badly flawed.
(D) We ought not allow ourselves to think that our thoughts are real.
(E) Human beings exist only because they think they exist.

Questions 13-24 are based on the following passage.

In this essay, a 19th century American Essayist discusses the virtues of walking.

I wish to speak a word for Nature, for absolute freedom and wildness, as contrasted with a freedom and culture merely civil--to
Line regard man as an inhabitant, or a part and
5 parcel of Nature, rather than a member of society. I wish to make an extreme statement, if so I may make an emphatic one, for there are enough champions of civilization: the minister and the school committee and every one of you

10 will take care of that.
I have met with but one or two persons in the course of my life who understood the art of Walking, that is, of taking walks--who had a genius, so to speak, for sauntering, which word
15 is beautifully derived "from idle people who roved about the country, in the Middle Ages, and asked charity, under pretense of going a la Sainte Terre," to the Holy Land, till the children exclaimed, "There goes a Sainte-
20 Terrer," a Saunterer, a Holy-Lander. They who never go to the Holy Land in their walks, as they pretend, are indeed mere idlers and vagabonds; but they who do go there are saunterers in the good sense, such as I mean.
25 Some, however, would derive the word from sans terre without land or a home, which, therefore, in the good sense, will mean, having no particular home, but equally at home everywhere. For this is the secret of successful
30 sauntering. He who sits still in a house all the time may be the greatest vagrant of all; but the saunterer, in the good sense, is no more vagrant than the meandering river, which is all the while sedulously seeking the shortest course to
35 the sea. But I prefer the first, which, indeed, is the most probable derivation. For every walk is a sort of crusade, preached by some Peter the Hermit in us, to go forth and reconquer this Holy Land from the hands of the Infidels.
40 It is true, we are but faint-hearted crusaders, even the walkers, nowadays, who undertake no persevering, never-ending enterprises. Our expeditions are but tours, and come round again at evening to the old hearthside from
45 which we set out. Half the walk is but retracing our steps. We should go forth on the shortest walk, perchance, in the spirit of undying adventure, never to return-- prepared to send back our embalmed hearts only as relics to our
50 desolate kingdoms. If you are ready to leave father and mother, and brother and sister, and wife and child and friends, and never see them again--if you have paid your debts, and made your will, and settled all your affairs, and are a
55 free man--then you are ready for a walk.
To come down to my own experience, my companion and I, for I sometimes have a companion, take pleasure in fancying ourselves knights of a new, or rather an old, order--not
60 Equestrians or Chevaliers, not Ritters or Riders, but Walkers, a still more ancient and honorable class, I trust. The Chivalric and heroic spirit which once belonged to the Rider seems now to reside in, or perchance to have subsided into,
65 the Walker--not the Knight, but Walker, Errant. He is a sort of fourth estate, outside of Church and State and People.
We have felt that we almost alone hereabouts practiced this noble art; though, to
70 tell the truth, at least if their own assertions are to be received, most of my townsmen would

fain walk sometimes, as I do, but they cannot.
No wealth can buy the requisite leisure,
freedom, and independence, which are the
75　capital in this profession. It comes only by the
grace of God. It requires a direct dispensation
from Heaven to become a walker. You must be
born into the family of the Walkers. Some of
my townsmen, it is true, can remember and
80　have described to me some walks which they
took ten years ago, in which they were so
blessed as to lose themselves for half an hour in
the woods; but I know very well that they have
confined themselves to the highway ever since,
85　whatever pretensions they may make to belong
to this select class. No doubt they were elevated
for a moment as by the reminiscence of a
previous state of existence, when even they
were foresters and outlaws. (For source reference, see
endnote ³)

13.　The author refers to "champions of
civilization" (line 8) in order to

(A)　add the weight of established authority
to his personal opinion
(B)　suggest that religion and education are
necessary to protect society
(C)　establish a contrast between his view
and the prevailing ideas of society
(D)　point out how hypocritical teachers and
ministers are
(E)　set up a contrast between freedom and
wildness

14.　In line 17, the word "pretense" most nearly
means

(A)　costume
(B)　beforehand
(C)　sponsorship
(D)　statement
(E)　disguise

15.　The author's discussion of the origins of the
word "sauntering" in the second paragraph is
used to

(A)　establish the author's historical
knowledge
(B)　demonstrate the futility of getting a true
derivation
(C)　distract the reader from the author's
true destination
(D)　point out how controversial trips to the
Holy Land once were
(E)　lead the reader better to understand the
author's viewpoint on walking

16.　The "expeditions" the author refers to in line
43 are meant to refer to

(A)　walks
(B)　crusades
(C)　adventures
(D)　retractions
(E)　guided tours

17.　The author mentions the "spirit of undying
adventure" (lines 47-48) in order to

(A)　appeal to the religious instincts of
crusaders and vagabonds
(B)　draw a contrast between short walks
and walks that never end
(C)　describe how he thinks we should all
embark on even brief walks
(D)　undermine the stubborn notions of
walking held by people with hard
hearts
(E)　suggest that we would all be better off
dying during a walk than in any other
way

18.　Lines 50-55 ("If you are ready to... then you
are ready for a walk.") show how much the
author

(A)　dislikes his friends and family
(B)　equates walking with freedom
(C)　believes that he is ready for a walk
(D)　romanticizes the importance of money
(E)　accepts that we must all die sooner or
later

19.　In the paragraph that begins "To come down
to my own experience..." (line 56), the
author mentions knights primarily to

(A)　debunk the myth that knights were
brave
(B)　demonstrate the heroic nature of the
walker
(C)　show how little ministers and walkers
have in common
(D)　argue that chivalry and heroism are
dead in modern society
(E)　suggest that he and his companion
would rather ride than walk

20. According to the author, a "Walker," as discussed on lines 61-65, is a person who

    (A) subsides into frequent errors
    (B) believes that only heroes have honor
    (C) used to ride but now feels the need to walk
    (D) exists beyond the normal bounds of society
    (E) cannot take pleasure in walking without a companion

21. In line 72, the word "fain" could be replaced by

    (A) eagerly
    (B) pretend to
    (C) slowly
    (D) tirelessly
    (E) practice to

22. The reference to "the grace of God" in lines 75-76 serves to emphasize that

    (A) all walks are really miniature holy crusades
    (B) the author believes himself outside the bounds of the Church
    (C) faith in God helps develop the temperament necessary to become a walker
    (D) the money needed to be a true walker comes only from Heaven
    (E) one cannot become a walker, one must be born that way

23. The author suggests that some of his "townsmen" (line 79) once

    (A) experienced the blessing of a true walk
    (B) enjoyed more rights than they do now
    (C) lived in a place with no paved roads
    (D) belonged to a select class
    (E) made money as foresters

24. The "select class" that the author refers to in line 86 includes

    (A) most of his townsmen
    (B) ministers of the Church
    (C) only the wealthiest of men
    (D) the family of Walkers
    (E) idlers and vagabonds

Questions 6-7 are based on the following passage.

The Fungi (singular: fungus) are a large group of organisms ranked as a kingdom within the Domain Eukaryota. Fungi occur in all
Line environments on the planet and include
5 important decomposers and parasites. Parasitic fungi infect animals, including humans, other mammals, birds, and insects, with consequences varying from mild itching to death. Other parasitic fungi infect plants,
10 causing diseases and making trees more vulnerable to toppling. The vast majority of vascular plants are associated with mutualistic fungi, called mycorrhizae, which assist their roots in absorption of nutrients and water. (For source reference, see endnote [4])

6. The passage implies that "decomposers" (line 5) differ from parasites because they

    (A) attack only plants or animals instead of both plants and animals
    (B) lead only to mild itching or toppling but not death
    (C) are not really fungi at all but a different sort of rot
    (D) assist plants rather than damaging them
    (E) occur in different environments

7. The term "mutualistic" in the last sentence is meant to show that some fungi

   (A) use plants to assist them in getting water
   (B) cooperate with animals to harm plants
   (C) are useful to plants rather than harmful
   (D) do their damage by toppling a plant's roots
   (E) survive by robbing plants of their nutrients

Questions 8-9 are based on the following passage.

There are moments when the wheels of life, even of such a life as yours, run slow, and when mistrust and doubt overshadow even the
Line most intrepid disposition. In such a moment,
5 towards the ending of your days, you said to your son, M. Alexandre Dumas, 'I seem to see myself set on a pedestal which trembles as if it were founded on the sands.' These sands, your uncounted volumes, are all of gold, and make a
10 foundation more solid than the rock.

8. This passage is most likely

   (A) the end of an essay-like obituary
   (B the beginning of an historical novel
   (C) a passage from a philosophy textbook
   (D) part of a meditation on the meaning of life
   (E) the introduction to an autobiography

9. The final sentence of the passage (lines 8-10) are intended by the author as

   (A) an argument that all human effort is futile
   (B) a rebuff of the quote in the previous sentence
   (C) an extension of what was said to M. Alexandre Dumas
   (D) a digression on the alchemical science of turning lead into gold
   (E) a way of making the speaker feel even worse about dying than he already does

Questions 10-18 are based on the following passage.

The following passage discusses the origin and revival of the Olympic Games.

The origin of the ancient Olympic Games has been lost, although there are many legends surrounding its beginnings. One of these
Line legends associates the first Games with the
5 ancient Greek concept of *ekeicheiria*, or Olympic Truce. The first recorded celebration of the Games in Olympia was in 776 BC, although this was certainly not the first time

they were held. The Games were then mostly a
10 local affair, and only one event was contested, the stadion race, in which contestants ran 192 meters, or the length of one stadium.

The Games slowly became more important throughout ancient Greece, reaching their
15 zenith in the sixth and fifth centuries BC. The Olympics were of fundamental religious importance, contests alternating with sacrifices and ceremonies honoring both Zeus (whose colossal statue stood at Olympia), and Pelops,
20 divine hero and mythical king of Olympia famous for his legendary chariot race, in whose honor the games were held. The number of events increased to twenty, and the celebration was spread over several days. Winners of the
25 events were broadly admired and were immortalized in poems and statues. The Games were held every four years, and the period between two celebrations became known as an Olympiad. The Greeks used Olympiads as one
30 of their methods to count years.

The Games gradually lost in importance as the Romans gained power in Greece. When Christianity became the official religion of the Roman Empire, the Olympic Games were seen
35 as a pagan festival threatening Christian hegemony, and in 393 AD the emperor Theodosius outlawed the Olympics, ending a thousand year period of Olympic contests.

The Olympic Games did not die in 393.
40 Already in the 17th century a sports festival named after the Olympic Games was held in England. Over the next few centuries, similar events were organized in France and Greece, but these were all small-scale and certainly not
45 international. The interest in reviving the Olympics grew when the ruins of ancient Olympia were uncovered by German archaeologists in the mid-19th century.

At the same time, Pierre, Baron de
50 Coubertin, searched for a reason for the French defeat in the Franco-Prussian War (1870-1871). He thought the reason was that the French had not received proper physical education, and sought to improve this. Coubertin also thought
55 of a way to bring nations closer together, to have the youth of the world compete in sports, rather than fight in war. In his eyes, the revival of the Olympic Games would achieve both of these goals. (For source reference, see endnote [5])

10. Which of the following statements best describes an important difference between the ancient Olympic Games, as discussed in the second paragraph, and the revival of the Olympic Games as discussed in the fourth paragraph?

(A) The revival was mostly a result of the rediscovery of ancient Greek temples.
(B) The Olympic Games were originally held in Greece while the revival took place in France.
(C) The Franco-Prussian war brought an end to the imperial dynasty that originally outlawed the Olympics.
(D) The original games were held for religious reasons while the revival was more for political and military reasons.
(E) While both games featured pagan festivals, the revival added a number of modern athletic events.

11. The author's claim that "The first recorded celebration of the Games... was certainly not the first time they were held" (lines 6-9) is backed up by what other assertion made in the passage?

(A) "The origin of the Olympic Games has been lost." (lines 1-2)
(B) "there are many legends surrounding its beginnings" (lines 2-3)
(C) "The Games were then mostly a local affair." (lines 9-10)
(D) "only one event was contested" (line 10)
(E) "The Games slowly became more important throughout ancient Greece" (lines 13-14)

12. Which of the following best describes the relationship that the second paragraph bears to the first paragraph?

(A) It extends the chronology of the first paragraph further back into Olympic history.
(B) It suggests that the ideas discussed in the first paragraph are dubious.
(C) It continues the discussion of the ideas brought up in the first paragraph.
(D) It demonstrates a specific case of a general idea raised in the first paragraph.
(E) It introduces a completely new idea unrelated to the first paragraph.

13. In line 16, the author uses the word "fundamental" to mean

(A) foundational
(B) magnificent
(C) orthodox
(D) primary
(E) unimpeachable

14. "The emperor Theodosius outlawed the Olympics" (lines 36-37) because

(A) Christianity had its own method of counting years
(B) the thousand-year cycle of Olympiads had run its course
(C) Romans no longer understood the significance of Greek holidays
(D) the colossal statue of Zeus had been toppled during the Roman invasion
(E) the religious connotations of the Olympic celebrations undermined Christian authority

15. In line 39, the author's claim that "The Olympics did not die in 393" is based on the fact that

(A) Olympic festivals continued to be held throughout the Middle Ages
(B) certain Greeks maintained the ancient tradition despite the law against it
(C) the ancient calendar of Greece continued to count four-year periods based on the Olympiad
(D) the Olympic Games were solely revived by the Baron de Coubertin after the Franco-Prussian War
(E) there was eventually a new festival named after the Olympic Games

16. The passage suggests that one reason that "The interest in reviving the Olympics grew" (lines 45-46) was because

(A) Baron de Coubertin believed that an international athletic competition would promote peace
(B) the Franco-Prussian War pointed out how little the French knew about ancient European culture
(C) the unearthing of the colossal statue of Zeus fulfilled an ancient prophecy
(D) France wanted to hide its defeat in the Franco-Prussian War by winning at sports
(E) the Prussians felt that German archaeologists were not receiving sufficient physical training

17. In the final paragraph, the author suggests that Baron de Coubertin became interested in athletics because he

   (A) had been a life-long devotee of comprehensive physical education
   (B) practiced an ancient pagan religion that had been passed down from Olympic times
   (C) was one of the founders of an international organization against war
   (D) wanted to understand why the French had lost the Franco-Prussian War
   (E) had read about the discovery of the temple ruins in Olympia

18. The author's primary purpose for writing this passage was probably to

   (A) prove that the modern Olympic Games are very different from the ancient version
   (B) demonstrate the ways the Franco-Prussian War transformed the Olympic Games
   (C) contend that one of the legends about the origins of the Olympic Games is the most plausible
   (D) trace the development of the Olympic Games from its ancient origins to its modern revival
   (E) suggest that modern athletes are more interested in training for war than ancient Greeks were

Questions 19-24 are based on the following passage.

The author of the following passage is a well-known French mystery writer, and here he introduces his novel The Yellow Room.

It is not without a certain emotion that I begin to recount here the extraordinary adventures of Joseph Rouletabille. Down to the
Line present time he had so firmly opposed my
5 doing it that I had come to despair of ever publishing the most curious of police stories of the past fifteen years. I had even imagined that the public would never know the whole truth of the prodigious case known as that of The
10 Yellow Room, out of which grew so many mysterious, cruel, and sensational dramas, with which my friend was so closely mixed up, a terrible adventure of which Joseph Rouletabille had told me he wished to be forever forgotten.
15 The Yellow Room! Who now remembers this affair, which caused so much ink to flow fifteen years ago? Events are so quickly forgotten in Paris. Has not the very name of the Nayves trial and the tragic history of the death
20 of little Menaldo passed out of mind? And yet the public attention was so deeply interested in

the details of the trial that the occurrence of a ministerial crisis was completely unnoticed at the time. Now The Yellow Room trial, which
25 preceded that of the Nayves by some years, made far more noise. The entire world hung for months over this obscure problem - the most obscure, it seems to me, that has ever challenged the perspicacity of our police or
30 taxed the conscience of our judges. The solution of the problem baffled everybody who tried to find it. It was like a dramatic rebus with which old Europe and new America alike became fascinated. That is, in truth - I am
35 permitted to say, because there cannot be any author's vanity in all this, since I do nothing more than transcribe facts on which an exceptional documentation enables me to throw a new light - that is because, in truth, I do not
40 know that, in the domain of reality or imagination, one can discover or recall to mind anything comparable, in its mystery, with the natural mystery of The Yellow Room.
   That which nobody could find out, Joseph
45 Rouletabille, aged eighteen, then a reporter engaged on a leading journal, succeeded in discovering. But when, at the Assize Court, he brought in the key to the whole case, he did not tell the whole truth. He only allowed so much
50 of it to appear as sufficed to ensure the acquittal of an innocent man. The reasons that he had for his reticence no longer exist. Better still, the time has come for my friend to speak out fully. You are going to know all; and, without further
55 preamble, I am going to place before your eyes the problem of The Yellow Room as it was placed before the eyes of the entire world on the day following the enactment of the drama at the Chateau du Glandier.

19. The primary purpose of the passage is to

   (A) lay out the evidence that Joseph Rouletabille found to help acquit an innocent man
   (B) reveal the motives that led the author to write a book about The Yellow Room
   (C) remind the reader of the sensation of the mystery of the Yellow Room to build anticipation for the story
   (D) discuss the differences between the public trial and the private account of Joseph Rouletabille's actions
   (E) argue that the Yellow Room trial deserves to be considered the most amazing spectacle of the century

20. Why did the author "despair of ever publishing the most curious of police stories of the past fifteen years" (lines 5-7)?

(A) The story was already copyrighted by another author.
(B) Joseph Rouletabille wished to have the story buried in his past.
(C) The outcome of The Yellow Room mystery was still not known.
(D) The law prevented revealing the details of a trial where the accused was acquitted.
(E) The author didn't want to tell the story until he knew all of the facts.

21. The author refers to the "the prodigious case" (line 9) in order to demonstrate

(A) the kind of impact The Yellow Room created
(B) how wasteful the entire adventure turned out to be
(C) why so many sensational dramas grew out of it
(D) the fact that fifteen years had passed since the story was first told
(E) justify his taking up the matter again even though everyone has forgotten about it

22. In lines 22-24, the author mentions that "the occurrence of a ministerial crisis was completely unnoticed at the time" in order to show

(A) how many important people were tied up in the scandal
(B) the importance of the trial's outcome for the stability of the government
(C) that the Nayves trial overshadowed The Yellow Room mystery
(D) why society was in such an uproar at the time
(E) how much the trial distracted the public's attention

23. The author's claim that "there cannot be any author's vanity in all this" (lines 35-36) is intended primarily to

(A) point out how understated the literary tone of the book is
(B) take a position of false modesty regarding the story's sensationalism
(C) conceal the fact that he has only written the book at the request of the acquitted man
(D) emphasize the fact that he's telling a completely true story
(E) reveal the essential humility of the book's hero, Joseph Rouletabille

24. In lines 47-51, the author points out that Joseph Rouletabille did not reveal the whole truth as he knew it during the trial primarily to

(A) demonstrate the moral character of the reporter
(B) apologize in advance for an incomplete record
(C) generate interest for his own telling of the story
(D) prove that his hero saved a man's life
(E) criticize his hero's actions at the time

Questions 7-19 are based on the following passages.

The author of passage 1 discusses Papaun languages. In passage 2, a different author discusses Native American languages. Both passages are current encyclopedia entries.

Passage 1

The term *Papuan languages* refers to those languages of the western Pacific which are neither Austronesian nor Australian. The
Line majority of the Papuan languages are spoken
5 on the island of New Guinea (which is divided between the countries of Papua New Guinea and Indonesia), with a few spoken in the Solomon Islands, and a number in various islands of Indonesia, in particular Halmahera,
10 Timor, Alor and Pantar. One Papuan language is spoken in Australia, in the eastern Torres Straits. It can be seen that the term 'Papuan languages' is not meant to imply any unity. There is a great deal of diversity amongst the
15 Papuan languages and it has not yet been shown that they are all related. In fact, they fall into a large number of family groupings.

Although there has been relatively little study of the Papuan languages compared with
20 Australian or Austronesian languages, a number of distinct genetic groups have been identified by linguists. These genetic groups are referred to as phyla. The largest phylum posited for the Papuan region is the Trans-New
25 Guinea phylum, consisting of a large number of languages running mainly along the highlands of New Guinea, from the Indonesian province of Irian Jaya (the western half of the island) through to Papua New Guinea (the eastern
30 half).

One commonly used classification system for Papuan language phyla includes isolate languages, for which no genetic affiliation is known. This scheme is based on the work of
35 linguist S.A. Wurm and others. Other linguists, including William A. Foley, have identified over sixty language families, suggesting that the grouping of certain languages into phyla by earlier linguists may have been based on
40 structural or other similarities, which may or may not indicate genetic relationships. Since perhaps only a quarter of Papuan languages have been studied in detail, linguists' understanding of the relationships between
45 them will likely continue to be revised. (For source reference, see endnote [6])

Passage 2

Native American languages are the indigenous languages of the Americas, spoken from Alaska and Greenland to the southern tip of South America. The Native American
50 languages consist of dozens of distinct language families as well as many language isolates; proposals to group these into higher-level families have been made by some linguists, but are not generally accepted.

55 Archeological and DNA evidence suggests that the Americas were peopled by migrants from Siberia about 13,000 years ago. From Alaska, the descendants of those first migrants went on to people the rest of North and South
60 America. The language spoken by these early migrants, and the process by which the current diversity of Native American languages emerged, are a matter of speculation. Some evidence suggests that the ancestors of the Na-
65 Dene and Eskimo-Aleut speakers arrived separately from Siberia some time after the earliest settlers.

Several Native American languages have developed their own writing systems, including
70 the Mayan languages and Nahuatl, the language of the Aztecs. These and many other Native American languages later adapted the Roman alphabet or Canadian Syllabics. Aleut was first written by missionaries in the Cyrillic
75 Alphabet, and later in the Roman alphabet.

Subsequent to the arrival of Christopher Columbus in the Americas in 1492, Spanish, English, Portuguese, French, and Dutch were brought to the Americas by European settlers
80 and administrators, and constitute the official languages of the independent states of the Americas, although Bolivia, Paraguay and Peru have one or more Native American languages as an official language in addition to Spanish.
85 Several indigenous Creole languages developed in the Americas from European languages. (For source reference, see endnote [7])

7. Passage 1 and Passage 2 are similar in that both

   (A) take an objective approach to their subjects
   (B) are written by scientists with narrow specialties
   (C) use metaphor as a basis for describing languages
   (D) discuss the same set of languages only in different terms
   (E) tend to view native languages from a European bias

8. The author of Passage 1 differs most from the author of Passage 2 because the former

(A) disclaims any expert knowledge
(B) avoids drawing any certain conclusions
(C) fails to distinguish between fact and speculation
(D) relies primarily on unscientific sources
(E) appears uncertain about important details

9. The first sentence of Passage 1 implies that the term Papuan languages

(A) has been misunderstood by most linguists
(B) does not refer to any clearly understandable concept
(C) has a double origin in both Australia and Austronesia
(D) can be understood in part by knowing what they are not
(E) will often be misused to refer to languages spoken in Australia

10. In line 13, "unity" most nearly means

(A) agreement
(B) harmony
(C) connection
(D) unanimity
(E) membership

11. In context, the phrase "family groupings" (line 17) is meant to imply that Papuan languages

(A) have a common origin
(B) are not all directly linked
(C) are spoken only by direct relatives
(D) all bear a resemblance to one another
(E) can be understood by any family member

12. Passage 1 indicates that knowledge about Papuan languages

(A) is far from complete
(B) can only be acquired by native speakers
(C) has been perfected by S.A. Wurm
(D) will be developed only with government funding
(E) has largely been proven false

13. The two passages differ in that, unlike Passage 2, Passage 1

(A) attempts to trace the development of the languages being discussed
(B) focuses on classification of the languages being discussed
(C) relies primarily on archeological and chemical evidence for its conclusions
(D) looks at only one language instead of an entire language group
(E) was more clearly written by a specialist in the field of linguistics

14. In lines 55-57, the author of Passage 2 shifts from

(A) an introduction of important terms to a consideration of general theories
(B) vague speculation to hard scientific data
(C) describing uncertainty and disagreement to discussing consensus
(D) a chronological to an archeological approach to the subject
(E) a hostile to a sympathetic stance

15. The statement in lines 60-63 ("The languages spoken ... a matter of speculation") implies that

(A) the way in which Native American and Papuan languages are related is unknown at this time
(B) there is no consensus among linguists about the origins of Native American languages
(C) there are those who doubt that native languages spread in the way commonly accepted
(D) the interpretation of the surviving writings of early missionaries cannot yet be completed
(E) there is some doubt about whether the Native languages are really as diverse as they seem

16. The phrase "later adapted" (line 73) indicates that

(A) a spoken language may be represented by more than one writing system
(B) missionaries feel that it is important to impose their writing system on natives
(C) the locals readily accepted the transformation of their languages brought about by Europeans
(D) European settlers had little difficulty translating native languages as long as they were written
(E) the Roman alphabet and Canadian Syllabics are written the same way

17. In line 85, "Creole" most likely means

(A) of mixed origin
(B) developed locally
(C) administrative
(D) written but not spoken
(E) officially recognized

18. Which statement about language is most strongly supported by both passages?

(A) Written language results from the efforts of outsiders to civilize a native population.
(B) Common classification systems include adaptations of the Roman alphabet.
(C) Only written languages can be fully understood by linguists.
(D) Most native languages were corrupted by the arrival of European explorers.
(E) Isolate languages defy attempts to tie languages together into high-level family groupings.

19. Which generalization best characterizes the conclusions drawn by both passages?

(A) Native peoples all speak languages that are difficult for scientists to study accurately.
(B) A complete study of all languages is required before a solid linguistic theory can be developed.
(C) Languages spoken by peoples who live in areas close to each other are not always related.
(D) The relationship between native languages extends from North and South America to Australia and the Pacific islands.
(E) Linguists feel that it is important to understand the relationships between all spoken and written languages.

7) A
8) B
9) D
10) C
11) B
12) A
13) B
14) C
15) B
16) A
17) A
18) E
19) C

CRITICAL READING LESSON 3

FURTHER PRACTICE

Focused practice, and careful analysis of your performance on homework and practice tests are the most important factors in improving your Critical Reading score. Lesson 3 is all about practice. Complete the Critical Reading sections listed below, and start to pay attention to your timing. If you're finishing ahead of time, you surely need to slow down. Try to balance speed and accuracy.

Practice reading only the first and last sentences of each paragraph in the textbook style passages (to save time and avoid filling your brain with unimportant details). After you finish each section, go back and take a slow, careful look at anything you missed, or anything you weren't sure about but got right anyway. Pay special attention to the wording of the Reading Comprehension answer choices. You want to figure out why you missed the question and how to get it right the next time.

HOMEWORK: CRITICAL READING LESSON 3

Review the chapter and focus on reading techniques before trying these Reading Comprehension problems. Also, any time you see a vocabulary word you don't know, add it to your list.

Pay special attention to the wording of the questions and answer choices!

Practice with these problems from *The Official SAT Study Guide:*

Practice Test	Section	Questions
3	3	1-24
	7	1-24
	9	1-19
4	3	1-24
	7	1-24
	9	1-19

All test, section, question and page numbers refer to *The Official SAT Study Guide (2004)*

Be sure to carefully score the sections from *The Official SAT Study Guide* and review the questions you miss. Figure out why you missed each question and how you can get it right the next time!

WRITING

The Writing section of the SAT consists of three Multiple-Choice question types — Error Identification, Sentence Improvement, and Paragraph Improvement — as well as an Essay question.

The essay is worth approximately 1/4 of the Writing score. How much the essay affects your final score depends to a certain extent on your performance on the Multiple-Choice questions. Take a look at the Writing section scoring table at the end of any test in *The Official Guide to the New SAT* if you want to see how the scores actually play out.

WRITING LESSON 1

THE ESSAY

Hate writing essays? Uncomfortable with the idea of a 25-minute essay? Fear not. The essay is not that tough. We'll show you how to maximize your essay score.

The essay is always the FIRST section of the test.

THE FORMAT

One of the criteria for a high essay score is good organization. You've probably had the 5-paragraph paper format driven into your head by now. Your SAT essay should be similar, but simpler.

While no specific format is required, we recommend a 4 – 5 paragraph essay because it promotes good organization. Basically, you need to state your point, support it with a couple of examples, and wrap up with a conclusion. Our recommended format is as follows:

PARAGRAPH 1 – INTRODUCTION

Make sure to answer the essay question that is asked. In fact, it's often useful to repeat the question word for word and then answer it. You may even want to start the essay with "I agree that..." or "I disagree with the statement..."

Mention the examples (or evidence) that you're going to use in the order you're going to use them. Two pieces of evidence is about right.

This paragraph should be about 3 – 5 sentences long.

PARAGRAPH 2 – EXAMPLE 1

Clearly state your first example or piece of evidence. Explain why it is a good example. Don't assume the reader has any knowledge of the subject matter you're writing about; be sure to explain completely.

This paragraph should be 4 – 5 sentences long.

PARAGRAPH 3 – EXAMPLE 2

Start with a transition word or phrase to link this paragraph with the one above. Transition phrases include: "furthermore", "in addition", "another example", etc.

Clearly state your second example or piece of evidence. Explain why it is a good example. Remember – you can't assume the reader has any knowledge of the subject matter you're writing about, so be sure to explain completely.

This paragraph should be 4 –5 sentences long.

PARAGRAPH 4 – EXAMPLE 3 – A COUNTEREXAMPLE (OPTIONAL)

A third example or counterexample is really optional. If you are a fast and accurate writer, you should consider adding this fourth paragraph, but you can still get a perfect score without it.

Use a counterexample: something that those arguing against your point might use. Show why this argument would be inappropriate, and, therefore, why it actually supports your point.

Start with a transition word or phrase to link this paragraph with the one above. Remember, if you use a counterexample, you should use transition words that make this clear. Transition phrases you might use include: "on the other hand…", "there are those who…", "one could argue…", etc.

This optional paragraph should be 4 – 5 sentences long.

PARAGRAPH 5 – CONCLUSION

Clearly restate your point, but use different words from those in the introduction to clarify your point even further. Use conclusion language, such as "As this essay clearly shows…"

Mention the two or three examples you used.

If possible, tie your idea to a slightly broader point.

This concluding paragraph should be 3 – 5 sentences long.

THE QUESTIONS

Here's an example of a typical essay question:

> "Decisive action in the face of challenging situations is paramount. It is necessary to act quickly and robustly lest we allow danger to intensify or opportunity to slip away. Those who waver shall be destroyed or left behind."
>
> Adapted from an imaginary text: *Forge Ahead, Facts Be Damned*

Is decisive action a better approach than a slow, careful, reasoned analysis of the facts? Plan and write an essay in which you develop your point of view on this issue. Support your position with reasoning and examples taken from your reading, studies, experience, or observation.

Most of the questions for the SAT essay, like the example above, ask you to agree or disagree with a particular point of view. Remember this: There is no right answer! These questions are chosen so that you can clearly argue either side of the point.

ANSWER THE QUESTION!

Read the question extremely carefully. It is crucial that you answer the question they're asking. If you write on a different topic, you will get no points! Zero. Zip. Zilch. Nada. This policy is even stated in all capitals in the instructions. (There are two rationales for this policy. First, they want to know that you can follow directions and focus on the topic at hand. Second, they want to make sure you haven't simply memorized a very good essay on a random subject.)

PICK A SIDE AND STICK TO IT.

Rule number one is: **DON'T WAFFLE!** Pick one side and defend it. Avoid a "sometimes yes, sometimes no" essay. While it is *possible* to score extremely well using a "yes and no" approach, it is harder to write a good essay.

Yes, it's true—the optional paragraph 4 talks about a counterexample that you debunk. It is appropriate to show that you have thought about the other side of the argument. Just clearly stand on only one side of the argument.

BRAINSTORMING

You should spend about 5 minutes brainstorming ideas and organizing your essay. Here's what you need to do:

BE PREPARED.

Yep, just like the Boy Scouts®, you too can be prepared.

- **Choose a favorite book.**

  Some books or plays have myriad themes and ideas. Pick a book that's complex and rich with ideas. Review the character names, situations and themes. You may be able to use an example from this book.

  Be careful, though. Don't try to force in an inappropriate example from one book simply because you've reviewed it. If it works for the essay you're assigned, great. If not, forget it.

- **Choose a bit of history.**

  Some events or periods of history also have myriad themes and ideas. Pick an event or time period that is complex and rich with ideas. Review pertinent events, situations and themes. You may be able to use an example from this bit of history.

  Again, be careful. Don't try to force in an inappropriate example from one bit of history simply because you've reviewed it. If it works for the essay you're assigned, great. If not, forget it.

BRAINSTORM BOTH SIDES

Don't lock yourself into one point of view before you brainstorm ideas! You may actually believe in one side of an argument, but be able to come up with better examples for the other side of the argument.

Make *For* and *Against* lists, and come up with as many ideas as you can in a few short minutes.

Here's an example of *For* and *Against* lists based on the sample question listed earlier in this lesson:

For	Against
Must act quickly in times of war or terrorist attack: Pearl Harbor.	Rash decisions are bad decisions: Romeo kills himself quickly when he thinks Juliet is dead.
Must make fast decisions on tests and quizzes: too much time on one question means you miss others.	If all death row inmates were put to death immediately, some innocent people would be killed: in several recent cases DNA evidence proved convicted murderers were innocent.
Business opportunities might slip away: eBay got there first and succeeded.	
If you don't ask someone for a date quickly, someone else might and you'll miss the chance.	Careful planning of the D-Day invasion, along with intricate deceptions like fake planes and tanks, led to its ultimate success.
Cuban missile crisis: quickly implementing blockade prevented Russians from completing nuclear missile sites in Cuba.	

Choose whichever side has better evidence.

Remember that arguments in favor of the opposing point of view can be used to your advantage. Refer back to the description of optional paragraph 4.

WRITING TIPS: IMPROVING THE ESSAY

After you've done some brainstorming, quickly decide which two or three examples you're going to use, and put them in order from strongest to weakest. Here are some other tips to help maximize your score:

USE ACTION VERBS

Most often, test takers get into trouble by overusing forms of the verb "to be" (is, are, were, being, etc.) Instead, use actions verbs. The essay graders are trained to look for action verbs and reward their use.

Instead of:	Use:
His considerations were…	He considered…
Edna's decision to…	Edna decided to…
Rosina's greeting was…	Rosina greeted…
Is	Reveals, shows, exemplifies

USE THE ACTIVE VOICE

If the subject of the verb is doing the action, a sentence is in the **active voice**.

> Ex) The lion ate the popcorn.

In this instance, the subject of the verb, the lion, is doing the eating.

If the subject is being acted upon, the sentence is in the **passive voice**.

> Ex) The popcorn was eaten by the lion.

In this instance, the subject, the popcorn, is being eaten. The object, the lion, is doing the eating.

Sentences in the active voice are generally better than sentences in the passive voice. Avoid using the passive voice in your essay.

MAKE IT CLEAN AND SIMPLE

Your sentences should be more sophisticated than "see Spot run," but not much.

- **Use clauses properly, or write separate sentences.**

  It's actually best to use a variety of sentence structures, but don't create long, run-on sentences because you think they sound impressive.

  One way to vary sentence structure is to use two clauses. You may remember that a clause is a complete idea with a subject and a verb. Clauses can be dependent or independent, but you don't really need to worry about that. Just remember that separate clauses must be separated:

  You can use a semicolon to separate clauses:

  > Ex) Amir installed the electrical panel; Mark brought the tools from the truck.

  Or you can separate clauses with a comma and a connecting word:

  > Ex) Amir installed the electrical panel, *and* Mark brought the tools from the truck.

You only need one connecting word. Don't use two connecting words!

> NO: *While* Amir installed the electrical panel, *and* Mark brought the tools from the truck.

- **Keep descriptive prepositional phrases to a minimum.**

   While it is important to use descriptive words in your essay, avoid using too many prepositional phrases all strung together.

VARY YOUR SENTENCE STRUCTURE

Often, essay writers get stuck in the same basic sentence mode for an entire paragraph or essay. For example, if you are writing an essay about the character of Huck from *Huckleberry Finn*, you might start three or four sentences with "Huck is..." or "Huck realized..." or "Huck's discovery..." or "Huck said..." While one or two such uses might be appropriate, starting three or four sentences the same way is considered redundant and tedious.

Instead, use different structures for different sentences.

Instead of:	Use:
Huck is viewed by others as...	Others view Huck as...
Huck made a bad decision when...	Poor choices lead to Huck's problems when...

Furthermore, try to vary the length and complexity of your sentences. Try using a mixture of *simple* sentences (with only one subject and verb), *compound* sentences (with two independent clauses), and *complex* sentences (with one main clause and one subordinate clause).

USE VOCABULARY CAREFULLY

Don't try to sound intelligent by using tough vocabulary words you don't FULLY understand. Choosing inappropriate words will cost you points. It's much better to use simple vocabulary clearly and concisely than to try to throw in big words.

On the other hand, if you DO understand some tough vocabulary, and you KNOW the word is appropriate, go ahead and use it.

LENGTH OF THE ESSAY

Basically, you just need to write enough to clearly state your point and provide adequate examples. However, while there is no required length, it is virtually impossible to fully develop an argument with an essay that is too short.

The answer sheet provides two pages on which to write your essay. Depending on how small you write, you should fill at least one full page, and probably about half or more of the second page. If you write extremely fast, or your writing is fairly large, two full pages is an acceptable amount, but don't go over two pages. You must stay within the essay boxes. The essay readers will not consider any part of your essay that falls outside the boxes.

WRITE LEGIBLY

Have you ever gotten a letter or card from you grandmother and struggled to figure out what the scribbling actually says, or received comments on a paper from a teacher, but couldn't understand what they were trying to say because he or she wrote so illegibly? (We all have… no offense to grandmothers, who generally rule!) It can be frustrating to say the least. First, if you can't figure it out, you simply won't know what the writer is trying to tell you. Second, even if you can figure it out, trying to decipher someone else's poor handwriting can interrupt the natural flow and progression of the words you're reading. The SAT essay is the same.

Remember that someone has to read your essay. Readers are trained not to take handwriting into consideration, but *if they can't read what you wrote, they can't give you a good score!* If your handwriting is horrible, write extremely carefully. Either printing or cursive writing is acceptable, so use whichever is the most legible.

Keep in mind the fact that, for most people, writing in script or cursive is a bit faster than printing. You've got to balance speed and legibility. If you are a slow writer to begin with, practice writing clearly in cursive… it may buy you some time.

Review the chapter and focus on brainstorming and structure before trying these essays.

Be sure to answer the question!

Practice with these problems from *The Official SAT Study Guide:*

Practice Test	Section	Questions	Page number
1	1	Essay	389
2	1	Essay	517

All test, section, question and page numbers refer to *The Official SAT Study Guide (2004)*

Some students find it understandably difficult to score their practice essays. Your English teacher, SAT instructor or tutor might be able to help. Be sure they fully understand the scoring guidelines set out in *The Official SAT Study Guide* before they review your practice essays. Learn from your content, grammar and style mistakes, and figure out how you can get a higher score the next time!

Additional Practice:

Essay Homework Drill 1

The essay gives you an opportunity to show how effectively you can write. Develop your ideas convincingly, and carefully express your point of view precisely, logically and clearly.

Write an essay on the topic assigned below. You have twenty-five minutes to plan and write your essay. DO NOT WRITE ON ANOTHER TOPIC OR YOU WILL BE GIVEN A SCORE OF ZERO.

Carefully consider the issue presented in the following excerpt and the assignment below.

> Alumni are the life blood of any institution of higher learning. Through contributions to academic, sports, cultural, and social programs, alumni provide colleges and universities with the resources needed to foster the development of students for generations to come. Absent preferential treatment of alumni children, alumni participation would dwindle to a level unhealthy to individual institutions and the educational system as a whole.

Assignment: Should colleges and universities give children of alumni special preference in the admissions process? Plan and write your essay, developing your own point of view on this topic. Support your point with examples from your studies, experience, literature, current events or personal observation.

WRITING LESSON 2

WRITING: THE MULTIPLE-CHOICE QUESTIONS

There are two Multiple-Choice writing sections.

The first section contains 35 Multiple-Choice questions of three different types. They appear in the following order:

1-11 Sentence Improvement questions (11 total)
12-29 Error Identification questions (18 total)
30-35 Paragraph Improvement questions (6 total)

Just because they appear in that order doesn't mean you have to do them in that order. Error Identification questions are the fastest (and often the easiest) writing questions. Sentence Improvement questions take a little more time, and Paragraph Improvement questions take the most time. So...

❶ Do Error Identification questions first!

❷ Move to Sentence Improvement questions second.

❸ Finally, finish up with Paragraph Improvement questions.

The second Multiple-Choice Writing section is all Sentence Improvement.

Note!
Paragraph Improvement questions are NOT in order of difficulty. Error Identification and Sentence Improvement questions are in approximate order of difficulty.

The Multiple-Choice Writing section is all about grammar, usage and word choice.

The first three Writing lessons in this book focus on grammar and the common errors. After that, we'll take a look at tackling the specific question types.

GRAMMAR, USAGE, AND WORD CHOICE PART I

It probably took you several years of school to get through every last bit of American English grammar. With that in mind, this section might seem rather daunting, but don't be fooled. The SAT doesn't test all that much grammar. The vast majority of questions are based on only 6 or 7 basic grammar rules. There are 6 or 7 more that appear occasionally. There are very few questions that deal with grammar rules that fall outside that range.

GRAMMAR BASICS

This manual assumes some basic understanding of grammar. You need to know the difference between a noun and a verb, an adjective and an adverb. You need to know how to spot the subject and object of a verb. You need to be able to pick out prepositions and pronouns. If you don't know these things, pick up a basic grammar book and start from the beginning.

SUBJECT – VERB – OBJECT: GETTING RID OF THE GARBAGE

The three most basic parts of any sentence are: the subject, which performs the action; the verb, which indicates the action; and the object, which receives the action. (When a sentence is in the passive voice, the subject is acted upon by the object... but we'll get to that later.)

Ex) Picasso painted pictures.
(subj)   (verb)   (obj)

Many questions test grammar rules based on these basic parts of a sentence, but the test writers fill the sentence with all sorts of other junk to make these questions confusing.

PREPOSITIONAL PHRASES ARE *OFTEN* JUNK

Prepositions are words, such as "of", "with", "from", "during" and "above," that show the relationship of a noun or pronoun to some other part of a sentence.

Ex) The book *on* the shelf...

The preposition "on" tells us the relationship between the shelf and the book. Prepositions most often tell the relative position of objects, but they can do other thing as well.

Ex) The color *of* money...

Prepositional phrases are phrases with a preposition followed by a noun or pronoun.

Prepositional phrases are *usually* garbage! It is often helpful to cross them off.

Now let's take a look at our Picasso sentence again, this time clogged with prepositions:

> Ex) Picasso painted pictures **during** his blue period **from** 1900 to 1904 and **during** his rose period **from** 1905 to 1906.

Cross off the prepositional phrases to simplify the sentence…

> Ex) Picasso painted pictures ~~**during** his blue period **from** 1900 to 1904 and **during** his rose period **from** 1905 to 1906~~.

… and we're back to our original subject, verb and object.

Be careful! Sometimes prepositions are important, usually when a question is testing idioms or parallelism. See the idiom and parallelism sections for more information.

DESCRIPTIVE PHRASES OR CLAUSES ARE *OFTEN* JUNK

The people who write the SAT also like to clog sentences with descriptive phrases and subordinate clauses.

> Ex) Picasso, who was born in Malaga, Spain in October of 1881, painted pictures.

The entire phrase "who was born in Malaga, Spain in October of 1881" simply describes Picasso in more detail. Get rid of it to look at subject-verb-object.

> Ex) Picasso~~, who was born in Malaga, Spain in October of 1881,~~ painted pictures.

Notice that this descriptive phrase is separated from the rest of the sentence by a comma at the beginning and the end. This can make it easy to spot.

A good point to remember is that a subject and its verb are never separated by a single comma! If there is one comma between a subject and its verb, you must either delete the single comma or add a second comma to set off a descriptive phrase.

There can certainly be errors within descriptive phrases or clauses, so check for errors in those sections before you cross them off.

SUBJECT – VERB AGREEMENT

It's a simple concept, but hard to spot on the test unless you know what to look for: **Singular subjects take singular verbs. Plural subjects take plural verbs**. One thing to remember is that, unlike nouns, singular verbs often end in the letter "s" while plural verbs do not. Here's how the SAT tries to trick you:

GARBAGE BETWEEN THE SUBJECT AND VERB

Sometimes the subject and verb are separated from each other by lots of words or phrases. To add insult to injury, the SAT might place a noun that is not the subject right next to the verb, making you think that it is the subject.

- **The MAIN subject of a sentence can NEVER be part of a prepositional phrase**

  Try ignoring or crossing out prepositional phrases. As you've learned, prepositional phrases are usually garbage.

  > Ex) The main *focus* (singular subject) of the related discussions *was* (singular verb) the devastating effect of the hurricane.

Note that the plural noun *discussions* is placed right next to the verb, but the subject, *focus*, is actually singular.

CONFUSING SUBJECTS

In addition to hiding subjects in distant corners of sentences, the SAT also throws in subjects that seem plural but are really singular, or seem singular but are really plural. Here are the things to look out for:

- **Compound Subjects**

  When two or more subjects are joined with an "and", the subject is considered plural:

  > YES: Enrique and Sam *own* (plural) turtles.

- **As Well As, In Addition To**

  These are both really just modifying phrases. They describe words, but DON'T make a singular subject plural.

  > YES: *John*, as well as Edna, *comes* (singular) here every day.
  > …or…
  > YES: My *car* in addition to most other people's cars *runs* (singular) on gasoline.

- **Either... Or, Neither... Nor**

  These confuse most people. The rule is actually quite simple: the verb agrees with the second noun (the one that follows the "or" or the "nor.")

  > YES: Either my cats or my dog ... *is* (singular) ... hungry.
  > ...or...
  > YES: Either my dog or my cats ... *are* (plural) ... hungry.

- **Groups**

  Words that refer to a group or a collection are usually singular, for example:

  > The Netherlands
  >
  > The United States
  >
  > The Sparks
  >
  > University
  >
  > Troop
  >
  > Army
  >
  > Flock
  >
  > Any team, company, school

  > YES: The Dodgers ... *is* (singular) ... a great team.
  > YES: Microsoft ... *wants* (singular) ... you to buy *its* products.

VERB FORM

Verb form questions deal with proper verb tense and proper form (such as past participles or gerunds).

The general rule for verb tense is to *be consistent*! Don't change tense in the middle of a sentence (or paragraph) unless there is a specific reason to do so.

If the sentence starts in the present tense, stay in the present tense (unless there's a specific reason to change).

If the sentence starts in the past tense, stay in the past tense (unless there's a specific reason to change).

If the sentence is talking about a past time period, the sentence must be in the past tense.

Also, keep the tense simple if you can. Some specific situations require slightly more complicated tense use.

PRESENT PERFECT TENSE

The present perfect tense uses the helping verb *has* or *have*, along with the past participle of the verb. For example, "I have run well so far this year," or "It has snowed every day this week!"

The present perfect indicates an action that started in the past and has continued right up to the present.

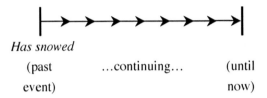

Has snowed

  (past   ...continuing...   (until

  event)   now)

The word "since" is often used to mean "continuously from the time when..." and therefore often indicates that present perfect should be used.

PAST PERFECT TENSE

The past perfect tense uses the helping verb *had*, along with the past participle of the verb. For example, "I had run well this year before I sprained my ankle," or "It had snowed heavily until about 4 pm, when it stopped suddenly."

The past perfect indicates a distant past event that happened earlier than another past event:

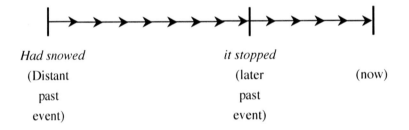

Had snowed   *it stopped*

(Distant   (later   (now)

  past   past

  event)   event)

CONDITIONALS AND HYPOTHETICALS

A conditional sentence expresses an idea or an action that is dependent on an imagined condition.

YES: If Paula had a jet, she would fly around the world.

The action of flying around the world is dependent on Paula's owning a jet, which she doesn't.

Conditional can be in the present, the future, or the "habitual present."

Present: If he had a candy bar, he would eat it.

Future: If I have a candy bar tomorrow, I might / will eat it.

Habitual: When / If I have a candy bar, I eat it.

This is all pretty straight forward, but in walks the subjunctive mood, and things get a wee bit trickier. Subjunctive mood conditional (you don't need to know the name) uses *were* and *would*, sometimes with the word *if*, sometimes not:

> YES: *Were* the subjunctive case to walk into the room, things *would* get uncomfortably weird.
> ...or...
> YES: If the subjunctive case *were* to walk into the room, things *would* get uncomfortably weird.
> ...or...
> YES: Things *would* get uncomfortably weird *were* the subjunctive case to walk into the room.
> ...or...
> YES: Things *would* get uncomfortably weird if the subjunctive case *were* to walk into the room.

Notice that when the word *were* is followed by a verb, the verb is always the infinitive. (*Were* doesn't have to be followed by a verb: If I *were* faster, I *would* have won the race.)

> The important thing to remember is that *would* always goes with *were* in subjunctive conditionals.

BEING IS *ALMOST* ALWAYS WRONG

The word *being* is almost always wrong! *Being* is the present participle (the -ing form) of the verb *to be*, and it is very difficult to use properly.

If you see the word *being* in an answer choice, be *extremely* reluctant to choose it.

In a few instances, *being* is actually acceptable. For instance, if the word *being* must be parallel with a second instance of the word *being* that cannot be changed, then you must use it.

> Ex) Being first across the finish line in the Olympics marathon is more impressive than <u>being last in a potato-sack race</u> at a family reunion picnic, but the latter is usually more fun.

If *being* appears in every answer choice, then you must choose it. This happens occasionally.

If *being* is used as a noun to indicate an object or person that exists, for example *human being,* then it's fine.

Also, in some phrases, such as *for the time being, all things being equal, still being,* the word *being* is also acceptable, but even these phrases are wordy and there is usually a better alternative.

PRONOUNS

Pronoun issues fall into three basic categories: Agreement, Case and Ambiguity.

> *Whenever* a pronoun appears in a Writing question, you should check it carefully! Pronoun errors are very common.

PRONOUN AGREEMENT

A pronoun has to agree in person and number (singular or plural) with the noun it refers to (the antecedent). Singular nouns take singular pronouns and plural nouns take plural pronouns.

The test writers usually make this difficult in two ways:
- **Separating the noun and pronoun with lots of garbage.**

> NO: The government of Blurvania, an imaginary province, always adjusts *their* census numbers to show a small proportion of the population living below the poverty line.

The *government* is singular, so the pronoun should be *its.*

> YES: The government of Blurvania, an imaginary province, always adjusts *its* census numbers to show a small proportion of the population living below the poverty line.

- **Using confusing nouns that seem plural but are really singular or seem singular but are really plural.**

> NO: Each of the contestants donned *their* hat at the appropriate cue from the show's producer.

The subject *each* is singular. The sentence should read:

> YES: Each of the contestants donned *his (or her)* hat at the appropriate cue from the show's producer.

Any pronoun that ends in ...*one*, ...*body*, or ...*thing* is singular.
Here's a list of other singular pronouns:

one	anyone	someone	no one
none	everyone	anybody	somebody
nobody	everybody	anything	something
nothing	everything	any	each

PRONOUN CASE

Case refers to whether a pronoun is used as a subject (subjective case), or a direct or indirect object (objective case). Subject pronouns include I, you, he, she, it, we, and they. Object pronouns, which act as objects of a verb or a preposition, include: me, you, him, her, it, us and them.

The test writers usually make these questions difficult by using compound subjects and objects connected by the word "and":

> Ex)   Bob and *I / me* went to the bank.

> Ex)   The medal was awarded to John and *she / her*.

To solve these, simply get rid of the other subject or object: the "Bob and" or the "John and":

> Ex)   ~~Bob and~~ *I / ~~me~~* went to the bank.

> Ex)   The medal was awarded to ~~John and~~ ~~*she*~~*/ her*.

PRONOUN AMBIGUITY

Pronouns must refer to a specific noun. If there are two singular nouns in a sentence, for example, the pronoun *it* might refer to either noun:

> NO: Henry exchanged stamp collections with Wilfred and he got the better deal.

The question is, which "he" got the better deal? Henry or Wilfred? It is unclear in this sentence.

Better versions of this sentence might be:

> YES: Henry exchanged stamp collections with Wilfred and Henry got the better deal.
> ...or...
> YES: Henry got the better deal when he exchanged stamp collections with Wilfred.

In the second example, since Wilfred can't really exchange stamps with himself, the *he* must refer to Henry.

NOUN-TO-NOUN AGREEMENT

The SAT sometimes tests noun-to-noun agreement as well, usually creating an error in which two people or objects are said to become one single thing.

> NO: Eduardo and Celine are studying to become a lawyer.
> NO: Students are required to write their papers on a computer.

What are the problems here? Well, how can two people become a single lawyer? Do you expect all the students to write their papers on one single computer? Not exactly reasonable sentences, are they? Here's how they should read:

> YES: Eduardo and Celine are studying to become lawyers.
> YES: Students are required to write their papers on computers.

Review the chapter and focus on the common errors before trying these Grammar problems.

Practice with these problems from *The Official SAT Study Guide:*

Practice Test	Section	Question
1	7	3, 7, 9, 12, 13, 14, 16, 19, 20, 21, 22, 23, 26
	10	1, 4, 11, 12

All test, section, question and page numbers refer to *The Official SAT Study Guide* (2004)

Be sure to carefully score the sections from *The Official SAT Study Guide* and review the questions you miss. Figure out why you missed each question and how you can get it right the next time!

Additional Practice:

Grammar Homework Drill 1

For the following sentences, underline the main subject and verb only.

1. Whether or not Edwin knew of the impending strike by airline employees, his flight from Phoenix to New York on one of the discount carriers was about to be delayed.

2. The carpet salesman who helped us in the store last week said that we could get a discount on the lime green shag carpet since no one else wanted to buy it.

3. Four times in the past week, the alarm on my neighbor's brand new convertible, which is parked right outside my window, went off at an annoying late hour.

4. To add insult to injury, after waiting on hold for customer service for nearly an hour, the service agent, who must really be a horrible person, hung up on me as soon as I complained about the company's products.

5. While I don't normally stray so far from the marked path, the wonderful sound of falling water from the awe-inspiring triple waterfall lured me so far afield that I almost didn't find my way back to the lodge before the sun dipped beneath the horizon.

For the following sentences, choose the italicized word or phrase that contains correct subject-verb agreement.

6. In retrospect, the plight of the birds of the upper Andes *demand* / *demands* greater attention and the allocation of more resources.

7. Erma, as well as Hank, *walk* / *walks* to work every day, rain or shine.

8. The Netherlands, located in the midst of several other distinct nations, *has* / *have* a completely unique culture.

9. Neither his warmest jacket nor his favorite albums *was* / *were* anywhere to be found, and Johan began to suspect his sister had taken them all with her to college.

10. While not entirely well organized, the Flivinian army troop *surpass* / *surpasses* all others when it comes to the stylishness of their berets.

11. After he had lunch with his friend George, Basil *was strolling / strolled / strolls* along the Third Street Promenade, window-shopping.

12. My uncle Dick always says that if pigs were able to fly, the president *would be / is / had been* in danger during hunting season.

13. My fortunes have turned since *my being / I was / I have been* made chairman of the social committee.

14. Standing in the rain at the bus stop, Lizbeth realizes that it *had been / was / has been* raining non-stop for nearly a week.

15. Since being a rock star is much harder on the human body than *to teach / having taught / being a teacher*, some insurance companies want to raise health insurance premiums for rock stars.

16. The committee knew that the presentation was to be given by Jake and *I / me*.

17. The museum wanted more information about the massive collection of pre-Columbian artifacts, but only two weeks before the exhibition, *it / they* had received no contact from the organizers.

18. If Eddie Izzard were to compete with Jay Leno in a head-to-head comedy competition, surely *they / he / Eddie* would win.

19. Despite an increasing mountain of evidence to the contrary, Omar and *she / her*, noted experts in the field of interior design and not planetary sciences, stood by their position that the earth was shaped like a giant snowflake because they felt the crystalline structure was more aesthetically pleasing.

20) The company's board of directors walked a fine line between proper management and self-serving supervision, since *he / it / they* increased executive and board salaries more than tenfold.

Answers:

1. his flight...was
2. the salesman...said
3. the alarm...went off
4. the agent...hung up
5. the sound...lured
6. demands
7. walks
8. has
9. were
10. surpasses
11. strolled
12. would be
13. I was
14. has been
15. being a teacher
16. me
17. it
18. Eddie
19. she
20. it

WRITING LESSON 3

THE COMMON ERRORS PART II

PARALLELISM

Parallelism is a general term that applies to rules that require different parts of a sentence to be in the same form. Parallelism is tested in several ways.

LISTS

Lists can be two words or phrases connected by an "and," or a series of several words or phrases separated by commas. All items in a list must be parallel, in the same basic form. Lists can consist of all nouns, all verbs in the same form, all prepositional phrases, etc. You can't combine types in a list. Here's an example of incorrect parallelism:

> NO: Nearly everyone likes eating chocolate, pretzels and eating chips.

Notice that the three things in the list above are **either** "eating chocolate", "pretzels" and "eating chips" **or** "chocolate", "pretzels" and "eating chips." In either case, the items are a mixture of nouns and verbs. The main list items have to be all nouns, all verbs or all modifiers in the same basic form. You can fix this sentence in two ways:

> YES: Nearly everyone likes eating chocolate, pretzels and chips.
> ...or...
> YES: Nearly everyone likes eating chocolate, eating pretzels and eating chips.

The second sentence is a bit redundant, so the first is preferable, though the second is still grammatically correct.

It sometimes helps to think of lists as branches. Each branch must be in the same form:

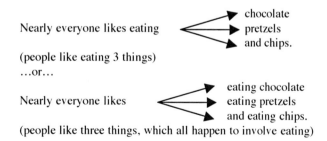

Nearly everyone likes eating
- chocolate
- pretzels
- and chips.

(people like eating 3 things)
...or...

Nearly everyone likes
- eating chocolate
- eating pretzels
- and eating chips.

(people like three things, which all happen to involve eating)

- **Watch out for Gerunds**

   Gerunds are –ing forms of verbs that can be used as nouns. While gerunds are technically parallel to other nouns in lists, you should avoid them if there is a good noun alternative.

   > NO: Ed was known for his compassion for and *acknowledging* of those less fortunate than himself.

   While "acknowledging" is a gerund, and therefore technically a noun, there is a better option: "acknowledgement." This one is better:

   > YES: Ed was known for his compassion for and *acknowledgement* of those less fortunate than himself.

COMPARISONS

If two items, ideas or actions are compared, they must also be parallel. Look for *than* and *as*…[something]…*as*, which indicate comparisons.

> NO: Henrietta likes soccer more than playing darts.

In this case, *soccer* is the sport being compared to *playing darts*, but they're not in the same form (even though *playing* is a gerund acting as a noun).

> NO: Erika has as many games as George.

In this case, the subject-verb combination *Erika has* is being compared to *George*, but you can't compare a subject-verb combination to a noun. It must be subject-verb to subject-verb.

The correct comparisons are:

> YES: Henrietta likes soccer more than darts.
> …or…
> YES: Henrietta likes playing soccer more than playing darts.
>
> YES: Erika has as many games as George has.
> …or…
> YES: Erika has as many games as George does.

Comparisons must not only be parallel in form, but also parallel in content.

Here's an example of a bad comparison:

> NO: The Iron Pony's inventory of performance motorcycle gear is much larger than most of their competitors.

Sound fine? So what's the problem here? Well, the example above actually compares *inventory* to *competitors*. That's not parallel. Instead, compare *inventory* to *inventory*:

> YES: The Iron Pony's inventory of performance motorcycle parts is much larger than most of their competitors' inventories.
> …or…
> YES: The Iron Pony's inventory of performance motorcycle parts is much larger than most of their competitors'.

Note that in the second example, only an apostrophe was added. Because *competitors'* is possessive, it implies the idea of *inventory*.

LIKE, SUCH AS, AND AS

These comparison words merit some special attention.

- **"Like" means "similar to"**

  "Like" is used to compare two similar nouns.

  > YES: Your flip-flops are *like* mine.

  DON'T use like to show an example:

  > NO: I enjoy sci-fi movies *like* the original *Star Wars*.

  (This is wrong because it indicates that this person enjoys movies similar to, but NOT including, *Star Wars*.)

- **"Such as" means "for example"**

  "Such as" is used to show an example of something.

  > YES: I enjoy sci-fi movies *such as* the original *Star Wars*.

- **"As" compares verbs**

  "As" is used to compare verbs, or subject-verb combinations.

  > YES: You should think *as* I do.

  (Here the sentence is comparing actions: Thinking to thinking.)

  Don't use *like* to compare verbs or actions:

  > NO: Walk like I walk.

  > YES: Walk as I walk.

A note on the pro-verbs "do" and "does":

Just as a pronoun can replace a noun, the words "do" and "does" can replace verbs and verb phrases. They are called "pro-verbs" (not to be confused with proverbs, which are short sayings that express a basic truth).

"Do" and "does" can also be used as helping verbs that create emphasis (I do like chocolate) or introduce a question (Do you like chocolate?)

MODIFYING PHRASES

Before we get to the rules about modifying phrases, let's recall the important differences between a *phrase* and a *clause*.

A *phrase* is a group of words that forms an idea but not a complete sentence. A phrase DOES NOT have a subject-verb combination:

Ex) Looking at the bank...
Ex) Wondering what to do next...
Ex) Completed ahead of schedule...

Note that each of these phrases implies a question:

Who is looking at the bank?
Who is wondering what to do next?
What was completed ahead of schedule?

A *clause* is a group of words that DOES contain a subject and a verb:

Ex) While Ed was looking at the bank...
Ex) I wondered what to do next...
Ex) Although it was completed ahead of schedule...

Each of these clauses has a subject, which can be a noun or pronoun: *Ed*, *I*, and *it*.

A phrase must be placed right next to the thing it modifies.

The SAT usually tests this rule by placing phrases, called introductory phrases, at the beginning of a sentence. These introductory phrases are usually followed by commas. Instead of following the phrase with the word it modifies (usually a noun), the test writers stick some other noun right after the phrase. Let's take a look:

NO: Archived in massive underground storage vaults, government librarians keep detailed indexes of the secret files.

So what's wrong? Well, the introductory phrase is "Archived in massive underground storage vaults." This phrase implies a question: what is archived? Well, according to this sentence, the "librarians" are archived, because "librarians" is the first noun that follows the phrase.

To check for this error, place the noun that follows the phrase in front of the phrase. You may have to add a helping verb like "was" or "were":

Ex) Librarians [were] archived in massive underground storage vaults...

Does this make any sense? Not unless you're a twisted megalomaniacal super-villain in a James Bond film called "Repositorian" about your attempt to take over the world by controlling all the information available in libraries. Which you might be...

... but we doubt it.

To correct the error, you have three choices:

- **Change the phrase so it modifies the noun that follows.**

    YES: Archiving secret files in massive underground storage vaults, government librarians keep detailed indexes.

    (Check it: "Librarians were archiving secret files..." Yep, makes sense.)

- **Place the noun that should be modified by the phrase right next to it.**

    YES: Archived in massive underground storage vaults, secret files are indexed in detail by government librarians.

    (Check it: "Files were archived..." Yep, makes sense.)

- **Turn the phrase into a clause.**

    YES: When the secret files were archived in massive underground storage vaults, government librarians kept detailed indexes.

Note that the sentence now starts with a clause, which doesn't need to be next to something it modifies… it has its own subject-verb combination.

Sometimes the nasty SAT writers will try to play another trick on you. They'll put a possessive word that looks like the correct noun right after a phrase, but the possessive is really just modifying a noun that is incorrectly placed. Let's take a look at this trick:

> NO: Attempting to write exactly what she felt, Anna's journal revealed some of her deepest fears.

Note that *Anna's* is NOT a noun… it's used as a possessive adjective modifying *journal*. So if we use our test, according to this sentence, "*Anna's journal* was attempting to write exactly what she felt…" Now that's a pretty impressive journal!

The tricky part is that we know *Anna* "is attempting to write," so at first glance it seems like the sentence is correct. Here are two correct versions:

> YES: Attempting to write exactly what she felt in her journal, Anna revealed some of her deepest fears.
> …or…
> YES: Attempting to write exactly what she felt, Anna revealed some of her deepest fears in her journal.

IDIOMS

Idioms, as far as the SAT goes, refer most often to specific prepositions that fit with specific verbs. For example, you "associate *with*" other people; you don't "associate *to*" other people. You "worry *about*" things; you don't "worry *over*" things.

Every time you see a preposition in an underlined section, check to see if it is the right preposition for the situation!

Please note that some verbs can take several different prepositions, depending on the intended meaning. Also, prepositions are often separated from the verb by other words. For example, "Mr. Herman *believed* "Moby Dick" *to be* the greatest story ever told." *Believed… to be* is the proper idiom.

A list of common idioms that might appear on the SAT follows. There are lots more, so please add to this list as you see more examples of idioms.

ability **to** (do something)	Neither.....**nor**.....
as.....**as**.....	not only......but also
associate **with**	not so much.....**as**.....
attributed **to**	permitted **to** (do something)
believed **to be**	prohibit **from** (doing something)
both.....**and**.....	regard.....**as**.....
consider (doesn't take "to be")	required **to** (do something)
contrast.....**with**.....	responsibility **to** (do something)
credited **with**	responsible **for** (some thing or action)
different **from**	see.....**as**.....
distinguish.....**from**......	so.....**as to be**
(distinguish) between.....**and**.....	so.....**that**.....
either.....**or**.....	superior **to**
estimated **to be**	targeted **at**
forbid **to** (do something)	the same.....**as**.....
from.....**to**	think of.....**as**.....
hypothesis **that**	try **to** (do something)
Just as.....**so too**	worry **about**
more.....**than**.....	
native **of** (referring to a person)	
native **to** (referring to a plant or animal)	

CLAUSES, CONNECTORS, AND COMMAS

The SAT likes to test your understanding of clauses, connectors and proper comma usage. A clause, you remember, contains a subject and a verb, and can stand alone as an idea (as opposed to a phrase, which doesn't have a subject-verb combination).

If you have two clauses in a sentence, they must be separated by a comma and a connecting word, or by a semicolon. Let's say that again:

> **Clauses require a comma and a connecting word**
> ...or...
> **a semicolon with no connector.**

You can also turn two independent clauses into two separate sentences.

Connecting words, also called conjunctions, come in two forms: Coordinating conjunctions and subordinating conjunctions. For all practical purposes on the SAT, you DON'T need to know the difference between coordinating and subordinating conjunctions. They follow the same basic rule, but we've listed them separately because our grandmothers would have wanted it that way. They always were sticklers for grammar.

Coordinating conjunctions join two independent clauses:

and	but	or
yet	for	so

NO: Eric went to the electronics store thinking he would only look but he made an impulse purchase.
…and…
NO: Eric went to the electronics store thinking he would only look, he made an impulse purchase.

In these two examples, the sentences lack either a comma or a connector to join the two phrases "Eric went to the electronics store thinking he would only look" and "he made an impulse purchase."

Here's how to fix them:

YES: Eric went to the electronics store thinking he would only look, but he made an impulse purchase.
…or…
YES: Eric went to the electronics store thinking he would only look; he made an impulse purchase.
…or…
YES: Eric went to the electronics store thinking he would only look. He made an impulse purchase.

In the first case, we added a comma. In the second case we changed the comma to a semicolon with no connection word. In the third case, we turned the two clauses into separate sentences.

Please note! If two independent clauses are nicely balanced and short, it is sometimes acceptable to leave out the comma, but it is *always* acceptable to include a comma:

YES: Eric went to the store and he made a purchase.
…or…
YES: Eric went to the store, and he made a purchase.

This short, balanced clause issue is only occasionally tested on the SAT.

Subordinating conjunctions join a dependent clause and an independent clause:

after	if	the first time
although	if only	though
as	in order that	unless
as if	now that	until
as long as	once	when
as though	rather than	whenever
because	since	where
before	so that	whereas
even if	than	wherever
even though	that	while

Subordinating conjunctions may come between the two clauses or before the first clause:

> YES: Tess likes chocolate, while I prefer vanilla.

> YES: Although the box was dropped from a great height, the air conditioning unit inside was not damaged.

Please note! The word *however* is NOT considered a connecting word! *However* is NOT a substitute for the conjunction *but*. If you use *however* you also need to separate the clauses with a semicolon (and separate the *however* with a comma):

> NO: The price is exorbitant, however I'll pay it because I like the painting.

> YES: The price is exorbitant, but I'll pay it because I like the painting.
> …or…
> YES: The price is exorbitant; however, I'll pay it because I like the painting.

ADVERBS VS. ADJECTIVES

Sometimes the test writers will put in an adjective where there should be an adverb. Adjectives can only modify nouns. Adverbs can modify verbs (*laughing heartily*), adjectives (*extremely cold*) or other adverbs (*very slowly*). Remember that *most* adverbs end in *–ly*.

> NO: The pick-up traveled swift along the country road.

The word *swift* is actually trying to describe how something *traveled*; therefore it should be an adverb, *swiftly*.

Occasionally, adverb errors involve the placement of the adverb. In general terms, any modifier should be as close to the thing it modifies as reasonably possible. Take a look at this example:

> NO: Tyrone types his class notes every evening after he gets home from school diligently.

In this case, *diligently* refers to the action *types*, but it is placed so far away from *types* that it seems to modify *gets home* instead. The sentence should read:

> YES: Tyrone diligently types his class notes every evening after he gets home from school.

REDUNDANCY AND DOUBLE NEGATIVES

We all know that it's preferable to avoid repeating yourself if not absolutely necessary, avoid saying the same thing twice, and even avoid reiterating redundantly again and again!

The SAT occasionally creates errors by inserting redundant words or phrases, or introducing double negatives. Keep an eye out for the following errors:

REDUNDANCIES

Some words or phrases already include certain meanings that shouldn't be repeated. Here are some phrases that are considered redundant:

Redundancy:	Should be:
Biography of his life	Biography
Close proximity	Proximity
Repeat again	Repeat
4 pm in the afternoon	4 pm

> NO: Many of Cornell's alumni who had attended the school donated to the annual fund drive.

If the sentence is talking about *alumni*, we already know they went to Cornell. The sentence should read:

> YES: Many of Cornell's alumni donated to the annual fund drive.

DOUBLE NEGATIVES

- **Can't or can hardly**

  The proper uses are *can't* or *can hardly*, **not** *can't hardly*.

  > NO: I can't hardly wait for the holidays.

  > YES: I can hardly wait for the holidays.
  > ...or...
  > YES: I can't wait for the holidays.

- **Scarcely any / Hardly any**

  The proper uses are *scarcely any* or *hardly any* or *no* or *none*, not *scarcely no, scarcely none, hardly no* or *hardly none:*

  > NO: I spent scarcely no time on that assignment.
  > ...or...
  > NO: I have hardly seen none of my friends all summer.
  >
  > YES: I spent scarcely any time on that assignment.
  > ...or...
  > YES: I spent no time on that assignment.
  > ...or...
  > YES: I have hardly seen any of my friends all summer.
  > ...or...
  > YES: I have seen none of my friends all summer.

- **Both... as well as**

  As well as already implies both. *Both* needs to have *and* (see Idioms earlier in this lesson).

  > NO: Both scientists as well as philosophers were fascinated by the discovery of water on Mars.
  >
  > YES: Both scientists and philosophers were fascinated by the discovery of water on Mars.
  > ...or...
  > YES: Scientists as well as philosophers were fascinated by the discovery of water on Mars.

Review the chapter and focus on the common errors before trying these Grammar problems.

Practice with these problems from *The Official SAT Study Guide:*

Practice Test	Section	Question
1	7	3, 5, 6, 8, 10, 11, 15, 17, 18, 24, 28, 29
	10	2, 3, 5, 6, 7, 9, 10, 13, 14

All test, section, question and page numbers refer to *The Official SAT Study Guide (2004)*

Be sure to carefully score the sections from *The Official SAT Study Guide* and review the questions you miss. Figure out why you missed each question and how you can get it right the next time!

Additional Practice:

Grammar Homework Drill

In the following sentences, circle the italicized portion of the sentence that is most parallel with the rest of the sentence.

1. Everyone I know has favorite pastimes, which might include surfing, playing video games, and *to go to / going to* the movies.

2. Wending your way through a beautiful forest can be more relaxing than *a luxurious spa / going to a luxurious spa / to go to a luxurious spa.*

3. Overall the dining experience at Joe's is absolutely fabulous, and even the menu at Joe's is more enticing than *Clown Town / Clown Town's / the salads of Clown Town.*

4. I want to live in New Zealand more than *you / you have / you do.*

5. Erika was somewhat vain and liked people to notice her striking good looks rather than her intelligence, sensitivity and *generosity / giving generously.*

In the following sentences, choose the italicized word or group of words that correctly uses an introductory phrase or clause.

6. *Helping / Because he helped* at the shelter, the food distribution process went much more smoothly.

7. Falling to the ground, *Krista's knees were scraped / Krista scraped her knees.*

8. *Confused / Since he was confused* by what he saw, his actions belied apprehension.

9. *Swinging the bat hard / Flying swiftly from the bat,* the shortstop's smartly hit ball was destined to make it over the fence.

10. Reginald's face registered utter glee, *an emotion he hadn't felt / he hadn't felt it* in a long time.

In the following sentences, choose the best idiom to complete the meaning of the sentence.

11. Just as the sky will never fall, *so / so too* will the mountains never float.

12. Karina knew that the birch tree was *a native of / native to* North America as well as other continents.

13. Watching the news every night on TV, one cannot help but worry *on / about* the state of the world today.

14. Beauty is in the eye of the beholder, but unfortunately many contrast beauty *to / with* intelligence.

15. In my opinion, dark chocolate is vastly superior *to / than* milk chocolate.

16. Despite waking up in a strange bed, *Wilma / but Wilma* loves being in the tropical resort.

17. I was positive that I knew how to work the complicated *machinery, however / machinery; however*, I reread the directions just to be sure.

18. *Even if / Because* the odds are against them, millions of people will gamble at casinos this year in hopes of winning.

19. Vast tracts of land are available in some of the remote regions of *Siberia, / Siberia;* some investors are bold enough to purchase it.

20. *Since not / Not* many people know that the bison should never be called a buffalo, so many zoos include this information on the display in front of the bison's pen.

21. Not following in his father's footsteps, John-John spoke *slow / slowly* and with great care.

22. The Chamber of Commerce *could not / could* hardly believe the drop in tax revenue the city experienced after the administration's disastrous monetary policies, which encouraged companies to move their headquarters offshore, had begun to effect the emergency services budget.

23. The National Science Review Board had invited both academic scientists *as well as / and* industry experts to the discussions on waterway pollution.

24. Do not travel *swift and reckless / swiftly and recklessly* into the dark night.

Answers:

1. going to
2. going to a luxurious spa
3. Clown Town's
4. you do
5. generosity
6. Because he helped
7. Krista scraped her knees
8. Since he was confused
9. Flying swiftly from the bat
10. an emotion he hadn't felt
11. so too
12. native to
13. about
14. with
15. to
16. Wilma
17. machinery; however,
18. Even if
19. Siberia;
20. Not
21. slowly
22. could
23. and
24. swiftly and recklessly

WRITING LESSON 4

THE COMMON ERRORS PART III

PUNCTUATION

COMMAS

- **Never separate a subject-verb combination by a single comma**

  You can insert phrases, set off by commas at the beginning and end of the phrase, in between subjects and verbs, but a single comma is not allowed:

  > NO: Edgar, though taller than most other players couldn't dunk the basketball.

  > YES: Edgar, though taller than most other players, couldn't dunk the basketball.

- **Commas are used to separate items in a list**

  Commas must separate more than two items in a list. The comma between the last two items is optional, but it will usually appear on the SAT.

SEMICOLONS

Semicolons only have two legitimate uses:

- **Separating clauses with no connecting word**

  See the Clauses, Connectors and Commas section in The Common Errors Part II for a full explanation.

- **Separating items in a list IF the items in the list have commas within them.**

  This is a bit of an odd one. Occasionally, items in a list will contain phrases set off by commas. If this is the case, separating the list items with commas makes the sentence confusing. Here's an example:

  > NO: American landmarks include Mount Rushmore, with the faces of four presidents carved in it, Hells Canyon, the deepest canyon in the country, Niagara Falls, a famous honeymoon destination, and Boston Harbor, where early patriots dumped a shipload of tea into the water.

In this case, commas separate each item in the list, but that would mean, for example, that "Hells Canyon" is one landmark, while "the deepest canyon in the country" is another landmark. In fact, "the deepest canyon in the country" is a phrase modifying "Hells Canyon." To avoid this confusion, separate the items in the list with semicolons:

> YES: American landmarks include Mount Rushmore, with the faces of four presidents carved in it; Hells Canyon, the deepest canyon in the country; Niagara Falls, a famous honeymoon destination; and Boston Harbor, where early patriots dumped a shipload of tea into the water.

APOSTROPHES

Apostrophes indicate contractions and possession.

- **Contractions**

  You are becomes *you're*
  He has becomes *he's*
  You are becomes *you're*
  They could have becomes *they could've*

> Please Note! Contractions *could've, should've, would've* are often misspelled *could of, should of, would of.* Don't make that mistake!

- **Possessives**

Apostrophes are used to make nouns possessive.

For nouns that don't end in *S*, simply add an apostrophe *S*.

Jack's new son...
The museum's collection...
A snowball's chance...

For *plural* nouns ending in *S*, just add an apostrophe. *Singular* nouns ending is *S* typically take an apostrophe *S*.

The doctors' recommendations... (plural)
The cows' favorite type of grass... (plural)
The witness's code of ethics... (singular)

Please note! Possessive pronouns DON'T use apostrophes.

My, mine	Our, ours
Your, yours (singular)	Your, yours (plural)
His, her, hers, its	Their, theirs

THAT VS. WHICH

You should know the different usages of the words *that* and *which*. In general, *that* is used to describe a subset of a larger group. *That* **does not** take a leading comma:

> Ex) Hamburgers *that* have cheese taste better than those *that* don't.

> Ex) The outfit that I wore yesterday is very hip.

Note that not all hamburgers have cheese. Only some do. Not all outfits are hip, just the one I wore yesterday.

Which is used to describe an entire thing or an entire group. *Which* is **almost always** set off with a leading comma:

> Ex) Hamburgers, which are very popular in the United States, are usually made of beef.

> Ex) My car, which is in the driveway, needs a wash.

Note that hamburgers in general are popular. My whole entire car is in the driveway. (Note: This also implies that I have only one car. If the sentence read, "My car that is in the driveway needs a wash," the sentence would have indicated I have more than one car.)

Which can also introduce a question or be used as the object of a preposition without a leading comma. It is usually used as the object of a preposition to avoid ending a sentence with a preposition:

> Ex) Which exit should I take?

> Ex) I do not know the book of which you speak.

WORD CHOICE

Diction, or word choice, is occasionally tested on the SAT. A diction error is generally created by substituting a word that sounds or looks like the correct word, but is, in fact, logically wrong. Here are some common ones:

LIE VS. LAY

People often confuse the words *lie* and *lay*.

Lie has two meanings:

1) To say something that is not true, or

2) To be, or place oneself, in a horizontal position.

Lie is what someone or something does to itself. *Lie* is intransitive, which means it never takes an object. *So you NEVER lie something else down!*

> YES: You should *lie* down if you have a headache.

Lay means to put or set down. *Lay* is what someone or something does to something else. *You lay something else down.*

> YES: *Lay* down that book and *lie* down to go to sleep.

Lie and *lay* have different verb forms for several tenses, with some annoying overlaps:

Present Tense	Past Tense	Past Participle	Present Participle
lie (fib)	lied	(has / had) lied	(is) lying
lie (lie down)	lay	(has / had) lain	(is) lying
lay	laid	(has / had) laid	(is) laying

Note the annoying overlap. The past tense of *lie* is *lay*, which is exactly the same as the present tense of *lay*.

SIT VS. SET

Sit and *set* are similar to lay and lie.

Sit is what someone or something does to itself.

> YES: The cat decided to *sit* on the newspaper when I started to read.

Set is what someone or something does to something else.

> YES: Don't *set* that hot plate down on the table; use the trivet.

IT'S VS. ITS

It's is ALWAYS the contraction of *it is*.

> YES: He told me *it's* a great day for a game of Frisbee golf.

Its is ALWAYS the possessive form of the pronoun *it*.

> YES: The dog ate *its* dinner in about three seconds.

THEY'RE VS. THEIR VS. THERE VS. THERE'S

They're is ALWAYS the contraction of *they are*.

> YES: *They're* coming to the concert tonight, right?

Their and *theirs* are ALWAYS the possessive forms of the pronoun *they*.

> YES: I haven't seen *their* new car yet.

> YES: My cat won best of show, but *theirs* didn't even win a ribbon.

There indicates location.

> YES: *There* is my uncle in the second row!

There's is ALWAYS the contraction of *there is*.

> YES: There's a good chance the storm will come ashore tonight.

BRING VS. TAKE

You *bring* something to a place; you *take* something from a place. The word you choose depends on your location:

> If you are **at home**:

> NO: I'm glad I took my Physics book home today.

> YES: I'm glad I brought my Physics book home today.

> If you are **at school**:

> NO: I should bring my Physics book home today.

> YES: I should take my Physics book home today.

IMMIGRATE VS. EMIGRATE

People *immigrate to* a country, but *emigrate from* a country.

> NO: My ancestors emigrated to the United States.

> YES: My ancestors immigrated to the United States.

> NO: My ancestors immigrated from Africa.

> YES: My ancestors emigrated from Africa.

INDETERMINATE VS. INDECISIVE

Indeterminate means not definite.

Indecisive means unable to make a decision. Ideas and inanimate objects can't be indecisive.

> NO: We waited an indecisive period of time.

> YES: We waited an indeterminate period of time.

COULD'VE VS. COULD OF

It is NEVER correct to say *could of*. Because the contraction *could've* sounds like the incorrect usage *could of*, people often make this mistake. Could've always means *could have*.

STYLE

Occasionally style counts on the SAT, especially on the Sentence Improvement and Paragraph Improvement sections. If there are two answer choices that have no grammatical errors, choose the one that is stylistically better.

SHORT AND CONCISE

In general, the shorter and more concise a sentence is, the better it is. This doesn't mean that all the shortest answers are correct, but you should carefully consider short answers. English is a dish best served without excess garnish, at least on the SAT.

ACTIVE VS. PASSIVE VOICE

If the subject of the verb is doing the action, a sentence is in the **active voice**.

> Ex) The toddler bit the shoe.

In this instance, the subject of the verb, the toddler, is doing the biting.

If the subject is being acted upon, the sentence is in the **passive voice**.

> Ex) The shoe was bitten by the toddler.

In this instance, the subject, the shoe, is being acted upon. The object, the toddler, is doing the biting.

Sentences in the active voice are generally better than sentences in the passive voice.

Now that we've reviewed the common errors, let's look at how to tackle the specific questions.

Remember, you should always do the Error Identification questions FIRST (even though they don't appear at the beginning of the section).

Error Identification questions ask you to find an error in grammar or usage. These questions have four underlined portions labeled A, B, C and D that may consist of a single word or several words. Each question contains one single error or no error at all.

Answer choice (E) always represents no error.

Ex)   <u>While using</u> your bare hands to serve food <u>might be</u>
        A   B

common practice in some places, regulations in my city

<u>requires all</u> cafeteria workers <u>to wear</u> gloves. <u>No error</u>.
   C   D   E

A note on "sounds wrong":

Most people go through the Error Identification section and look for the underlined portion that "sounds wrong." While this might get you the correct answer some of the time, or even most of the time, it's ultimately not the best approach. The SAT is rife with grammatically correct answers that "sound wrong," and also grammatically or stylistically incorrect answers that "sound right." Don't rely on "sound" alone. (It can be a useful tool during step ❶ that follows, but only for the relatively easy questions.)

THE PROCESS

It is extremely helpful to develop a process for answering Error Identification questions. If you follow a specific process, you will be much less likely to miss one of the common errors, and you won't waste time reading and re-reading the questions looking for what "sounds" right or wrong.

Approach the Error Identification questions with a three-step process. We've included a flow chart at the end of the section if you like that sort of thing.

❶ Read the sentence through completely. If you spot a glaring error, and you know for sure it's wrong, choose it and move on. If you don't see an error immediately, or if you're not sure, go to step 2.

❷ Look closely at each underlined portion and check for common errors. You really want to target your approach to the specific errors that are tested on the SAT. So, depending on what type of words are actually underlined, you want to look for different errors:

IF A VERB IS UNDERLINED

Check subject verb agreement, verb form and parallelism.

IF A PRONOUN IS UNDERLINED

Check pronoun agreement, case and parallelism.

IF A PREPOSITION IS UNDERLINED

Check for proper idiom usage and parallelism.

IF AN INTRODUCTORY PHRASE IS UNDERLINED

Check that it modifies the noun that follows.

IF A NOUN IS UNDERLINED

Check for parallelism, noun to noun agreement, proper modifying phrases and word choice.

IF AN ADVERB OR ADJECTIVE IS UNDERLINED

Check for proper modifier usage. Adjectives modify nouns; adverbs modify verbs, adjectives, and other adverbs.

IF A PUNCTUATION MARK IS UNDERLINED

Check for clauses and connector errors, proper comma use, and proper apostrophe use.

❸ Find the error? If so, choose it. If everything looks fine, choose (E) No error. Move on to the next question.

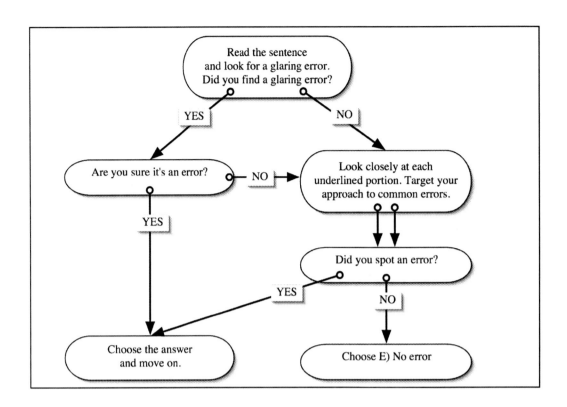

Review the chapter and focus on the common errors before trying these Error Identification problems.

Practice with these problems from *The Official SAT Study Guide:*

Practice Test	Section	Question
1	7	1, 4, 25, 27
	10	8
2	7	12-29
3	6	12-29

All test, section, question and page numbers refer to *The Official SAT Study Guide (2004)*

Be sure to carefully score the sections from *The Official SAT Study Guide* and review the questions you miss. Figure out why you missed each question and how you can get it right the next time!

Additional Practice:

Error Identification Homework Drill 1

The following questions test your ability to spot errors in grammar and usage. Each sentence contains one error or no error at all, but never more than one error. If there is an error, it is underlined and labeled with a letter. Select the single underlined portion that represents a grammatical or usage error, or choose E if the sentence is correct as is. Follow the rules of standard written English.

12. The city water supply <u>was found</u> to be
    A
    contaminated because of the three year old

    water filters <u>and they were</u> intended <u>for</u> use
                   B   C
    only <u>temporarily</u>. <u>No error</u>
         D   E

13. Even though Carla <u>had already</u> called the
                       A
    bank and <u>been assured</u> that the error on her
             B
    statement <u>would be</u> corrected, the
              C
    withdrawal <u>is still</u> shown on the following
               D
    month's balance. <u>No error</u>
                      E

14. Mr. and Mrs. Esuabana, <u>after</u> working
                           A
    many years <u>for the same company</u>, were
               B
    finally teaming up to become <u>a partner</u> in
                                 C
    their own <u>arts-and-crafts business</u>.
              D
    <u>No error</u>
    E

15. The coach knew <u>that</u>, despite the many
                    A
    strong players <u>he had</u> on the bench, he
                   B
    could neither substitute <u>for</u> his injured
                             C
    quarterback <u>and</u> replace the retired kicker.
                D
    <u>No error</u>
    E

16. <u>One</u> of my mother's favorite sayings <u>was</u>
    A   B
    that <u>you</u> could go as far as one wanted
         C
    <u>if only</u> one tried hard enough. <u>No error</u>
    D   E

17. <u>For</u> the summer job his father got Pedraum
    A
    when <u>he got back</u> from school, he had to
    B
    get up before sunrise, <u>arrive</u> no later than
    C
    seven o'clock, and <u>would return</u> home
    D
    sometimes as late as ten o'clock at night.

    <u>No error</u>
    E

18. Although the <u>resort's brochure</u> had
    A
    promised a breakfast buffet <u>of</u> unequaled
    B
    variety, the <u>actual</u> choice of items was
    C
    limited to bacon, waffles, and

    <u>a chef making omelets</u>. <u>No error</u>
    D   E

19. <u>After leaving</u> the Beatles, John Lennon
    A
    wrote songs <u>that</u> many in the music
    B
    industry felt <u>has surpassed</u> his work <u>with</u>
    C   D
    the Beatles. <u>No error</u>
    E

20. <u>Of</u> the eight competitors to make it to the
    A
    final event, only five of them <u>swum</u> in the
    B
    race because the others <u>had all contracted</u>
    C
    the same strain of food poisoning

    <u>from eating</u> in the same restaurant.
    D
    <u>No error</u>
    E

21. Many historians <u>have pointed out</u>
    A
    that <u>were</u> it not for the invention of the
    B
    steam engine and <u>the spread of trains</u>
    C
    across the North American continent,

    there <u>will be</u> no conquest of the Western
    D
    frontier. <u>No error</u>
    E

22. According to certain developmental

    psychologists, couples <u>who</u> have only
    A
    one child are unable to provide the

    interpersonal challenges <u>needed</u> for their
    B
    offspring <u>to become</u> <u>a socially-adept adult</u>.
    C   D
    <u>No error</u>
    E

23. In his letter to the editor last month, the

    new PTA President asserted <u>that</u> the use of
    A
    certain tests to determine students'

    abilities <u>are</u> usually <u>mandated</u> more
    B   C
    <u>for political than for educational</u> reasons.
    D
    <u>No error</u>
    E

24. Textile experts agree that the <u>intricate</u>
    A
    woven Persian rugs, <u>all of which</u> are made
    B
    by hand, cannot be duplicated <u>even</u> by the
    C
    most sophisticated <u>of automated</u> looms.
    D

    <u>No error</u>
    E

25. Both economists and economic historians

    claim <u>that</u> whenever the government
    A
    <u>chooses to ban</u> the sale of a product
    B
    <u>for which</u> a consumer demand exists, a
    C
    black market, however dangerous,

    <u>will spring up</u> to fill that demand. <u>No error</u>
    D   E

26. Many experts on automobile safety knew

    of the hazards <u>built into</u> many passenger
                      A
    vehicles long before *Unsafe at Any Speed*

    was published, yet it was not until <u>then</u>
                                          B
    that <u>regulations addressing</u> the problem
          C
    <u>was enacted</u> by Congress. <u>No error</u>
      D   E

27. Natasha's English teacher <u>was</u> fond of
                                 A
    telling her that <u>one could not</u> succeed in
                      B
    life without first learning enough <u>about</u>
                                          C
    oneself to find a way <u>in which</u> to succeed at
                            D
    even the most boring schoolwork.

    <u>No error</u>
      E

28. Joshua's childhood <u>fascination about</u> the
                          A
    mysteries of the ancient Egyptian

    pyramids helped <u>him</u> later <u>to establish</u> a
                      B   C
    lucrative <u>career as a consultant</u> to museums
                C
    of Middle Eastern art. <u>No error</u>
                              E

29. Scientists claim that, <u>genetically</u>
                            A
    speaking, there <u>are only</u> very minor
                      B
    differences that <u>separated</u> the chimpanzee
                      C
    <u>from</u> the human being. <u>No error</u>
      D   E

Answers

WRITING LESSON 5

SENTENCE IMPROVEMENT PART I

Sentence Improvement questions present a sentence with a portion — or sometimes the entire sentence — underlined, followed by five choices (A, B, C, D, and E) for either replacing the underlined portion or leaving it as it is. Answer choice (A) is always **exactly** the same as the underlined portion in the Sentence Improvement question.

You are asked to select the best answer. If the underlined portion of the sentence contains no error, and there is not a stylistically better answer, choose (A).

The Sentence Improvement questions seem a bit more difficult and time consuming than the Error Identification questions for most students. This is due to the structure of the question: You are asked to find the *best* answer among a sea of wrong answers. These questions can test *several* grammatical concepts in various answer choices, and the answers are often rife with errors. But Sentence Improvement questions don't have to be harder. You just need to know what to look for.

REPEATED ERRORS

Often, grammatical errors are repeated in two, three or even four incorrect answer choices. Once you've discovered an error, you can eliminate all the answer choices that repeat the error.

See if you can spot the error in the original sentence, then eliminate all the answers that repeat the error:

Ex)   While the giraffe might be one of the tallest creatures currently walking the earth, <u>for sheer bulk, they don't rival the blue whale, which can weigh up to 135 metric tons.</u>

(A)   for sheer bulk, they don't rival the blue whale, which can weigh up to 135 metric tons.
(B)   they don't rival the bulk of the blue whale, which can weigh up to 135 metric tons.
(C)   for sheer bulk, they don't rival the blue whale that can weigh up to 135 metric tons or more.
(D)   for sheer bulk, it doesn't rival the blue whale, which can weigh up to 135 metric tons.
(E)   for sheer bulk, it doesn't rival the blue whale, which can top out at up to 135 metric tons.

Notice anything wrong in the original? It's one of the common errors, pronoun agreement. *The giraffe* is singular, so the pronoun *they* doesn't agree. The pronoun should be *it.*

Cross off anything that repeats the error:

> (A) ~~for sheer bulk, *they* don't rival the blue whale, which can weigh up to 135 metric tons.~~
> (B) ~~*they* don't rival the bulk of the blue whale, which can weigh up to 135 metric tons.~~
> (C) ~~for sheer bulk, *they* don't rival the blue whale that can weigh up to 135 metric tons or more.~~
> (D) for sheer bulk, it doesn't rival the blue whale, which can weigh up to 135 metric tons.
> (E) for sheer bulk, it doesn't rival the blue whale that can top out at up to 135 metric tons.

Now you've only got two answers to deal with! In this case, answer choice (E) contains a *That vs. Which* error, and uses a redundant phrase *tops out at up to*, so (D) is the correct answer.

USE THE ANSWERS TO SPOT THE DIFFERENCES

The answer choices themselves can be your best guide to errors. Differences among the answer choices can often point out which grammar rules a question is trying to test. **Look for a pattern of answer choices** that present two or three alternatives. For example, if two answer choices use the pronoun *it*, two use *they* and one uses *you*, it's a pretty good bet that the question is testing pronoun agreement.

Let's look at an example:

> Ex) Last year Paul was given a good-citizen award from the local newspaper, <u>and since then is an insufferable braggart.</u>
>
> (A) and since then is an insufferable braggart.
> (B) where ever since he brags insufferably.
> (C) and he has been an insufferable braggart ever since.
> (D) he has been bragging insufferably since then.
> (E) since that time he has bragged insufferably.

Note the differences in the answers. Each answer choice seems quite different, but there are noticeable patterns of alternatives:

Answers (A) and (C) start with *and*, the others don't.

Answers (A) and (B) are in present tense. Answers (C), (D), and (E) all use the helping verb *has* in some way.

Just from these two differences, we can spot the correct answer. Since there are two clauses in this sentence, it needs a comma and a connector (or a semicolon, which is not an option here because the comma is not underlined, so you can't change it). Therefore, we need the word *and*. Cross off (B), (D), and (E).

> (A)   and since then is an insufferable braggart.
> (B)   where ever since he brags insufferably.
> (C)   and he has been an insufferable braggart ever since.
> (D)   he has been bragging insufferably since then.
> (E)   since that time he has bragged insufferably

Paul was awarded last year, and both remaining answers indicate something taking place *since* then. The present tense is not appropriate. Cross off (A). Answer choice (C) is correct.

Note! Differences in answer choices can be red herrings! (Red herrings are things that deflect your attention from the central issue.) There are often words or phrases that are equally acceptable, so a difference between two answer choices doesn't *always* indicate an error in one.

> (A)   Because he gave me a new cap…
> (C)   Since he gave me a new cap…

One definition of *since* is *because*, so they can be used interchangeably in many cases.

Once again, following a specific process can help you efficiently tackle these questions.

THE PROCESS

This process is slightly more complex than the two-step Error Identification process, but it's not rocket science. We've already gotten a hint of it from the examples above. We've included a flow chart at the end of this section, too, if you like that sort of thing.

Remember that *Clear and Concise* answer choices are often correct. Take a close look at the shorter answer choices and give them a fair shake.

---

❶ Read the original sentence, looking for common errors. If you find an obvious error, go to step ❷. If not, go to step ❸.

❷ Eliminate all answer choices that repeat the same error. (Be aware that alterations in other parts of the underlined portion may change the "error" you originally spotted and make it correct.) If you have eliminated all but one answer choice, go to step ❹. If not, proceed to step ❸.

❸ Look for differences in the remaining answer choices. Use the differences to determine errors. If you have eliminated all but one answer choice, go to step ❹. If not, return to step ❸ and use the differences in the remaining answers again.

❹ You're down to one answer! Choose it and move on to the next question.

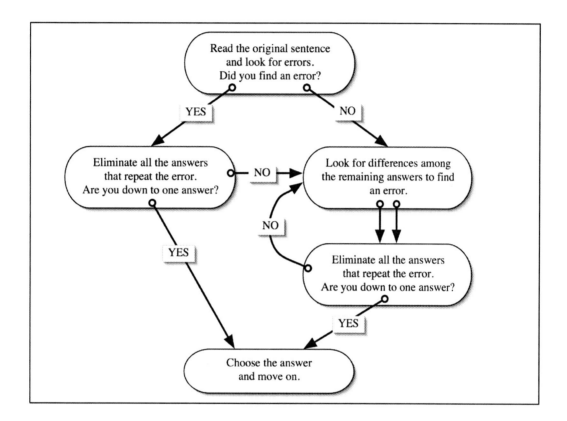

Review the chapter and focus on the common errors before trying these Sentence Improvement problems.

Practice with these problems from *The Official SAT Study Guide:*

Practice Test	Section	Questions
1	2	9-24
	5	6-24
	8	7-19
2	2	9-24
	5	6-24
	8	7-19

All test, section, question and page numbers refer to *The Official SAT Study Guide* (2004)

Be sure to carefully score the sections from *The Official SAT Study Guide* and review the questions you miss. Figure out why you missed each question and how you can get it right the next time!

Additional Practice:

Sentence Improvement Homework Drill 1

The following questions test your understanding of correct and effective expression. The answer choices represent five ways of expressing the underlined portion of each sentence. Choose the answer that you think represents the best expression of the underlined portion. Your choice should be clear and concise, and should avoid awkwardness and ambiguity. Choice A is exactly the same as the original.

1. The movie was nearly three-quarters completed <u>at that time during which the projector</u> malfunctioned and the audience could not see the rest.

    (A) at that time during which the
    (B) during the time the projector
    (C) at which time the projector
    (D) and that was when the projector
    (E) when the projector

2. Unable to overcome her fear of flying, <u>the airplane was forced to return to the gate when Nancy asked to be let off the flight.</u>

    (A) the airplane was forced to return to the gate when Nancy asked to be let off the flight.
    (B) so that the airplane was forced to return to the gate when Nancy asked.
    (C) Nancy's request to be let off the flight meant that airplane was forced to return to the gate.
    (D) Nancy's flight was forced to return to the gate when she asked to be let off.
    (E) Nancy asked to be let off the flight, and the airplane was forced to return to the gate.

3. The five starting basketball players were late for the game <u>because, when his car wouldn't start, the captain, who was everyone's ride, was late picking up the team.</u>

(A) because, when his car wouldn't start, the captain, who was everyone's ride, was late picking up the team.
(B) because the captain, who was everyone's ride, his car wouldn't start and he was late picking up the team.
(C) when the captain, who was everyone on the team's ride, couldn't get his car to start.
(D) and that was because the captain's car, which was the team's ride, wouldn't start so he was late picking everyone up.
(E) since the captain, whose car wouldn't start and who was everyone on the team's ride, was late picking them up.

4. Construction on the new city hall had to be halted when a crack was discovered in the foundation, <u>and this was the base upon which the entire structure was to be built.</u>

(A) and this was the base upon which the entire structure was to be built.
(B) and that was supposed to have been the base upon which the entire structure was to be built.
(C) upon which the entire structure had been supposed to have been built.
(D) the base upon which the entire structure was to be built.
(E) a structure upon which base the entire structure was to be built.

5. Equestrians know that the health of a horse can be judged both by the soundness of its hooves <u>and also the condition of its teeth.</u>

(A) and also the condition of its teeth.
(B) as well as the condition of its teeth.
(C) and by the condition of its teeth.
(D) but as well by the condition of its teeth.
(E) and the condition of its teeth as well.

6. As a response to the greater complexity of the information age, many teachers are attempting to prepare students to use computers for <u>a multitude of tasks, but they also recognize that it is first necessary to impart the fundamentals</u> of reading, writing, and arithmetic.

(A) a multitude of tasks, but they also recognize that it is first necessary to impart the fundamentals
(B) a multitude of tasks, but they are also recognizing that it is still necessary to first impart the fundamentals
(C) a multitude of tasks while also recognizing that imparting the fundamentals is still necessary
(D) a multitude of tasks, but also they recognize as well that it is still first necessary to impart the fundamentals
(E) multitudinous tasks while also recognizing that it is first necessary to impart the fundamentals

7. Writing a good novel means having not only a strong story <u>but they also need to develop well their characters.</u>

(A) but they also need to develop well their characters.
(B) but writers also need to develop well their characters.
(C) but also developing well the novel's characters.
(D) but as well the writers have to develop their characters.
(E) but also well-developed characters.

8. Car experts often warn that, as far as keeping a new automobile running well goes, <u>changing the oil frequently is just as important as having routine maintenance checks</u> done by the dealer.

(A) changing the oil frequently is just as important as having routine maintenance checks
(B) changing the oil frequently is just as important as the routine maintenance checks done by the dealer
(C) an oil change is just as important as having the routine maintenance checks
(D) an oil change is just as important for the routine maintenance checks
(E) one must change the oil frequently as well as having the important routine maintenance checks

9. The "AM" in AM radio <u>standing for amplitude modulation, meaning the radio signal</u> is produced by varying the height rather than the length of the radio wave.

    (A) standing for amplitude modulation, meaning the radio signal
    (B) standing for amplitude modulation, which means that the radio signal
    (C) is meaning to stand for amplitude modulation, because the radio signal
    (D) stands for amplitude modulation, meaning that the radio signal
    (E) stands for amplitude modulation, whose meaning is that the radio signal

10. Keen observers of city politics often point out that <u>the mayor, he is one of the finest leaders ever to run the city government.</u>

    (A) the mayor, he is one of the finest leaders ever to run the city government.
    (B) the mayor, who is one of the finest leaders ever to run the city government.
    (C) the mayor is one of the finest leaders ever to run the city government.
    (D) the mayor, he can be said to be one of the finest leaders ever to run the city government.
    (E) the mayor, one of the finest leaders ever to run the city government.

11. <u>No quarks have ever been observed directly,</u> quantum physicists maintain that they are in fact among the set of fundamental particles.

    (A) No quarks have ever been observed directly,
    (B) Even though no quarks have ever been observed directly,
    (C) Even though no quarks had ever yet been observed directly,
    (D) Despite the fact that no quantum physicist had ever directly observed a quark yet,
    (E) The fact that no quarks have ever yet been observed directly,

1.1 NASA officials warned that a few of the intricate parts that help operate the Hubble Telescope <u>may be wearing</u> out before astronauts are able to replace them.

    (A) may be wearing
    (B) may have been wearing
    (C) may have weared
    (D) may be worn
    (E) may worn

2.1 Unless they contain the proper features, <u>office workers who sit at their desks all day can find that their chairs cause back pain.</u>

    (A) office workers who sit at their desks all day can find that their chairs cause back pain.
    (B) office workers' chairs, which sit at their desks all day, can find that they cause back pain.
    (C) chairs that cause back pain can be found by office workers, if they sit at their desks all day.
    (D) chairs that office workers sit at all day, when they're at their desks, they can cause back pain.
    (E) the chairs of office workers who sit at their desks all day may cause back pain.

3.1 As he stood at the foot of Mt. Vesuvius gesturing upwards, <u>the words the tour guide spoke were greeted by his audience with quiet awe.</u>

    (A) the words the tour guide spoke were greeted by his audience with quiet awe.
    (B) the audience greeted the tour guide's spoken words with quiet awe.
    (C) the tour guide spoke words that were greeted by his audience with quiet awe.
    (D) the greeting of the audience to the words the tour guide spoke was one of quiet awe.
    (E) the tour guide spoke greeting words of quiet awe to his audience.

4.1 Ivan's friends consider him an expert on the cultural treasures of Moscow <u>since he is supposed to of spent his childhood years living there.</u>

    (A) since he is supposed to of spent his childhood years living there.
    (B) because, supposedly, his childhood years were spent through by living there.
    (C) as a result of his supposed having lived there through his childhood years.
    (D) since he supposedly lived there through his childhood years.
    (E) since he is supposed to have spent his living childhood years there.

5.1 Caroline's story about her trip down the Amazon River started out as a simple description but quickly turned into a cautionary tale about entering into the unknown unprepared.

(A) but quickly turned into a cautionary tale about entering into the unknown unprepared.
(B) but was quickly turned into a cautionary tale of unpreparedly entering among the unknown.
(C) but, quickly turning into a cautionary tale, is about entering unpreparedly upon the unknown.
(D) but is about a cautionary tale of entering the unknown, quickly, unpreparedly.
(E) but that was quickly being turned into a cautionary tale about entering unprepared into the unknown.

6.1 Even the most well trained sprinter would not attempt to running a marathon without further preparation.

(A) would not attempt to running a marathon
(B) would not attempt to run a marathon
(C) would not attempt to ran a marathon
(D) would not attempt marathon run
(E) would not attempt to have ran a marathon

7.1 To prevent premature aging and daily weariness, one can get the advice of a trained nutritionist who can advise you how to eat for maximum health and energy.

(A) one can get the advice of a trained nutritionist who can advise you how to eat for maximum health and energy.
(B) a trained nutritionist can advise one on how one should eat for maximum health and energy.
(C) advise can be given by a trained nutritionist to one about how one could eat for maximum health and energy.
(D) one can get the advice of a trained nutritionist about eating for maximum health and energy.
(E) a trained nutritionist can give advice on how to eat for maximum health and energy.

8.1 While scuba diving may allow one to see sights deeper underwater than snorkeling can, the greater also are the dangers that it presents.

(A) the greater also are the dangers that it presents.
(B) it also has greater dangers that it presents.
(C) also greater dangers are presented.
(D) present also are greater dangers.
(E) it also presents greater dangers.

9.1 The giant Redwoods of California are known to live many centuries, in a few cases several millennia.

(A) in a few cases several millennia.
(B) several millennia are a few cases.
(C) in a few cases it is several millennia.
(D) a few of the cases are of them living several millennia.
(E) as well as, in a few cases, to be several millennia.

10.1 Because of their uniqueness and rarity, collectors of American antiques particularly prize finding nineteenth-century typewriters with keyboards arranged in alphabetical order.

(A) collectors of American antiques particularly prize finding nineteenth-century typewriters with keyboards arranged in alphabetical order.
(B) American antiques collectors prize the particular finding of nineteenth-century typewriters with keyboards arranged in alphabetical order.
(C) nineteenth-century typewriters with keyboards arranged in alphabetical order are particularly prized by collectors of American antiques.
(D) typewriter keyboards of nineteenth-century alphabetical order arrangement are particularly prized by collectors of American antiques.
(E) keyboards arranged in alphabetical order on nineteenth-century typewriters are a particular prizing of collectors of American antiques.

11.1 Some fly-fishing experts claim that <u>lures made with a single color of thread is most likely to attract</u> younger fish.

   (A) lures made with a single color of thread is most likely to attract
   (B) lures that are made with a single color of thread is most likely to attract
   (C) it is the single-color thread lures that is most likely to attract
   (D) lures made with a single color of thread are most likely to attract
   (E) a lure made with single colors are most likely to attract

12.1 Even though they agreed on just about everything, Leigh-Ann and Baxter, surprisingly, <u>were not a friend who ever</u> considered going out on a date.

   (A) were not a friend who ever
   (B) were not friends that ever
   (C) were not friends who ever
   (D) who were friends that never
   (E) never was friends who

13.1 Clarissa has lived most of her adult life <u>in a top-floor apartment, however she would prefer to live, otherwise.</u>

   (A) in a top-floor apartment, however she would prefer to live, otherwise.
   (B) in a top-floor apartment; otherwise, however, she would prefer to live.
   (C) in a top-floor apartment; however otherwise she would prefer to live.
   (D) in a top-floor apartment however, otherwise, she would prefer to live
   (E) in a top-floor apartment; however, she would prefer to live otherwise.

14.1 <u>It has been cloudy all day, and it might still be possible to see the lunar eclipse tonight.</u>

   (A) It has been cloudy all day, and it might still be possible to see the lunar eclipse tonight.
   (B) Despite the fact that it has been cloudy all day, but it might still be possible to see the lunar eclipse tonight.
   (C) It might still be possible, though it has been cloudy all day, for seeing the lunar eclipse tonight.
   (D) Although it has been cloudy all day, it might still be possible to see the lunar eclipse tonight.
   (E) It has been cloudy all day, it might still be possible to see the lunar eclipse tonight.

Answers

1. E
2. E
3. C
4. D
5. C
6. A
7. E
8. A
9. D
10. C
11. B
1.1 D
2.1 E
3.1 C
4.1 D
5.1 A
6.1 B
7.1 D
8.1 E
9.1 A
10.1 C
11.1 D
12.1 C
13.1 E
14.1 D

WRITING LESSON 6

PARAGRAPH IMPROVEMENT PART I

On the SAT, one Paragraph Improvement passage is followed by six questions. Passages are usually ten to fifteen sentences long and usually contain two to four paragraphs. Each sentence in the passage is numbered, and most questions refer to one or more specific sentences by number.

The passage in each Paragraph Improvement section is **poorly written**. It is meant to mimic an early draft of an essay a student might write. Your job is to make the passage better.

Paragraph Improvement questions come in several different flavors. Some simply ask you to correct grammatical problems based mostly on the common errors we've already discussed. Many require you to combine sentences or make the passage more *Clear and Concise*, or ask you to choose proper connecting or transition words. Others are Reading Comprehension style questions about content, often asking you about the main idea or focus of the passage or a single paragraph. Yet others ask you to re-order sentences or phrases.

CONTINUITY

It's all about the flow, baby! Unlike Error Identification and Sentence Improvement questions, Paragraph Improvement questions don't float around in a vacuum unaffected by their surroundings. The various sentences that make up each passage are supposed to flow smoothly and fit together. They need to relate.

Each paragraph is supposed to introduce a single idea that supports the main gist of the passage. Paragraphs should follow one another in logical fashion, connecting ideas with appropriate transition words and phrases. Transitions should indicate whether a paragraph is going to go along with or diverge from the paragraph before.

But there's more to continuity than just connecting ideas. Verb tense and pronoun use must be consistent from paragraph to paragraph, too. You can't suddenly switch from past tense to present tense unless you have a good reason. You can't suddenly switch from third person (he, she, it) to second person (you). Yep, even paragraphs need to be parallel.

STAY ON TOPIC

These passages are usually fairly narrow in scope. There will be one overriding topic or point, and each paragraph should contain one single idea that goes along with the main topic and is also supported by evidence, examples, or discussion.

Note that most Paragraph Improvement questions include the phrase *in context*. If a sentence, clause or phrase strays significantly from the single idea of a paragraph, it should either be deleted or altered to fit the topic. For example:

> BAD: **(1)** Paula went into the sales meeting prepared to make her best pitch. **(2)** She believed the stationery products she was selling to be the best made and the greatest value to the customer. **(3)** She felt confident as she turned on her laptop computer for the presentation. **(4)** Her laptop had the largest hard drive money could buy. **(5)** As the computer booted up, she smiled at the potential clients and handed out samples of the products.

See a sentence that doesn't quite fit? Well, what is this paragraph really about? Paula's confident sales pitch, right? What the heck does the size of the hard drive on her computer have to do with the sales pitch? Nothing! Sentences (3) and (5) did mention the laptop, but only in the context of the sales presentation. Adding unrelated information about the laptop itself is simply out of scope of the paragraph. So, eliminate sentence (4):

> BETTER: **(1)** Paula went into the sales meeting prepared to make her best pitch. **(2)** She believed the stationery products she was selling to be the best made and the greatest value to the customer. **(3)** She felt confident as she turned on her laptop computer for the presentation. **(4)** ~~Her laptop had the largest hard drive money could buy.~~ **(5)** As the computer booted up, she smiled at the potential clients and handed out samples of the products.

CLEAR AND CONCISE

The test writers love to include redundant, unnecessarily wordy and confusing information in their paragraphs. Because *Clear and Concise* writing is considered better, you should choose *Clear and Concise* answer choices whenever possible, provided that they are grammatically and stylistically correct.

Usually *Clear and Concise* errors deal with redundancy. **Keep a sharp eye out for redundant constructs and eliminate them when possible.**

Adding detail or description is acceptable provided it is not redundant and the information is relevant to the topic.

INTRODUCE IDEAS BEFORE DISCUSSING THEM

There is also a logical order in which ideas should appear. First, ideas or evidence should be introduced and explained. Only after they've been introduced can they be further discussed and analyzed.

Errors are often created by placing sentences in the wrong order. When asked to re-order sentences, make sure that ideas, evidence and information is established before it is discussed. For example:

> BAD: **(1)** In the book, Henry tells the story of his cross-country trip with a woman named Fern and her daughter. **(2)** Over the course of their extensive journey, the three visit every state capitol in the 48 contiguous states. **(3)** Coming into his own as a writer in his mid-fifties, Jake Henry wrote a compelling nonfiction tale called *Motel Volkswagen* about developing relationships in confined quarters.

What's wrong? The problem here is that the reader doesn't know what book we're talking about until the third sentence. The first sentence starts with the phrase *In the book*, which suggest the reader should already know which book. The third sentence actually introduces the book, so it should come first.

> BETTER: **(1)** Coming into his own as a writer in his mid-fifties, Jake Henry wrote a compelling nonfiction tale called *Motel Volkswagen* about developing relationships in confined quarters. **(2)** In the book, Henry tells the story of his cross-country trip with a woman named Fern and her daughter. **(3)** Over the course of their extensive journey, the three visit every state capitol in the 48 contiguous states.

CONNECTING WORDS AND TRANSITIONS

Paragraph Improvement questions often focus on transitions and connecting words. These words can change the direction of a passage or send it merrily on its way. They can indicate cause and effect, set up a time sequence, or introduce a counterexample. Connecting words can drastically change the meaning of a sentence or paragraph. You need to choose the word or phrase that fits the context of the passage as a whole:

> Ex) While Jonathan read the newspaper, he nibbled on a bowl of grapes.

> Ex) After Jonathan read the newspaper, he nibbled on a bowl of grapes.

Notice the difference *while* and *after* make. In this case, it's all about time. If these were answer choices, the passage would indicate whether or not Jonathan ate the grapes at the same time as he read the newspaper. Here's another example:

> Ex) Which is the best version of sentence (1)?
> *Because of accepted norms of behavior, Edwina raised chickens in her bedroom.*
>
> (A) (As it is now)
> (B) Without accepted norms of behavior, Edwina raised chickens in her bedroom.
> (C) In accordance with accepted norms of behavior, Edwina raised chickens in her bedroom.
> (D) In contrast with accepted norms of behavior, Edwina raised chickens in her bedroom.
> (E) By flouting accepted norms of behavior, Edwina raised chickens in her bedroom.

Notice how much the choice of words changes the meaning of the sentence. These examples deal with assigning causality (*because of*, *by flouting*) or relationship (*in contrast with*, *without*, *in accordance with*). Let's look at each of the examples:

(A) Since it should be fairly self-evident that raising chickens in your bedroom is *not* standard behavior, saying that Edwina does so *because of* those norms just isn't logical.

(B) says *without accepted norms of behavior*. This seems to indicate that there aren't any norms. But that doesn't make sense either.

(C) is much like the first. Norms of behavior *do not* include raising chickens in your bedroom.

(D) looks good. It suggests what we assume to be true: That raising chickens in your bedroom is *in contrast with* behavioral norms.

(E) *by flouting norms of behavior* suggests that this is the way she raised chickens. The relationship is backwards. A better version of (E) might be: Edwina flouted accepted norms of behavior by raising chickens in her bedroom.

Watch out for words that indicate time periods, causality, continuity or contrast. They must fit logically with the passage. Here are a few to pay attention to:

Time	Causality	Continuity	Contrast
When	Because	In fact	Contrary to
Then	Since	Obviously	But
Since	Therefore	For example	However
After	Thus	As you can see	Despite
First	So	Naturally	While

THE PROCESS

The test writers will tell you that you need to slowly and carefully read each entire passage before you answer any questions. They might suggest that while you do this, you'll need to simply ignore all the bad writing so you can get the gist of the whole passage.

Hmmm. Read extremely carefully, but ignore all the mistakes. And do this at the end of a high-pressure timed section in which you're probably running out of time. Sounds like a recipe for disaster to us. Fortunately, there is a better way.

First and foremost, ***don't read the whole passage***. It's a waste of precious time for most people.

The way you read the passage depends to a great extent on the question type.

> Note! The methods that follow are suggested guidelines that will help you spot the answers in almost all cases. Still, you need to be flexible. A few of the questions may require reading more of the passage to fully understand context. Paragraph transitions are particularly important, so reading a sentence or two from a paragraph above or below the sentence in question might be appropriate.

Do general questions last!

If you get to a question that asks about the entire passage, save it until you've answered all the other questions first. You'll probably read most or all of the passage in the course of answering the other questions. That will make it easier to skim over the entire passage if you need to in order to answer the general questions.

> Note! Any time you skip questions, make sure you fill in the correct question numbers on the answer sheet. Be very careful.

SINGLE-SENTENCE QUESTIONS: TWO ABOVE, TWO BELOW

In general, when a question asks you to deal with a *single-sentence or a portion of a single-sentence*, you need to read about two sentences above and two sentences below the sentence you're dealing with. Be aware that paragraph transitions are often extremely important, so you may want to read the last sentence of the preceding paragraph, or the first sentence of the next paragraph, depending on the particular question.

MULTIPLE-SENTENCE QUESTIONS: TWO ABOVE, TWO BELOW

Often, questions ask for the best rewrite of *two adjacent sentences*. You may be asked to combine the two sentences, or make sure that the two sentences are not redundant. The process is the same as for one-sentence questions: Read two sentences above and two sentences below the selected sentences. This should be enough to help you understand the context and avoid repeating information.

PARAGRAPH QUESTIONS: ONE ABOVE, ONE BELOW

Other questions deal with entire paragraphs. Since context is important, read the last sentence or two of the preceding paragraph through to the first sentence or two of the following paragraph.

If paragraph questions ask how the paragraph fits into the passage as a whole, answer it last. It's really a general question.

REORDER PARAGRAPH QUESTIONS: ONE ABOVE, ONE BELOW

Questions frequently ask how to reorder existing sentences within paragraphs, or where to place an additional sentence in the passage. Since sentences can be moved around anywhere in a paragraph, you should read from the last sentence or two of the preceding paragraph through to the first sentence or two of the following paragraph.

These questions often deal with introducing facts, ideas or information before discussing them, or with logical chronological order. Connecting and transition words often help determine proper order.

READING COMPREHENSION STYLE QUESTIONS

Occasionally, Paragraph Improvement questions are really just like Reading Comprehension questions. These questions can be quite specific or very general. They might ask for the best concluding sentence to a passage or paragraph, or ask what role a sentence or a paragraph plays in the passage as a whole.

Ex)   The role of sentence x in the passage is best described as…

Ex)   In the second paragraph (sentences x-y), the author of the passage is primarily…

Ex)   The author of the passage uses all of the following strategies EXCEPT…

As mentioned earlier, you should do these general questions last. After you've answered the other questions, you'll probably have a pretty good idea of the passage as a whole, and a quick skim can refresh your memory.

Review the chapter and focus on correcting grammar, continuity and context while trying these Paragraph Improvement problems.

Practice with these problems from *The Official SAT Study Guide:*

Practice Test	Section	Questions
1	7	30-35
2	7	30-35

All test, section, question and page numbers refer to *The Official SAT Study Guide* (2004)

Be sure to carefully score the sections from *The Official SAT Study Guide* and review the questions you miss. Figure out why you missed each question and how you can get it right the next time!

Additional Practice:

Paragraph Improvement Homework Drill 1

The following essay represents an early draft that needs to be revised. For the questions that follow, select the answers that best rewrite the essay. You may be asked to improve organization, development, sentence structure, or word choice. Follow the rules of standard written English.

(1) The original idea behind the Electoral College was twofold, based on a combination of the Founders' concern to preserve the power of the states in determining the Chief Executive and their equally strong distrust of common American voters to make a wise, informed choice; however, a shift in basic values from an elitist politics to a truly all-inclusive democratic system has been going on since the Constitution was ratified. (2) American history is in many ways one of struggling to broaden democratic participation. (3) Over a third of all Amendments passed since 1800 have concerned the extension of voting rights in one way or another, succeeding in spreading the rights of political participation from the core group of property-owning white males to the rest of the adult population.

(4) But what of the Founders' concern for preserving state power? (5) Proponents of the Electoral College point out that our Constitution establishes a federal system. (6) In such a system, power is shared among the three branches of the national government, and it is also shared between the federal and state governments. (7) This dispersal of power is an essential component of the checks-and-balances system, taking into account the important fact that our nation comprises diverse regions with different moral, political, and economic sensibilities. (8) The federal system preserves the liberty of this diverse population of Americans by allowing differences to be expressed through the exercise of state power. (9) By guaranteeing that the states have a central role in the Presidential election, the Electoral College reflects and reinforces this core idea of federalism and maintains the delicate balance of power between the states and the federal government.

(10) It's undoubtedly true that the Electoral College gives states an important say in the selection of the Chief Executive, but at what cost? (11) One of these might be the different importance of certain states in the Presidential election. (12) There is a conventional wisdom, being that certain states are "safe" states for one party or another and that certain states are "swing" or "battleground" states. (13) The "safe" states on both sides don't matter much to the candidates, since the outcome of these "safe" states is hardly worth disputing - the candidate not on the safe side knows he can't possibly win it no matter how he campaigns, and the candidate on the safe side will win it no matter what - candidates are much better off spending limited time, money, and energy campaigning in the "battleground" states. (14) Because of this, the "battleground" states take on much greater importance in Presidential elections than do "safe" states.

30. Which of the following sentences would make the best introduction to the passage if inserted before sentence 1?

   (A) In order to be an informed voter, it is necessary to understand how the American political system operates.
   (B) After the Presidential election of 2000, many Americans realized that they didn't know how the Electoral College worked.
   (C) For over 200 years, America has chosen its highest elected official, the President of the United States, using a system that originated in Europe with the College of Cardinals that select the Pope.
   (D) Critics of the Electoral College claim that it isn't fair or democratic and that it's a relic of the past, while proponents argue that it still plays an important role in American democracy.
   (E) The only way that we're going to be able to get rid of the Electoral College is to understand exactly where it came from and why so many Americans like it.

31. In context, which of the following is the best way to revise and combine sentences 5 and 6 (reproduced below)?

   Proponents of the Electoral College point out that our Constitution establishes a federal system. In such a system, power is shared among the three branches of the national government, and it is also shared between the federal and state governments.

   (A) Proponents of the Electoral College point out that our Constitution establishes a system of power that is known as a federal system, in which it is shared among the three branches of the national government along with the state governments.
   (B) Proponents of the Electoral College point out that our Constitution establishes a federal system in which power is not only shared among the three branches of the national government but also between the federal and state governments.
   (C) While Proponents of the Electoral College point out that our Constitution establishes a federal system, it is one where power is shared between the three branches of government as well as among the federal and state governments.
   (D) Although in our Constitution power is shared among the three branches of the national government, proponents of the Electoral College point out that our system makes power shared among the federal and state governments as well.
   (E) Since, proponents of the Electoral College point out, our Constitution shares power as in a federal system, not only among the three branches of the national government, but also between the federal and state governments.

32. The underlined portion of sentence 2 (reproduced below) could best be revised in which of the following ways?

   American history is in many ways one of struggling to broaden democratic participation.

   (A) one of broadening
   (B) an historic struggle for broadening
   (C) the broadening historical struggle for
   (D) a history of the struggle to broaden
   (E) one of a struggling broadening of

33. In context, which of the following is the best version of sentence 12 (reproduced below)?

There is a conventional wisdom, being that certain states are "safe" states for one party or another and that certain states are "swing" or "battleground" states.

(A) (As it is now)
(B) Because of the conventional wisdom, certain states are "safe" states for one party or another while certain other states are "swing" or "battleground" states.
(C) For conventional wisdom divides states into "safe" – those that are certain to go for one party or another – and "swing" or "battleground."
(D) Some states are "safe" ones, says conventional wisdom, those states that are certain to go for one party or the other, while there are other states that are "swing" or "battleground" states.
(E) The conventional wisdom is that certain states are "safe" for one party or the other, while others, known as "swing" or "battleground" states, could go either way.

34. Which of the following portions of sentence 13 (reproduced below) could be eliminated to improve flow of the third paragraph without sacrificing needed information?

The "safe" states on both sides don't matter much to the candidates, since the outcome of these "safe" states is hardly worth disputing - the candidate not on the safe side knows he can't possibly win it no matter how he campaigns, and the candidate on the safe side will win it no matter what - candidates are much better off spending limited time, money, and energy campaigning in the "battleground" states.

(A) The "safe" states on both sides don't matter much to the candidates,
(B) since the outcome of these "safe" states is hardly worth disputing
(C) the candidate not on the safe side knows he can't possibly win it no matter how he campaigns
(D) the candidate on the safe side will win it no matter what
(E) candidates are much better off spending limited time, money, and energy campaigning in the "battleground" states

35. Which of the following would make the most logical concluding sentence for the third paragraph?

(A) So it seems that there are two different kinds of states in our federal system.
(B) Ultimately the Electoral College doesn't preserve the power of those "safe" states very well.
(C) So if the Electoral College doesn't preserve a justifiable form of state, what does it do?
(D) We should be able to conclude from this that the Electoral College helps reach the Founders' goal of keeping power out of the hands of the common people.
(E) It seems clear that we should get rid of this archaic system and replace it with the only alternative that makes any sense: nation-wide popular election of the President.

Answers

WRITING LESSON 7

PARAGRAPH IMPROVEMENT PART II

NO CHANGE

Unlike Error Identification and Sentence Improvement questions, Paragraph Improvement questions **DO NOT** have a default *No Change* answer.

On a few questions, you will have the option of picking (A) *Leave it as is* or (A) *(As it is now)*, but don't assume that answer choice (A) indicates *No Change*. You must carefully read every answer choice.

INTERPRETING THE QUESTION

Most Paragraph Improvement questions are cookie cutter questions that look like this:

> Ex) In context, which is the best version of the underlined portion of sentence *x*, reproduced below?

These questions are very straightforward.

Don't get lulled into a false sense of security. Not all questions are created equal. As always, you need to pay attention to the specifics of the question. Fortunately, if you read carefully, the questions themselves can steer you in the right direction. Here are some other question types:

LINKING QUESTIONS

Linking Questions are about continuity and transitions that fit the context of the passage.

> Ex) Which of the following revisions of the underlined portion of sentence *x*, reproduced below, would best link the first and second paragraph?

The language of this question tells you that you need to look for transition words that fit the context and properly introduce new ideas.

PARAGRAPH BREAK QUESTIONS

You may need to break up a paragraph that tries to do too many things. Remember, one basic idea per paragraph is enough!

> Ex) Where is the most logical place to start a new paragraph?

The language of this question tells you that you need to look for a place where the subject matter and point change.

NOT / EXCEPT QUESTIONS

NOT and EXCEPT questions have four right answers and only one wrong answer. Your job is to spot what's wrong or to eliminate all four answers that are right.

Always circle the word *NOT* or *EXCEPT* so that you don't forget what you're looking for!

> Ex) In context, which of the following revisions would (NOT) improve sentence *x* (reproduced below)?

PUNCTUATION

Finally, let's talk about punctuation issues on Paragraph Improvement questions. You should be very aware of punctuation, especially commas and semicolons that separate clauses.

PUNCTUATION IN THE ANSWER CHOICES

If there are differences in the punctuation of the answer choices, pay heed! Those differences usually signal an error. Remember that two clauses in the same sentence need either a comma and a connector, or a semicolon. You could also break up two clauses into separate sentences.

PUNCTUATION THAT CAN'T BE CHANGED

If there are punctuation marks in portions of the sentence that are not dealt with in the question, those marks must stay the same! This means you have to follow punctuation rules. Descriptive phrases that are set off by a comma at one end must be separated by a comma at the other end, too.

Review the chapter and focus on correcting grammar, continuity and context while trying these Paragraph Improvement problems.

Note that the homework assignment below includes Sentence Improvement and Error Identification questions from Practice Tests 3 and 4.

Practice with these problems from *The Official SAT Study Guide:*

Practice Test	Section	Questions
3	6	1-11, 30-35
	10	1-14
4	6	1-35
	10	1-14

All test, section, question and page numbers refer to *The Official SAT Study Guide* (2004)

Be sure to carefully score the sections from *The Official SAT Study Guide* and review the questions you miss. Figure out why you missed each question and how you can get it right the next time!

TIMED DRILLS

After you've finished all the lessons, try your hand at these timed drills. They are a great warm-up for the last few days before you take the SAT. Use them in conjunction with any sections you haven't completed in *The Official SAT Study Guide*.

Time yourself carefully and work on your pacing and your approach to tough questions. Remember that slowing down can not only improve your accuracy, but can also save time you might otherwise waste by rushing into a time-consuming method of solving a problem. However, don't allow yourself to get bogged down on one or two difficult questions. Keep moving steadily ahead.

For these Timed Drills, we recommend that you use an answer sheet from *The Official SAT Study Guide* to practice filling in the answers as you would on the real SAT. Answers appear at the end of the Timed Drills (except for the essay, of course).

Solve each of the following problems and choose the best of the choices given. Use any available space for scratch work, if necessary.

1. If $2x - 3 = x + 7$, what is the value of x?

    (A) $1\frac{1}{3}$

    (B) $3\frac{1}{3}$

    (C) 4

    (D) 5

    (E) 10

2. If $x^6 = 3^{2x}$, then $x =$

    (A) 1

    (B) 2

    (C) 3

    (D) 6

    (E) 9

3. If a number is added to $x - 5$ so that it equals $x + 3$, what must that number be?

    (A) -2

    (B) 2

    (C) 5

    (D) 8

    (E) 15

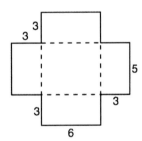

4.

    If the figure above is folded along the dotted lines to make a rectangular box, what is the volume of the box in cubic units?

    (A) 54

    (B) 90

    (C) 180

    (D) 216

    (E) 270

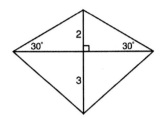

5.

    How many different ways can a single line segment be drawn in the figure above to create an equilateral triangle using the existing lines in the figure?

    (A) 0

    (B) 2

    (C) 3

    (D) 4

    (E) 8

6. A store is discounting an item that cost 60 dollars by 30 percent and an item that cost s dollars by 40 percent. If the dollar amount of the discount is the same for both items, what is the value of s?

    (A) 37.5

    (B) 42

    (C) 45

    (D) 58

    (E) 100

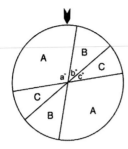

7.

Note: Figure not drawn to scale

A spinning wheel is divided into lettered sections as shown above, where $b = 60$ and $c = 15$. What is the probability that the wheel will stop with the marker pointing to a section labeled A?

(A) $\dfrac{1}{2}$

(B) $\dfrac{7}{12}$

(C) $\dfrac{13}{18}$

(D) $\dfrac{3}{4}$

(E) $\dfrac{9}{10}$

8. If x, y, and z are consecutive even integers greater than 2, which of the following must be true?

I. $x + y > z$

II. $z - 2 = x$

III. $y + 1 = z$

(A) I only
(B) II only
(C) I and II only
(D) II and III only
(E) I, II, and III

9. A line of colored lights consists of red and blue lights arranged using only these three sequences:

Sequence A: A single red light followed by four blue lights.

Sequence B: A single red light followed by five blue lights.

Sequence C: A single red light followed by six blue lights.

If the line of lights is made by following a pattern of A C B repeated 100 times, how many blue lights will there be between the 9th and 10th red lights?

(A) 5
(B) 6
(C) 9
(D) 11
(E) 15

10. If the equation $y = 2x^3 - \dfrac{6}{x}$ is graphed in the xy-plane, what is the y-coordinate of the point on this graph when $x = 3$?

(A) 16
(B) 20
(C) 36
(D) 48
(E) 52

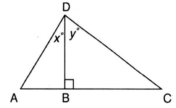

11.

NOTE: Figure not drawn to scale

In the triangle shown above, if $2x = y$, what is $\dfrac{AB}{CD}$?

(A) $\dfrac{1}{2}$

(B) $\sqrt{3}$

(C) $\dfrac{2}{\sqrt{3}}$

(D) 3

(E) It cannot be determined from the information given

12. If the line described by the equation
$y + z = 3x$ crosses the y-axis when $y = 3$,
what is the value of z?

   (A) -3
   (B) 0
   (C) $\dfrac{1}{3}$
   (D) 3
   (E) 9

13. $\{54, 18, 36, 62, x, 69, 38\}$

   If the median of the numbers in the set
   above is 2 less than the average (arithmetic
   mean) of the numbers, which of the
   following could be the value of x?

   (A) 3
   (B) 18
   (C) 36
   (D) 40
   (E) 42

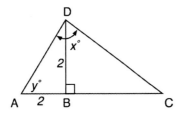

14.

   NOTE: Figure not drawn to scale

   In the figure above, $x = 75$ and $y = 45$.
   What is the area of Triangle ACD?

   (A) $2(1+\sqrt{3})$
   (B) 3
   (C) $3\sqrt{3}$
   (D) $2+\dfrac{2\sqrt{3}}{3}$
   (E) $4\sqrt{2}$

15. If p is the largest prime number less than 30
and c is the greatest common factor of 40
and 100, which of the following must be
true?

   I. $\dfrac{p}{c}$ is an integer

   II. $p - c > 0$

   III. c is a prime number

   (A) None of the above
   (B) I only
   (C) II only
   (D) II and III only
   (E) I, II, and III

16. If line j is described by the equation
$2x - 4y = -8$, which of the following
describes a line that is perpendicular to line
j?

   (A) $y = 5 - 2x$
   (B) $y = \dfrac{1}{2}x + 8$
   (C) $y = 2x + 6$
   (D) $y = -8x - 8$
   (E) $y = 4 - \dfrac{1}{2}x$

17. If $f(x) = 3x + 5$ and $g(x) = z - 2x$, what is
z, in terms of x, when $f(g(x)) = 11$?

   (A) $-6x + 5$
   (B) $x + 1$
   (C) $2x + 2$
   (D) $3x + 5$
   (E) $6x + 6$

18. A football team has a total of p players. If d
players play defense and b players play both
offense and defense, and every player plays
offense only or defense only or both, how
many players play offense?

   (A) $p - (d + b)$
   (B) $p - (d - b)$
   (C) $p - 2(d + b)$
   (D) $2p - 2(d + b)$
   (E) $(p - d) + (b - d)$

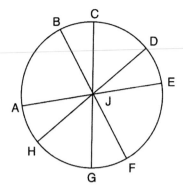

19.

NOTE: Figure not drawn to scale

The radius of the circle with center J shown above is 5. If the length of arc AC is 2π and the length of arc BE is 4π, what is the area of sector JEF?

(A) $\dfrac{\pi}{2}$

(B) π

(C) $\dfrac{5\pi}{2}$

(D) 5π

(E) It cannot be determined from the information given

20. A certain breakfast cereal contains both green and yellow marshmallows. The number of green marshmallows per box is supposed to be one-half the number of yellow marshmallows, but the machine that fills each box cannot count the marshmallows exactly. An inspector has determined that n is the average number of extra green marshmallows per box. If the inspector checks a box that has y yellow marshmallows, g green marshmallows, plus the average extra n green marshmallows, which of the following equations can be used to find the total number of marshmallows in that box?

(A) $y + g - n$

(B) $y + 2g + n$

(C) $\dfrac{1}{2}y + \dfrac{2gn}{n^2}$

(D) $\dfrac{3y}{2} + n$

(E) $\dfrac{2y}{n} + \dfrac{g}{n} + n$

Math Timed Drill 2 — 25 Minutes

Solve each of the following problems and choose the best of the choices given. Use any available space for scratch work, if necessary.

1. If $\dfrac{6+y}{3} = 4\dfrac{2}{3}$, what is the value of y?

(A) -4

(B) 2

(C) 6

(D) 8

(E) 14

2.

In the figure above, lines x and y are perpendicular and cut by line z as shown. If $a + c = 90$, what is the value of e?

(A) 45

(B) 90

(C) 110

(D) 120

(E) 135

3. In a neighborhood of 125 houses, 72 of the houses have a **garage** and the rest have no garage. There **are** 60 3-bedroom houses in the neighborhood, and the rest have 2 bedrooms. If one third of the houses with a garage have 3 **bedrooms**, how many of the 2-bedroom houses have no garage?

(A) 17
(B) 24
(C) 53
(D) 60
(E) 65

4. If the symbol ♣ describes a function $x ♣ y = \dfrac{2x}{2y-3}$, then what is the value of $5♣4$?

(A) $\dfrac{5}{8}$
(B) 1
(C) $\dfrac{5}{4}$
(D) 2
(E) $\dfrac{10}{3}$

5. If $ab = 2$, $bc = 3$, and $cd = 4$, what is the value of $\dfrac{b}{d}$?

(A) $\dfrac{1}{2}$
(B) $\dfrac{2}{3}$
(C) $\dfrac{5}{7}$
(D) $\dfrac{3}{4}$
(E) $1\dfrac{1}{3}$

6. In a class of 50 students, the ratio of boys to girls is 3 to 2. When the teacher puts the students in small groups, he makes sure every group has this same ratio. Which of the following CANNOT be the number of boys in a group?

(A) 5
(B) 6
(C) 9
(D) 12
(E) 15

7. The area of Square X is 20, and the area of Square Y is 50. If x is the length of a side of Square X and y is the length of a side of Square Y, what is xy?

(A) $2\sqrt{5}$
(B) $5\sqrt{2}$
(C) $10\sqrt{10}$
(D) $20\sqrt{5}$
(E) 100

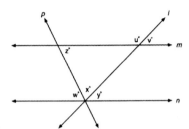

8.

In the figure above, $m \parallel n$. What is the value of z if $w = 50$?

(A) 40
(B) 50
(C) 75
(D) 110
(E) 130

The following questions require you to solve the problem and fill in the bubbles corresponding to your answers on the answer sheet. No (A) – (E) answer choices are provided.

9. If $x^2 + 10 = 25$, what is the value of x^4?

10. If Gavin started reading a book at the top of page 18 and finished at the bottom of page 31, how many total pages did he read?

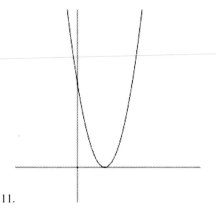

11.

The graph shown above is described by the function $y = (x-3)^2$. If a line is drawn that is described by the equation $y = 9 - 2x$, what is the greatest y-coordinate for a point where the line intersects the graph?

12. If $2x + 3y = 8$ and $x - y = 14$, what is the value of x?

13. Germain is cutting a piece of cylindrical pipe that is 18 inches long and has a radius of 1 inch. If he wants each piece to be cut the same length with no leftover pipe, and he wants pieces that are anywhere from 2 to 3 inches long, how many different ways could he cut the pipe?

14. A list of numbers consists of seven consecutive integers. If the sum of the numbers is 686, what is the second integer on the list?

15. If the ratio of the area of Circle A to the area of Circle B is 1 to 4, the radius of Circle A is what fraction of the radius of Circle B?

16. If g is a negative integer and $(g + 4)(g - 4) = 9$, what is the value of g?

17.
$3 = 1 ticket$

$5 = 2 tickets$

$10 = 5 tickets$

$25 = 13 tickets$

In a charity raffle, tickets can be purchased as shown above. What is the greatest number of tickets that can be bought for $78?

18. Shayla is arranging six statues on a shelf in her living room. Each statue is a different color. If Shayla wants the black statue to go on the far left and the red statue to go on the far right, how many different arrangements could she make with the six statues?

Math Timed Drill 3 — 20 Minutes

Solve each of the following problems and choose the best of the choices given. Use any available space for scratch work, if necessary.

1. Dividing a certain number by 3 gives the same result as subtracting 6 from the number. What is the number?

   (A) 2
   (B) 3
   (C) 6
   (D) 9
   (E) 18

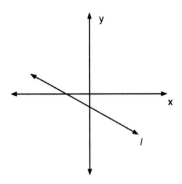

2.

Which of the following statements about line *l*, shown above, must be true?

I. The slope of the line is between 0 and 1

II. The y-intercept is negative

III. The equation of the line could be
$y = 4 - 2x$

(A) I only
(B) II only
(C) I and II only
(D) II and III only
(E) I, II, and III

	Cheese	Pepperoni	Special
Slice	$1.50	$1.80	$2.25
Whole Pizza	$10.00	$13.25	$15.50

3.

The menu above shows the prices for pizza at a restaurant. What is the greatest number of slices of pepperoni pizza that Alex can buy if she has $10?

(A) 1
(B) 5
(C) 6
(D) 8
(E) 10

4. An office has two printers, a slow one and a fast one. The slow printer can print 10 pages per minute. The fast printer can print 14 pages per minute. If the fast printer has exactly 210 pieces of paper, and the slow printer is used when the fast printer runs out of paper, how many minutes will it take to print 420 pages?

(A) 15
(B) 30
(C) 36
(D) 48
(E) 50

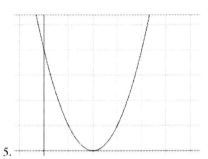

5.

The figure above shows the graph of the function $f(x) = (x-2)^2$. Which of the following gives the coordinates of the point where the graph crosses the y-axis?

(A) (0, 4)
(B) (0, 2)
(C) (4, 0)
(D) (1, 1)
(E) (-1, 2)

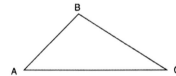

6.

NOTE: Figure not drawn to scale.

In the triangle shown above, if angle *A* is one third the measure of angle *B* but twice the measure of angle *C*, what is the measure of angle *A?*

(A) 20
(B) 30
(C) 40
(D) 80
(E) 100

7. If $x^2 - y^2 = 1$ and $(z+3)^{-2} = \dfrac{1}{9}$, which of the following must be true?

(A) $xy = 0$

(B) $x + y = 1$

(C) $x + y + z = \dfrac{10}{9}$

(D) $x^2 + y^2 + z = \dfrac{10}{9}$

(E) $xyz = 0$

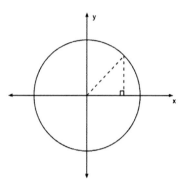

8.

The center of the circle shown on the xy-plane above is $(0, 0)$. An isosceles right triangle is made by drawing the dotted lines as shown. If the area of the triangle is 18, what is the area of the circle?

(A) $18\sqrt{2}\pi$

(B) 36π

(C) $36\sqrt{2}\pi$

(D) 72π

(E) 324π

9. If $\sqrt{x} + x^2 = 18$ and $\sqrt{x+5} > 2$, which of the following could be x?

(A) 1

(B) 4

(C) 7

(D) 9

(E) 25

10. If Francis is reading a chapter in her history textbook that begins at the top of page 323 and ends at the bottom of page 350, how many pages must Francis read in order to complete exactly half of the chapter?

(A) 14

(B) 15

(C) 27

(D) 28

(E) 30

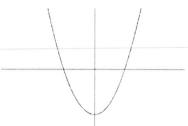

11.

If the graph above is described by the function $f(x) = x^2 + mx + b$, which of the following could be the value of b?

(A) -2

(B) 0

(C) $\dfrac{1}{2}$

(D) 3

(E) 9

12. If $3y < 2x < 0$, which of the following is greatest?

(A) $-3x$

(B) $-(3x+2y)$

(C) $4(2x)$

(D) 0

(E) $-2y$

13. Lelia bought a shirt on sale for $47.60. If the original price of the shirt was first reduced by 20 percent and then that sale price was reduced by 30 percent, what was the original price of the shirt?

(A) $26.65

(B) $59.96

(C) $79.33

(D) $85.00

(E) $95.20

14. A certain number is twice its greatest prime factor. If the greatest prime factor of this number is less than 10 but the number is greater than 10, what is the number?

(A) 9

(B) 10

(C) 14

(D) 16

(E) 18

15. If the greatest of seven consecutive integers is greater than 7 times the average of the integers, which of the following statements must be true?

I. All of the numbers are negative

II. One of the numbers is 0

III. The average of the numbers is ≤ 0

(A) I only
(B) III only
(C) I and III only
(D) II and III only
(E) I, II, and III

16. If 6 is the average of a set of s numbers, and 7 is the average of a set of v numbers, which of the following conditions guarantees that the sum of the s numbers is greater than the sum of the v numbers?

(A) $s > 7$
(B) $s > v$
(C) $2s = v$
(D) $s = v + 1$
(E) $v < s < 7$

Critical Reading Timed Drill 1 — 25 Minutes

Each of the following sentences has one or two blanks, which indicate that a word or group of words has been omitted. Answer choices A through E represent five words or groups of words that could fill the blank or blanks. Choose the word or group of words that best completes the meaning of the sentence as a whole.

1. To prevent astronauts' bodies from absorbing harmful ultraviolet rays, the exterior of the Space Shuttle is specially designed to ------- as much sunlight as possible.

(A) return
(B) transmit
(C) ascertain
(D) deflect
(E) erase

2. The shirt and tie Wanda bought her father for his birthday were -------, designed specially to be worn together with a matching suit.

(A) pragmatic
(B) incendiary
(C) complimentary
(D) consecutive
(E) outlandish

3. Even though they did not enjoy the daily quizzes, the students found the ------- of answering questions about the assigned readings ------- when it came to writing their term papers.

(A) necessity . . advantageous
(B) challenge . . confusing
(C) nuisance . . distracting
(D) imposition . . burdening
(E) hassle . . childish

4. Mr. Peterson is a painstaking chef, taking care to ------- prepare everything in advance so that nothing is left to ------- when it comes time for making the dish.

(A) scrupulously . . founder
(B) meticulously . . chance
(C) hastily . . unwrap
(D) assiduously . . return
(E) whimsically . . fancy

5. A good literary critic is both analytical and entertaining, making sure that the review is not only ------- but also ------- to read.

(A) judicious . . simple
(B) disparaging . . pleasurable
(C) informative . . enjoyable
(D) synthetic . . educational
(E) fallacious . . inspiring

6. The first *homo sapiens*, simple yet resourceful creatures, must have found very ------- ways to utilize the ------- materials that were available to them.

   (A) altruistic . . raw
   (B) clumsy . . natural
   (C) ingenious . . crude
   (D) uncomplicated . . technical
   (E) unforeseen . . acute

7. Owen is a skilled carpenter and a visionary architect, making him a ------- and farsighted house builder.

   (A) maladroit
   (B) duplicitous
   (C) reactionary
   (D) consummate
   (E) profligate

8. Although many people thought the poems read by Clarice were excessively -------, a few of the audience members were moved to tears despite the overt sentimentality of the verse.

   (A) saccharine
   (B) rancorous
   (C) stringent
   (D) boorish
   (E) cynical

The following passages are the basis for the questions below; if there are two passages, questions may ask about the relationship between the related passages. Answer the questions based on what is directly stated or what can be inferred from the passages and the italicized introduction, if provided.

Questions 9-10 are based on the following passage.

The term *aleatory* is not always applied to music where the composer does not maintain full control over the piece. In pieces where
Line certain decisions are left up to the performer,
5 but are not a matter of chance, the terms *indeterminate music* or *limited aleatory* are sometimes used. For example, a composer may indicate to the player a certain melodic idea by drawing a wavy line across the staff,
10 ornamented with arrows perhaps, approximately where the notes should fall, but will not actually notate the melody, or indicate a tempo. (For source reference, see endnote [8])

9. The example in lines 7-14 is intended to

   (A) describe the proper notation for an aleatory reference
   (B) demonstrate one way in which a piece may be aleatory
   (C) outline the basic structure of all aleatory decisions
   (D) demonstrate how little control composers have over the performance of their music
   (E) suggest why there are so many terms for the same musical concept

10. The author uses the phrase "not a matter of chance" (line 5) to indicate that

   (A) decisions left up to the performer are still limited by the composition
   (B) random processes have no place in musical composition
   (C) composers choose a certain notation for very specific reasons
   (D) the use of one of the three terms for *aleatory* has a definite reason
   (E) composers carefully select which musicians will be allowed to perform their pieces

Questions 11-12 are based on the following passage.

Today the site of Mayapan is far from one of the more impressive Maya sites. This is due, in part, to the fact that at the end of the revolt
Line the roofs of every building in the city were
5 burned or torn down. In a larger part, however, it is due to the fact that monumental architecture on the scale of Chichen Itza or Uxmal was simply never attempted at Mayapan. One central pyramid is a smaller
10 version of the "Castillo" at Chichen Itza; there were a few other moderately sized temples and a palace (of which only the foundations exist); otherwise Mayapan had little public architecture. (For source reference, see endnote [9])

11. The passage indicates that Mayapan is "far from one of the more impressive Maya sites" (lines 1-2) primarily because

(A) most of the larger monuments were torn down during the revolution
(B) architects from Chichen Itza sent troops to destroy the public buildings in Mayapan
(C) European conquerors skipped over Mayapan because it was not an imposing city
(D) Mayapan architects worked in less grandiose ways than other Mayan builders
(E) the Mayans buried in Mayapan's pyramids were of a very small stature

12. The passage is primarily concerned with Mayapan's

(A) revolutionary history
(B) conquering neighbors
(C) pyramid schemes
(D) tourist industry
(E) public structures

Questions 13-24 are based on the following passages.

The following passages are excerpts from novels written in the mid 19th century.

Passage 1

A green valley with a brook running through it, full almost to overflowing with the late rains, overhung by low stooping willows.
Line Across this brook a plank is thrown, and over
5 this plank Adam Bede is passing with his undoubting step, followed close by Gyp with the basket; evidently making his way to the thatched house, with a stack of timber by the side of it, about twenty yards up the opposite
10 slope.
    The door of the house is open, and an elderly woman is looking out; but she is not placidly contemplating the evening sunshine; she has been watching with dim eyes the
15 gradually enlarging speck, which for the last few minutes she has been quite sure is her darling son Adam. Lisbeth Bede loves her son with the love of a woman to whom her first-born has come late in life. She is an anxious,
20 spare, yet vigorous old woman, clean as a snowdrop. Her grey hair is turned neatly back under a pure linen cap with a black band round it; her broad chest is covered with a buff neckerchief, and below this you see a sort of
25 short bed gown made of blue-checkered linen, tied round the waist and descending to the hips, from whence there is a considerable length of linsey-woolsey petticoat. For Lisbeth is tall,

and in other points too there is a strong likeness
30 between her and her son Adam. Her dark eyes are somewhat dim now—perhaps from too much crying—but her broadly marked eyebrows are still black, her teeth are sound, and as she stands knitting rapidly and
35 unconsciously with her work-hardened hands, she has as firmly upright an attitude as when she is carrying a pail of water on her head from the spring. There is the same type of frame and the same keen activity of temperament in
40 mother and son, but it was not from her that Adam got his well-filled brow and his expression of large-hearted intelligence. (For source reference, see endnote 16)

Passage 2

To begin with the old rigmarole of childhood. In a country there was a shire, and
45 in that shire there was a town, and in that town there was a house, and in that house there was a room, and in that room there was a bed, and in that bed there lay a little girl; wide awake and longing to get up, but not daring to do so for
50 fear of the unseen power in the next room — a certain Betty, whose slumbers must not be disturbed until six o'clock struck, when she wakened of herself 'as sure as clockwork,' and left the household very little peace afterwards.
55 It was a June morning, and early as it was, the room was full of sunny warmth and light.
    On the drawers opposite to the little white dimity bed in which Molly Gibson lay, was a primitive kind of bonnet-stand on which was
60 hung a bonnet, carefully covered over from any chance of dust, with a large cotton handkerchief, of so heavy and serviceable a texture that if the thing underneath it had been a flimsy fabric of gauze and lace and flowers, it
65 would have been altogether 'scromfished' (again to quote from Betty's vocabulary). But the bonnet was made of solid straw, and its only trimming was a plain white ribbon put over the crown, and forming the strings. Still,
70 there was a neat little quilling inside, every plait of which Molly knew, for had she not made it herself the evening before, with infinite pains? And was there not a little blue bow in this quilling, the very first bit of such finery
75 Molly had ever had the prospect of wearing?
    Six o'clock now; the pleasant, brisk ringing of the church bells told that; calling every one to their daily work, as they had done for hundreds of years. Up jumped Molly, and ran
80 with her bare little feet across the room, and lifted off the handkerchief and saw once again the bonnet; the pledge of the gay bright day to come. Then to the window, and after some tugging she opened the casement, and let in the
85 sweet morning air. The dew was already off the flowers in the garden below, but still rising from the long hay-grass in the meadows

directly beyond. At one side lay the little town of Hollingford, into a street of which Mr.
90 Gibson's front door opened; and delicate columns, and little puffs of smoke were already beginning to rise from many a cottage chimney where some housewife was already up, and preparing breakfast for the breadwinner of the
95 family. (For source reference, see endnote [11])

13. In lines 14-17, the passage suggests that the elderly woman is watching

   (A) apathetically
   (B) composedly
   (C) with hope
   (D) expectantly
   (E) in awe

14. In line 20, "spare" most nearly means

   (A) lean
   (B) elderly
   (C) nervous
   (D) thrifty
   (E) extraneous

15. The author's lengthy physical description of Lisbeth Bede (lines 21-38) implicitly serves the purpose of

   (A) explaining her reasons for being so nervous
   (B) setting up Lisbeth as the novel's real hero
   (C) giving the reader a picture of Adam Bede
   (D) foreshadowing the old woman's early death
   (E) revealing the origin of Adam's intelligence

16. All of the following are used to describe Lisbeth Bede EXCEPT

   (A) a simile related to her work habits
   (B) a detailed account of her clothing
   (C) a comparison between her and her son
   (D) an analogy relating her to Nature
   (E) a reference to her early education

17. Which of the following is most likely the reason that the author speculates that it is from "too much crying" (lines 31-32) that Lisbeth's eyes are "somewhat dim"?

   (A) Adam Bede has been gone from his mother's house for a long time.
   (B) Adam Bede does not love his mother as much as she loves him.
   (C) Lisbeth's son was taken from her when he was just a baby.
   (D) Lisbeth has gone blind while watching the road for her son's arrival.
   (E) Lisbeth and Adam both have the same sensitive temperament.

18. In context, the word "scromfished" (line 65) from Betty's vocabulary most likely means

   (A) flimsy
   (B) hidden
   (C) squashed
   (D) trimmed
   (E) smelly

19. In Passage 2, the author uses two rhetorical questions (lines 69-75) to indicate

   (A) why the bonnet was special to Molly despite its plainness
   (B) the reasons for Betty's scornful attitude towards Molly
   (C) how right Betty was that Molly's bonnet was not being 'scromfished'
   (D) the source of Molly's fear of Betty
   (E) that Molly is an invalid child

20. According to Passage 2, Molly remains in bed until the clock struck six for which of the following reasons?

   I. To avoid disturbing Betty

   II. To prolong the joy of the day to come

   III. To postpone opening the window because of her fears

   (A) I only
   (B) II only
   (C) I and III only
   (D) II and III only
   (E) I, II, and III

21. Which of the following best represents Molly's expectations for how the day to come would be?

(A) Betty
(B) Her bonnet
(C) The smoking chimneys
(D) Mr. Gibson's front door
(E) The room next door

22. Which of the following is the greatest similarity between Molly in Passage 2 and Lisbeth Bede in Passage 1?

(A) Their ages
(B) Their family relationships
(C) The source of their fears
(D) The way they look out on the horizon
(E) The plainness and solidity of their clothing

23. Passage 1 and Passage 2 are most similar in structure because they both

(A) delve deeply into their characters' minds
(B) discuss the background of the story
(C) use analogies to describe the setting
(D) linger on physical descriptions
(E) convey a complex story with simple terms

24. The ending of Passage 2, "where some...of the family" (lines 93-95), would be an apt description of Lisbeth's morning if which of the following were true?

(A) Lisbeth Bede earned money by baking bread.
(B) Adam Bede lived with and supported his mother.
(C) Lisbeth's cabin had columns out front.
(D) The town of Hollingford was located in a green valley.
(E) Molly lived in the same town as Lisbeth.

Critical Reading Timed Drill 2 — 25 Minutes

Each of the following sentences has one or two blanks, which indicate that a word or group of words has been omitted. Answer choices A through E represent five words or groups of words that could fill the blank or blanks. Choose the word or group of words that best completes the meaning of the sentence as a whole.

1. It is not surprising that someone who changes his mind so often ------- a decision that would have major consequences for his future.

(A) complained about
(B) wavered on
(C) jumped into
(D) resolved for
(E) hinted at

2. Because no emergency plan had yet been developed, the city was ------- to handle a ------- of this sort.

(A) determined . . tragedy
(B) equipped . . disaster
(C) staggered . . contest
(D) primed . . crisis
(E) unprepared . . catastrophe

3. Nutritionists widely recognize the beneficial effects of eating garlic regularly, yet many doctors refuse to acknowledge its ------- properties.

(A) derisory
(B) remissive
(C) venomous
(D) munificent
(E) salubrious

4. Some researchers are so ------- that a cure can be found for cancer that it seems ------- that this dread disease will one day be eliminated.

(A) certain . . inevitable
(B) doubtful . . assured
(C) hopeful . . improbable
(D) resolute . . negligible
(E) trenchant . . predestined

5. Successful criminal lawyers are able to ------
    a guilty client's case without being ------- by
    the knowledge that they are arguing against
    the truth.

    (A) advocate . . inspired
    (B) emasculate . . assuaged
    (C) dispute . . disturbed
    (D) extemporize . . inspired
    (E) advance . . hampered

The following passages are the basis for the
questions below; if there are two passages,
questions may ask about the relationship between
the related passages. Answer the questions based
on what is directly stated or what can be inferred
from the passages and the italicized introduction,
if provided.

Questions 6-9 are based on the following passages.

Passage 1

It has been the office of art to educate the
perception of beauty. We are immersed in
beauty, but our eyes have no clear vision. It
Line needs, by the exhibition of single traits, to
5 assist and lead the dormant taste. We carve and
paint, or we behold what is carved and painted,
as students of the mystery of Form. The virtue
of art lies in detachment, in sequestering one
object from the embarrassing variety. Until one
10 thing comes out from the connection of things,
there can be enjoyment, contemplation, but no
thought. (For source reference, see endnote [12])

Passage 2

Western philosophers have distinguished
between two kinds of knowledge: a priori
15 knowledge and a posteriori knowledge. A
priori knowledge is gained or justified by
reason alone, without the direct or indirect
influence of experience. A posteriori
knowledge is any other sort of knowledge; that
20 is, knowledge the attainment of which requires
reference to experience. A fundamental
question in epistemology is whether there is
any non-trivial a priori knowledge. Generally
speaking rationalists believe that there is, while
25 empiricists believe that all knowledge is
ultimately derived from some kind of external
experience. (For source reference, see endnote [13])

6. The distinctions made in Passage 1, unlike
    those in Passage 2, serve to

    (A) advance the practice of good art rather
         than explain the sources of human
         knowledge
    (B) explain the passage's main concept
         rather than divide the world into
         distinct categories
    (C) make important ethical claims rather
         than ignore difficult moral questions
    (D) divide our attainment of knowledge
         rather than advance our understanding
         of art
    (E) confuse further the questions raised
         rather than clarify the situation

7. Both passages assume that

    (A) the reader has a strong background in
         both history and literature
    (B) human beings are innately drawn to
         pure contemplation
    (C) the only way to achieve knowledge is
         through perceptions
    (D) pure philosophy is the best road to
         understanding Form
    (E) certain aspects of human experience
         can be isolated from one another

8. The author of Passage 1 would most likely
    agree with which of the following discussed
    in Passage 2?

    (A) the fundamental questions of
         epistemology
    (B) the division of knowledge into two
         kinds
    (C) the perspective of the empiricists
    (D) the claims of the rationalists
    (E) the ideas of Western philosophers

9. Unlike the author of Passage 1, the author of
    Passage 2 does which of the following?

    (A) gives concrete examples
    (B) uses a controversial definition
    (C) describes conflicting viewpoints
    (D) makes morally questionable claims
    (E) relies on pure thought to understand the
         world

Questions 10-15 are based on the following passage.

*In this passage, the author discusses the ruins
of a cathedral destroyed during World War II.*

The city of Coventry, West Midlands,
England is unusual in that it has had three
cathedrals. The first was St. Mary's, a monastic
Line building, only a few ruins of which remain. The
5 second was St. Michael's, an Anglican
cathedral and now a ruined shell since the

Second World War. The third is the new St. Michael's rising like a phoenix from the ashes out of the destruction of the former and a celebration of 20th century architecture.

10 The original St Michael's Cathedral was largely constructed between the late 14th century and early 15th century but now stands ruined, bombed almost to destruction on
15 November 14, 1940 by the German Luftwaffe. Only the tower and spire along with the outer wall survived. Before 1918 it was the church of St Michael, the largest parish church in England, but in that year was elevated to
20 cathedral status after a revision of the diocese. The new St Michael's cathedral, built next to the remains of the old, was designed by Basil Spence.

The ruin of the older cathedral remains
25 hallowed ground. A cross made of nails from the cathedral was donated to the Kaiser Wilhelm Memorial Church in Berlin, which was destroyed by allied bomb attacks and is kept as a ruin also. A copy of a graphic by Kurt
30 Reubers that was drawn in 1942 in Stalingrad (now Volgograd) is shown in the cathedrals of all three cities as sign for reconciliation of the three countries that were once enemies.

Basil Spence (later knighted for this work)
35 insisted that instead of re-building the old cathedral, it should be kept in ruins as a garden of remembrance and that the new cathedral should be built alongside, the two buildings together effectively forming one church. The
40 selection of Spence for the work was a result of a competition held in 1950 to find an architect for the new Coventry Cathedral; his design was chosen from over two hundred submitted. (For source reference, see endnote [14])

10. In lines 1-3, the author implies that most towns in England

(A) were not bombed during the Second World War
(B) do not have as many as three cathedrals
(C) have monastic buildings that are in ruins
(D) were not around during the early 15th century
(E) are named for a single saint

11. In context, the author's claim that the new St Michael's rises "like a phoenix from the ashes out of the destruction of the former" (lines 8-9) is misleading because

(A) the two cathedrals are named for different saints both of whom were called Michael
(B) the original cathedral and the new one were designed by different people
(C) the bombing of the original St Michael's left more than just ashes
(D) the ground upon which the new St Michael's was built was never made hallowed ground
(E) the new cathedral is actually built alongside the old cathedral, not on the same site

12. The author implies that the most likely reason St Michael's was once "the largest parish church in England" (lines 18-19) is that

(A) its ancient origins drew a large number of parishioners before the German bombings
(B) the town of Coventry was unusual in that it had three cathedrals
(C) diocese politics led the building to become hallowed ground
(D) it was large enough to be considered a cathedral, but hadn't been categorized that way yet
(E) the construction of the church, beginning in the early 14th century, made it England's oldest as well as largest

13. According to the passage, the gift to the Kaiser Wilhelm Memorial Church was appropriate because both churches

(A) served the same religious community
(B) were attacked during the Second World War
(C) originally housed crosses made of nails
(D) survived repeated bombing raids
(E) were rebuilt out of wood nailed to stone

14. The author mentions that Basil Spence won a competition to design the rebuilt cathedral in order to emphasize that

(A) he was knighted because of his uncompromising stance on the design
(B) his design ideas spoke powerfully to the people rebuilding the cathedral
(C) little attention was paid by the media to the rebuilding of the cathedral
(D) only nobility understand architecture enough to recapture the brilliance of destroyed cathedrals
(E) he ignored the religious symbolism of the original in favor of popularity

15. The passage suggests that the presence of the Kurt Reubers graphic in three cathedrals represents

(A) the unifying symbolism of Christ's dying on the cross
(B) the ability of enemy governments to destroy historical landmarks
(C) the peaceful co-existence of three once-warring countries
(D) the similar design of all European cathedrals regardless of national origin
(E) the devastation brought on by allied bomb attacks during the Second World War

Questions 16-24 are based on the following passage.

The author of this passage briefly describes gene therapy.

Gene therapy is the insertion of genes into an individual's cells and tissues to treat diseases, and hereditary diseases in particular.
Line Gene therapy typically aims to supplement a
5 defective mutant allele—a member of a pair or series of genes that occupies a specific position on a specific chromosome—with a functional one. Although the technology is still in its infancy, it has been used with some success.
10 In the 1980s, advances in molecular biology had already enabled human genes to be sequenced and cloned. Scientists were looking for a method of easily producing proteins, such as insulin, the protein deficient in diabetics.
15 They investigated introducing human genes into bacterial DNA. The modified bacteria then produced the corresponding protein, which could be harvested and injected in people who could not produce it naturally.
20 Scientists have taken the logical step of trying to introduce genes straight into human cells, focusing on curing diseases caused by single-gene defects, such as cystic fibrosis, hemophilia, muscular dystrophy and sickle cell
25 anemia. However, this has been much harder

than modifying simple bacteria, primarily because of the problems involved in carrying large sections of DNA and delivering them to the right site on the genome, or genetic
30 material.
  In theory it is possible to transform either somatic cells (most cells of the body) or cells of the germ line (such as stem cells, sperm and eggs). All gene therapy in people has so far
35 been directed at somatic cells, whereas germ line engineering in humans remains a highly controversial prospect. For an introduced gene to be transmitted normally to offspring, it needs not only to be inserted into the cell, but also to
40 be incorporated into the chromosomes by recombination.
  Somatic gene therapy can be broadly split into two categories: ex vivo (in which cells are modified outside the body and then
45 transplanted back in again) and in vivo (in which genes are modified in cells still in the body). Recombination-based approaches in vivo are especially uncommon, because for most DNA constructs, recombination is a very
50 low probability event.
  The ex vivo approach was the first to be put into practice. In 1990 trials were run designed to treat children with an inherited immune deficiency, as well as children or adults with
55 high serum cholesterol. Cells were removed from the patients' bodies and incubated with vectors that inserted copies of the genes. Most gene-therapy vectors are viruses, although there are techniques for delivering DNA directly as
60 well. After modification, the cells were transplanted back into the patients where scientists hoped the cells would replicate and produce functional descendants for the life of the transplanted individual. (For source reference, see endnote [15])

16. The primary purpose of this passage is to

(A) describe how genes mutate
(B) explain gene therapy research
(C) argue for more research into molecular biology
(D) demonstrate the futility of fighting disease with gene therapy
(E) suggest a promising approach to genetic recombination

17. In line 9, "infancy" most nearly means

(A) newborn
(B) immaturity
(C) maturation period
(D) early stages
(E) viral

18. The purpose of the second paragraph (lines 10-19) is to

(A) describe the initial steps taken by early gene-therapy researchers
(B) explain how molecular biology has been replaced by DNA research
(C) demonstrate how complex the process of gene therapy has become
(D) introduce important terms that are used in the rest of the passage
(E) prove that gene therapy can be made to work as promised

19. In lines 32-34, the parenthetical phrases serve to

(A) define important terms
(B) clarify unexplained points
(C) provide alternative views
(D) digress on unrelated topics
(E) divide a complex sentence into simple parts

20. Which of the following is the most likely reason that "germ line engineering in humans remains a highly controversial prospect" (lines 35-37)?

(A) The majority of research funding currently goes to somatic gene therapy.
(B) Genetic recombination has a low likelihood of succeeding.
(C) The chromosomes of sperm and eggs cannot be modified ex vivo.
(D) Gene therapy in human subjects can lead to death or serious illness.
(E) There are religious objections to meddling with sperm and eggs.

21. The sentence in lines 37-41 ("For an introduced gene... by recombination") is intended by the author to

(A) show how the in vivo approach differs from the ex vivo approach
(B) demonstrate the difficulty of the germ line approach
(C) give an example of diseases caused by single-gene defects
(D) explain how germ DNA behaves differently than chromosomal DNA
(E) describe the difference between normal and abnormal offspring

22. The author develops the fifth paragraph (lines 42-50) by

(A) comparing and contrasting two approaches
(B) setting up two complementary lines of research
(C) invalidating an uncommon scientific claim
(D) providing definitions and interpreting their meaning
(E) drawing a distinction and discussing a problem

23. The "viruses" (line 58) mentioned in the last paragraph served to

(A) introduce genetic changes ex vivo
(B) recombine the chromosomes of sick children
(C) transmit immune-deficiency conditions
(D) deliver DNA directly to trial subjects
(E) nourish transplant organs

24. The hope of the scientists mentioned in the final sentence (lines 60-64) suggests that

(A) the clinical trials designed to treat children had little chance of success
(B) gene-therapy researchers still aren't sure if the ex vivo approach will work
(C) using virus vectors to treat immune deficiency was always known to be the best approach
(D) the scientists wished they had tried genetic recombination instead
(E) neither the in vivo nor the ex vivo technique is very likely to produce the hoped-for results

Each of the following sentences has one or two blanks, which indicate that a word or group of words has been omitted. Answer choices A through E represent five words or groups of words that could fill the blank or blanks. Choose the word or group of words that best completes the meaning of the sentence as a whole.

1. The director professed to be interested in ------- with the writer, but when it came time to staging the show, the two failed to work well together.

   (A) rebelling
   (B) promoting
   (C) intensifying
   (D) collaborating
   (E) experimenting

2. Tamara was able to ------- her message effectively by presenting her case in ------- manner, using an outline and providing clear instructions to her audience.

   (A) communicate . . an organized
   (B) undermine . . a methodical
   (C) exaggerate . . an efficient
   (D) transform . . a hyperbolic
   (E) explain . . a futile

3. Paradoxically, an intense fever may sometimes result in a ------- body temperature as the immune system attempts to ------- its effort to combat the illness.

   (A) decreased . . diffuse
   (B) raised . . challenge
   (C) steadied . . manipulate
   (D) mortifying . . boost
   (E) lowered . . intensify

4. Dr. Franklin relied on evidence of debatable accuracy, making her conclusions ------- as well.

   (A) rigorous
   (B) profound
   (C) rancorous
   (D) dubious
   (E) audible

5. The electorate was highly ------- on the issue of gun-control in this last election; some voters were strongly for it, the others strongly opposed.

   (A) polarized
   (B) classified
   (C) indulgent
   (D) favorable
   (E) undecided

6. The marriage counselor advises that in order to maintain the ------- needed to keep a relationship growing, spouses must avoid being ------- about their beliefs, especially the ones that they hold the most stubbornly.

   (A) fortitude . . moderate
   (B) haughtiness . . imprudent
   (C) profligacy . . unyielding
   (D) stability . . humble
   (E) flexibility . . rigid

The following passages are the basis for the questions below; if there are two passages, questions may ask about the relationship between the related passages. Answer the questions based on what is directly stated or what can be inferred from the passages and the italicized introduction, if provided.

Questions 7-19 are based on the following passage.

The author of this address to Congress discusses the importance of the reconstruction of the southern United States after the end of the Civil War.

Seldom has any legislative body been the subject of a solicitude more intense, or of aspirations more sincere and ardent. There are
Line the best of reasons for this profound interest.
5 Questions of vast moment, left undecided by the last session of Congress, must be manfully grappled with by this one. No political skirmishing will avail. The occasion demands statesmanship.
10   Whether the tremendous war so heroically fought and so victoriously ended shall pass into history a miserable failure, barren of permanent results, —a scandalous and shocking waste of blood and treasure, —a strife for empire, as
15 Earl Russell characterized it, of no value to liberty or civilization, —an attempt to re-establish a Union by force, which must be the merest mockery of a Union, —an effort to bring under Federal authority States into which

20 no loyal man from the North may safely enter,
    and to bring men into the national councils who
    deliberate with daggers and vote with
    revolvers, and who do not even conceal their
    deadly hate of the country that conquered them;
25 or whether, on the other hand, we shall, as the
    rightful reward of victory over treason, have a
    solid nation, entirely delivered from all
    contradictions and social antagonisms, based
    upon loyalty, liberty, and equality, must be
30 determined one way or the other by the present
    session of Congress. The last session really did
    nothing which can be considered final as to
    these questions. The Civil Rights Bill and the
    Freedmen's Bureau Bill and the proposed
35 constitutional amendments, with the
    amendment already adopted and recognized as
    the law of the land, do not reach the difficulty,
    and cannot, unless the whole structure of the
    government is changed from a government by
40 States to something like a despotic central
    government, with power to control even the
    municipal regulations of States, and to make
    them conform to its own despotic will. While
    there remains such an idea as the right of each
45 State to control its own local affairs—an idea,
    by the way, more deeply rooted in the minds of
    men of all sections of the country than perhaps
    any one other political idea—no general
    assertion of human rights can be of any
50 practical value. To change the character of the
    government at this point is neither possible nor
    desirable. All that is necessary to be done is to
    make the government consistent with itself, and
    render the rights of the States compatible with
55 the sacred rights of human nature.
        The arm of the Federal government is long,
    but it is far too short to protect the rights of
    individuals in the interior of distant States.
    They must have the power to protect
60 themselves, or they will go unprotected, spite
    of all the laws the Federal government can put
    upon the national statute book.
        Slavery, like all other great systems of
    wrong, founded in the depths of human
65 selfishness, and existing for ages, has not
    neglected its own conservation. It has steadily
    exerted an influence upon all around it
    favorable to its own continuance. And today it
    is so strong that it could exist, not only without
70 law, but even against law. Custom, manners,
    morals, religion, are all on its side everywhere
    in the South; and when you add the ignorance
    and servility of the ex-slave to the intelligence
    and accustomed authority of the master, you
75 have the conditions, not out of which slavery
    will again grow, but under which it is
    impossible for the Federal government to
    wholly destroy it, unless the Federal
    government be armed with despotic power, to
80 blot out State authority, and to station a Federal
    officer at every crossroad. This, of course,

cannot be done, and ought not even if it could.
The true way and the easiest way is to make
our government entirely consistent with itself,
85 and give to every loyal citizen the elective
    franchise—a right and power which will be
    ever present, and will form a wall of fire for his
    protection.
    (For source reference, see endnote [16])

7. In line 3, the "aspirations" mentioned by the
    author refer to

    (A) healing the wounds of the Civil War
    (B) punishing those who failed
    (C) establishing a Union by force
    (D) regaining the loyalty of the North
    (E) winning the political skirmishes

8. In line 14, "strife" could best be replaced by

    (A) argument
    (B) friction
    (C) rivalry
    (D) trouble
    (E) boon

9. The reference to Earl Russell's
    characterization of the Civil War (lines 15-
    16) serves to

    (A) illustrate the common point of view
         held by the author and many others
    (B) justify what the author thinks is his
         rightful reward for victory
    (C) describe one of the approaches the
         author is arguing for Congress to adopt
    (D) demonstrate how the members of
         Congress must think about the outcome
         of the war
    (E) lay out one of the undesirable outcomes
         of inaction by the present session of
         Congress

10. The author uses the phrase "on the other
     hand" (line 25) in order to

     (A) show how things might turn out if
          Congress ignores his recommendations
     (B) introduce the ideas that he hopes will
          be the outcome of Congress's
          deliberations
     (C) elaborate on the same point using
          different examples
     (D) switch his argument to the opposite
          side
     (E) demonstrate that he is about to discuss
          an equally unacceptable outcome

11. The author mentions the Civil Rights Bill and the Freedmen's Bureau Bill in lines 33-34 in order to

    (A) congratulate Congress on its extraordinary statesmanship
    (B) demonstrate the shortcomings of the previous session of Congress
    (C) prove that the Civil War was not fought and won in vain
    (D) draw a comparison between these new laws and a constitutional amendment
    (E) explain why he had always remained secretly loyal to the North

12. Opponents of the author's argument on lines 50-55 might best respond by pointing out that

    (A) making the government consistent with itself in the face of States' resistance would require the continued use of force
    (B) the character of the government had already been changed by the passage of the Civil Rights Bill and the Freedmen's Bureau Bill
    (C) everyone in the South thought it was desirable to change the character of the government into a more consistent one
    (D) every general assertion of human rights had a practical value if made in the right time and place
    (E) the tyranny of the Federal government would always be worse than the tyranny of State governments

13. Which of the following best describes the author's evaluation of the power of the Federal government?

    (A) The Federal government unjustifiably imposed its despotic will on the South.
    (B) The Federal government had not always used its power to achieve good results.
    (C) The power of the Federal government by itself was not enough to win the Civil War.
    (D) The Federal government is powerful but not all-powerful.
    (E) The Federal government should be granted unlimited power over the States.

14. The author responds to the idea that the Federal government can pass effective laws to secure human rights by pointing out that

    (A) it is impossible to get a solid majority in such a divided country
    (B) slavery would never have existed were it not for national statutes
    (C) individuals in far away locations will not benefit from Federal protection
    (D) it is undesirable to act on political ideas instead of practical necessity
    (E) the State governments already have effective laws securing human rights

15. According to the author, the Federal government would need to do which of the following to impose an end to slavery?

    I. Assume a despotic form of power

    II. Deny Southerners the right to vote

    III. Deport all but the most loyal of citizens

    (A) I only
    (B) III only
    (C) I and III only
    (D) II and III only
    (E) I, II, and III

16. In making his argument in the final paragraph (lines 63-88), the author

    (A) deplores the institution of slavery but resigns himself to living with it
    (B) makes an emotional case for using military means to destroy slavery
    (C) lays out a strategy for changing Southern culture into the true and correct culture
    (D) points out what cannot be done before revealing the best course of action
    (E) resigns himself to supporting the lesser of two evils in a bad situation

17. In line 66, "conservation" most nearly means

    (A) demise
    (B) arrogance
    (C) protection
    (D) environment
    (E) accumulation

18. The "wall of fire for his protection" (lines 87-88) that the author is referring to is

(A) a large, permanent police force
(B) a rational system of government
(C) education for the ex-slave
(D) revised religious ideas
(E) the right to vote

19. Which of the following best describes the attitude toward slavery revealed by the author in the last paragraph?

(A) Slavery is evil, but it is a necessary evil.
(B) Slavery cannot be eliminated by force.
(D) Slavery was lawfully based on a difference in intelligence.
(D) Slavery can be blotted out by the Federal government.
(E) Slavery is essential to maintaining State authority in the American system.

Writing Timed Drill 1 — 25 Minutes

This essay gives you an opportunity to show how effectively you can write. Develop your ideas convincingly, and carefully express your point of view precisely, logically and clearly.

Write an essay on the topic assigned below. You have twenty-five minutes to plan and write your essay. DO NOT WRITE ON ANOTHER TOPIC OR YOU WILL BE GIVEN A SCORE OF ZERO.

Carefully consider the issue presented in the following excerpt and the assignment below.

> To be, or not to be--that is the question:
> Whether 'tis nobler in the mind to suffer
> The slings and arrows of outrageous fortune
> Or to take arms against a sea of troubles
> And by opposing end them.
>
> *Hamlet* by William Shakespeare

Assignment: Should people continue to fight an unwinnable battle once they know it is unwinnable, or should they graciously accept defeat? Plan and write your essay, developing your own point of view on this topic. Support your point with examples from your studies, experience, literature, current events or personal observation.

Writing Timed Drill 2 — 25 Minutes

The following questions test your understanding of correct and effective expression. The answer choices represent five ways of expressing the underlined portion of each sentence. Choose the answer that you think represents the best expression of the underlined portion. Your choice should be clear and concise, and should avoid awkwardness and ambiguity. Choice A is exactly the same as the original.

1. European nations currently import more textiles from China than it does the United States.

(A) it does
(B) does from
(C) China does
(D) they do from
(E) China does it from

2. Mrs. Flannigan works in a factory run by Dexta Corporation, that produces tractors for farm use.

   (A) that produces
   (B) which produces
   (C) whom produces
   (D) it produces
   (E) a company who produces

3. The biology class I am taking this semester does not require as much homework as my math.

   (A) as my math
   (B) as math class required
   (C) as the math I am taking
   (D) than my math class does
   (E) as my math class does

4. The recent storm dumped three feet of snow on the highway leading to Rock Mountain Lodge, and makes it difficult to go skiing there this weekend.

   (A) and makes it difficult
   (B) that made it difficult
   (C) so making it difficult
   (D) thereby which made it difficult
   (E) which makes it difficult

5. After having spent many hours working on his presentation, the fact that the meeting at which he was to make it was cancelled was greatly frustrating to Mr. Hansel.

   (A) the fact that the meeting at which he was to make it was cancelled was greatly frustrating to Mr. Hansel
   (B) the meeting at which he was to make it was cancelled, greatly frustrating Mr. Hansel
   (C) the frustration of Mr. Hansel was great because the meeting at which he was to make it was cancelled
   (D) Mr. Hansel was greatly frustrated that the meeting at which he was to make it was cancelled
   (E) the greatly frustrating fact is that the meeting at which Mr. Hansel was to make it was cancelled

6. The most common cause of fires around the winter holidays are insufficiently watered Christmas trees and they catch fire because of dry needles in close contact with hot lights.

   (A) are insufficiently watered Christmas trees and they catch fire
   (B) is having insufficiently watered Christmas trees which catch fire
   (C) is insufficiently watered Christmas trees that catch fire
   (D) are catching fire by insufficiently watered Christmas trees
   (E) have insufficiently watered Christmas trees and they catch fire

7. According to U.S. Customs officials, JFK airport, which has the most international arrivals and departures in the country, serves nearly 600 incoming international flights per day.

   (A) which has the most international arrivals and departures in the country, serves
   (B) having the most international arrivals and departures in the country, and it served
   (C) that has the most international arrivals and departures in the country, is one that serves
   (D) which has the most international arrivals and departures in the country; it serves
   (E) where there are the most international arrivals and departures in the country, having served

8. After having learned to ride a bicycle at the age of fifty, the next thing Toby decided to attempt was skydiving.

   (A) After having learned to ride a bicycle at the age of fifty, the next thing Toby decided to attempt was skydiving.
   (B) When she learned to ride a bicycle at the age of fifty, Toby decides the next thing to attempt was skydiving.
   (C) Once she had learned to ride a bicycle, at the age of fifty, Toby, the next thing, decided to attempt skydiving.
   (D) The next thing Toby decides after having learned to ride a bicycle at the age of fifty was to attempt skydiving.
   (E) After having learned to ride a bicycle at the age of fifty, Toby decided the next thing she would attempt was skydiving.

9. <u>Knowing not only Latin and Sanskrit, but also ancient Aramaic and Etruscan</u>, many feel that Dr. Yogana is the world's leading expert on dead languages.

(A) Knowing not only Latin and Sanskrit, but also ancient Aramaic and Etruscan
(B) Since he is knowing Latin and Sanskrit as well as ancient Aramaic and Etruscan
(C) Because he knows not only Latin and Sanskrit but also ancient Aramaic and Etruscan
(D) By knowing not only Latin and Sanskrit but also ancient Aramaic and Etruscan
(E) Having knowledge of not only Latin and Sanskrit but ancient Aramaic and Etruscan as well

10. Isaac found many things he needed at the new downtown store – <u>the first thing was a new coat, then he found a pair of pants, finally a tie he liked</u>.

(A) the first thing was a new coat, then he found a pair of pants, finally a tie he liked
(B) firstly a new coat, then a pair of pants, and finally a tie he liked
(C) the first was a new coat, the second was a pair of pants, then finally a tie he liked
(D) finding first a new coat, then a pair of pants, and finally he found a tie he liked
(E) first a new coat, then a pair of pants, and finally a tie he liked

11. Although he needed help <u>from his father on math homework problems, while also needing help from his older sister in science projects, Germain was generally</u> a very independent young man who coped quite well with schoolwork.

(A) from his father on math homework problems, while also needing help from his older sister in science projects, Germain was generally
(B) from his father on math homework problems and from his older sister on science projects, Germain was generally
(C) on math homework problems from his father and in science projects from his older sister, Germain is generally
(D) from his father and older sister on math homework and science projects, respectively, Germain is generally
(E) Germain, who got help from his father on math homework problems and his sister on science projects, was generally

The following questions test your ability to spot errors in grammar and usage. Each sentence contains one error or no error at all, but never more than one error. If there is an error, it is underlined and labeled with a letter. Select the single underlined portion that represents a grammatical or usage error, or choose E if the sentence is correct as is. Follow the rules of standard written English.

12. <u>Once</u> a child has learned to walk <u>unaided</u> by
A   B
parents, other motor skills <u>were</u> quickly
                         C
learned <u>without as much</u> difficulty.
               D
<u>No error</u>
 E

13. Stalin, a Georgian <u>rather than</u> a Russian
                         A
<u>like</u> most other high-ranking Soviet
 B
officials, <u>rose</u> to the top of the
              C
Russian-dominated Communist Party,

<u>though not without difficulty</u> and heavy
              D
opposition. <u>No error</u>
          E

14. Despite millennia <u>of searching</u>, neither
           A
    scientists <u>or</u> philosophers can be certain
           B
    <u>about</u> how the universe <u>originated</u>.
     C   D
    <u>No error</u>
      E

15. Although young Michael <u>did not</u> make
                         A
    friends easily, he <u>was</u> an affable boy, and
                    B
    <u>they were</u> able to find playmates in the
     C
    new hometown <u>to which</u> his parents had
                    D
    moved. <u>No error</u>
            E

16. The blizzard was <u>supposed to of arrived</u> in
                       A
    the early afternoon, but even though the

    meteorologists <u>continued</u> to make dire
                      B
    predictions all evening, it <u>still hadn't</u>
                                 C
    struck <u>by</u> the next morning. <u>No error</u>
           D   E

17. Since he <u>was once</u> a critic himself,
               A
    Standish <u>defies</u> what the critics say about
              B
    his poetry, <u>deliberately</u> ignoring even
                    C
    their most valid assertions <u>about</u> the
                                   D
    sterility of his work. <u>No error</u>
                             E

18. Since she <u>has skied</u> during the one time
                 A
    when her daughter <u>caught</u> the winter flu,
                         B
    Mrs. Henberger now <u>feels</u> that she should
                          C
    no longer take vacations during January

    <u>when her children are</u> most likely to get
     D
    ill. <u>No error</u>
          E

19. Because King George III ruled England

    at a time <u>during which</u> Parliament
                  A
    <u>was much weaker</u> than it is today, he
          B
    <u>did not need to convince</u> those who
            C
    opposed him <u>of</u> the wisdom of fighting the
                  D
    American Colonists. <u>No error</u>
                          E

20. Though paleontologists agree <u>on</u> the time
                                  A
    period <u>in which</u> the dinosaurs <u>became</u>
              B   C
    extinct, they have not come <u>on consensus</u>
                                    D
    on the cause of the sudden disappearance of

    these gigantic creatures. <u>No error</u>
                                E

21. In Katie's senior year, <u>she was</u> the star
                              A
    pitcher for the school softball team,

    and no one could stop <u>she</u> and
                            B
    <u>her teammates</u> <u>from winning</u> a third
     C   D
    straight championship. <u>No error</u>
                             E

22. As the old saying goes, to err is human but

    <u>forgiving</u> is divine, yet <u>fewer</u> people
     A   B
    <u>are able</u> to forgive than <u>to blame</u>. <u>No error</u>
     C   D   E

23. The twins, considering <u>their</u>
                             A
    remarkable likeness to each other,

    <u>had such different personalities</u> that no
     B
    one <u>had</u> difficulty remembering which one
         C
    was <u>which</u>. <u>No error</u>
         D   E

24. <u>Although it</u> is common for scientific
       A

    theories to be discarded by experts even

    when many people believe them <u>fervently</u>,
                                         B

    but such a change <u>does not usually occur</u>
                               C

    without an important new discovery

    <u>that precipitates</u> a revolution in the field
         D

    in question. <u>No error</u>
                      E

25. Great painters <u>who</u> fail to achieve fame or
                     A

    financial success during <u>their lifetimes</u> are
                                    B

    often <u>known</u> to have struggled <u>about</u>
              C   D

    serious personal problems. <u>No error</u>
                                     E

26. Despite ample reason to accuse <u>my</u> sister
                                        A

    <u>and I</u> of breaking the lamp, our parents
     B

    <u>decided</u> to believe our story about the dog
     C

    <u>being responsible</u>. <u>No error</u>
         D   E

27. <u>During</u> the job interview, I <u>was been told</u>
      A   B

    that if I <u>was</u> to take the job, I would
                C

    have to visit a doctor for a complete

    <u>cardiovascular exam</u>. <u>No error</u>
         D   E

28. After a string of disappointments <u>dealt by</u>
                                            A

    various casting agents, the actor <u>decided</u> to
                                           B

    believe that <u>their</u> talent was perhaps not
                     C

    so great as she <u>had once believed</u>. <u>No error</u>
                          D   E

29. The Earth's fundamental ecosystem is

    <u>composed of</u> a <u>perpetual</u> cycling system of
         A   B

    oxygen and carbon-dioxide <u>that is routed</u>
                                    C

    back and forth <u>between</u> plant and animal
                        D

    life. <u>No error</u>
              E

The following essay represents an early draft that
needs to be revised. For the questions that follow,
select the answers that best rewrite the essay.
You may be asked to improve organization,
development, sentence structure, or word choice.
Follow the rules of standard written English.

---

(1) Prison reformers point out that college-study programs are cheap and effective means of reducing the number of prisoners who get arrested after their release; some are even saying that such programs are the most cost-effective way of dealing with the problem of recidivism. (2) It may be true that these programs are cheap, and that they do have the beneficial effect of reducing recidivism somewhat, but are they the cheapest and effectivest means?

(3) The only evidence for the cheapness of such programs is that educational programs have minimal costs because for the most part they are provided by community colleges and universities that offer moderately priced tuition. (4) No idea is given of how these "moderate" prices stack up against other prison programs like work-release, drug-therapy, counseling, etc. (5) College-study programs may be cheap, but can we accept the reformers' conclusion that they are the cheapest and most effective? (6) They seem unlikely.

(7) More to the point, their effect on the overall recidivism rate would be minimal. (8) Unfortunately, college study programs are aimed only at a significantly limited sub-set of the total prison population. (9) Since seventy percent of prisoners never finished high school, and another sixteen percent never attended at all, only fourteen percent of all prisoners, being the only ones to have finished high school and be ready to do college-level work, would be in a position to take advantage of college-study programs. (10) Because college-study programs would only be available to high-school graduates, that college-study programs could have only a minor effect on recidivism.

(11) If that prisoner who cannot take advantage of the college-study program will repeat offend at the same rate as always, known to be 60%, that still leaves over 51% of prisoners who will repeat offend. (12) And this is only from the non-college-study group. (13) It is presumable that some of the college-study prisoners would repeat

offend as well, bringing the level of this number up. (14) While it would be admirable to reduce the recidivism rate even a little bit, it hardly seems like what this provides counts as the most effective possible means. (15) This is particularly true since that result would be limited to a small portion of the total prison population.

30. Which of the following revisions is necessary to make sentence 2 (reproduced below) grammatically correct?

    It may be true that these programs are cheap, and that they do have the beneficial effect of reducing recidivism somewhat, but are they the cheapest and effectivest means?

    (A) Leave it as it is.
    (B) Delete "means."
    (C) Change "are they" to "is it."
    (D) Change "effectivest" to "most effective."
    (E) Insert "means" after "cheapest."

31. Which is the best way to deal with sentence 6 (reproduced below)?

    They seem unlikely.

    (A) Leave it as it is.
    (B) Change "They" to "The reformers."
    (C) Change "They seem" to "It seems."
    (D) Change "unlikely" to "uncertain."
    (E) Replace it with "We probably shouldn't."

32. In context, which of the following is the best replacement for the underlined portion of sentence 7 (shown below)?

    More to the point, their effect on the overall recidivism rate would be minimal.

    (A) the effect of these on
    (B) effectiveness of these to reduce
    (C) college-study programs effect on
    (D) the college-study programs would effect
    (E) the effect of college-study programs on

33. In context, what is the best change for sentence 10 (reproduced below)?

    Because college-study programs would only be available to high-school graduates, that college-study programs could have only a minor effect on recidivism.

    (A) Leave it as it is.
    (B) Delete "that."
    (C) Add "These reformers say" at the beginning.
    (D) Change "Because" to "It is a fact that."
    (E) Rephrase the sentence to begin with "Since college-study programs could have only a minor effect on recidivism."

34. In context, which is the best version of sentence 13 (reproduced below)?

    It is presumable that some of the college-study prisoners would repeat offend as well, bringing the level of this number up.

    (A) (As it is now)
    (B) It can be presumed how some of the college-study prisoners would repeat offend also, thus bringing up this number.
    (C) Presumably some of the college-study prisoners would also repeat offend, bringing this number higher.
    (D) This number would be brought up higher because one can presume that some of the college-study prisoners would repeat offend as well.
    (E) Not to mention the college-study group who, presumably, raise this number higher by repeat offending as well.

35. Which of the following is the most logical conclusion to follow sentence 15?

    (A) An even smaller portion of the prison population would limit the result further.
    (B) The college-study program is, therefore, likely to be an inexpensive success.
    (C) However, the policy of educating prisoners cannot be adequately judged by these facts.
    (D) Such a program is not a good policy for achieving an overall reduction of recidivism in America.
    (E) Consequently, it is an obvious waste of money to provide a college-study program to repeat-offending prisoners.

The following questions test your understanding of correct and effective expression. The answer choices represent five ways of expressing the underlined portion of each sentence. Choose the answer that you think represents the best expression of the underlined portion. Your choice should be clear and concise, and should avoid awkwardness and ambiguity. Choice A is exactly the same as the original.

1. Although seedless grapes have been widely available for many years, food scientists have also been attempting engineering a seedless apple.

    (A) been attempting engineering
    (B) been attempting to engineer
    (C) attempting to be engineered
    (D) made attempts to engineering
    (E) attempted at engineering

2. Schoolchildren in the area hoped that the snow that began to fall at eight o'clock would pile up, but it overnight turned to sleet and then rain.

    (A) but it overnight turned to sleet and then rain
    (B) but overnight it turns to sleet and then rain
    (C) but overnight it turned to sleet and then to rain
    (D) but overnight turning to sleet and then to rain
    (E) but, overnight, it turned to sleet and then raining

3. Many educational experts claim that intelligence cannot be measured by standardized tests, for, they say, true intelligence is displayed by resourcefulness and creativity that standardized tests are unable to examine.

    (A) for, they say, true intelligence is displayed
    (B) since they say that true intelligence was displayed
    (C) because true intelligence, they say, will display
    (D) despite the fact that, as they say, true intelligence is displayed
    (E) insomuch as, the educational experts say, true intelligence displays itself

4. If dogs had thumbs, they could more easily open doors and also to perform other tasks that only their masters can currently perform.

    (A) and also to perform
    (B) and they also are able to perform
    (C) which also would enable them to perform
    (D) and also they could perform
    (E) and could also perform

5. Engineers do not determine how much weight a bridge can hold, driving trucks over it until it breaks and then rebuilding it, but rather by using mathematical calculations.

    (A) can hold, driving trucks over it
    (B) holds, first driving trucks over it
    (C) will hold, to drive trucks over it
    (D) can hold by driving trucks over it
    (E) will be holding by driving trucks over it

6. The professor explained to the students about her grading procedures, that they would be tough but fair.

    (A) about her grading procedures, that they would be tough but fair
    (B) that they would be tough but fair, her grading procedures
    (C) her grading procedures, and which they would be tough but fair
    (D) because her grading procedures would be tough but fair
    (E) that her grading procedures would be tough but fair

7. Mark Twain is considered by many literary critics to have been both a great satirist and a realistic writer.

    (A) and a realistic writer
    (B) and a writer who wrote realistically
    (C) and to have been a realist
    (D) plus being realistic
    (E) as well as a realist

8. Even though the latitude, climate, and soil composition of both Washington State and France are very nearly identical, wine experts believe that the wine-growing regions of France produce better wine than those of Washington State.

(A) Even though the latitude, climate, and soil composition of both Washington State and France are very nearly identical, wine experts believe that the wine-growing regions of France produce better wine than those of Washington State.

(B) With very nearly identical latitude, climate, and soil, wine experts believe that the wine growing regions of France produce better wines than those of Washington State.

(C) Despite having very nearly identical latitudes, climates, and soil compositions, French wine is believed by wine experts to be better than Washington State wine.

(D) Wine experts believe that French wine-growing regions produce better wine than Washington State's despite very nearly identical latitudes, climates, and soil compositions being had by both places.

(E) Even though the latitude, climate, and soil composition of both Washington State and France are very nearly identical, wine experts believe that the wine-growing regions of France produce a better wine than Washington State.

9. Recent medical studies indicate that taking aspirin every day, it reduces the risk of having a heart attack.

(A) that taking aspirin every day, it reduces the risk of having a heart attack

(B) that reducing the risk of having a heart attack can be had by taking aspirin every day

(C) that taking aspirin every day reduces the risk of having a heart attack

(D) how taking aspirin every day, that it reduces the risk of having a heart attack

(E) by taking aspirin every day that one has a reduced risk of having a heart attack

10. Without any formal language training, the way I speak Spanish contains numerous grammatical errors.

(A) the way I speak Spanish contains numerous grammatical errors

(B) I speak Spanish in a way that contains numerous grammatical errors

(C) there are numerous grammatical errors in the way I speak Spanish

(D) my way of speaking Spanish contains numerous grammatical errors

(E) I spoke in a way of Spanish that contained numerous grammatical errors

11. Sociologists often claim that urban residents face so many daily choices and they cannot possibly be expected to handle the stress.

(A) and they cannot

(B) from which they cannot

(C) and which they cannot

(D) to which they cannot

(E) that they cannot

12. Using nothing more than a pencil, a string, and a tack, it is possible to duplicate very complex fractal patterns.

(A) it is possible to duplicate very complex fractal patterns

(B) very complex fractal patterns can be duplicated

(C) you can duplicate very complex fractal patterns

(D) one can be possible to duplicate very complex fractal patterns

(E) there exists the possibility of duplicating very complex fractal patterns

13. The Department of Homeland Security <u>hopes to establish not only a useful terrorism-alert system, but they also want to keep potential terrorists from entering the United States</u>.

   (A) hopes to establish not only a useful terrorism-alert system, but they also want to keep potential terrorists from entering the United States

   (B) is hoping to establish not only a useful terrorism-alert system, they also want to establish a way to keep potential terrorists from entering the United States

   (C) hopes to establish a useful terrorism-alert system as well as a way to keep potential terrorists from entering the United States

   (D) has a hope to establish both a useful terrorism-alert system and to find a way to keep potential terrorists from entering the United States

   (E) hopes to both establish a useful terrorism-alert system as well as to keep potential terrorists from entering the United States

14. Central High School has students <u>who, despite their varied ethnic background, has a common youth culture that they share</u>.

   (A) who, despite their varied ethnic background, has a common youth culture that they share

   (B) who, despite their varied ethnic backgrounds, share a common youth culture

   (C) who have a common youth culture that they share despite their varied ethnic background

   (D) with a shared common youth culture that is despite their varied ethnic backgrounds

   (E) sharing a common youth culture, which is despite their varied ethnic background

Math Timed Drill 1 Answers

1. E	8. A	15. C
2. C	9. A	16. A
3. D	10. E	17. C
4. B	11. E	18. B
5. B	12. A	19. C
6. C	13. A	20. D
7. B	14. D	

Math Timed Drill 2 Answers

1. D	8. B	15. $\frac{1}{2}$ or .5
2. E	9. 225	16. -5
3. A	10. 14	17. 40
4. D	11. 9	18. 24
5. D	12. 10	
6. A	13. 4	
7. C	14. 96	

Math Timed Drill 3 Answers

1. D	7. E	13. D
2. B	8. D	14. C
3. B	9. B	15. D
4. C	10. A	16. E
5. A	11. A	
6. C	12. B	

Critical Reading Timed Drill 1 Answers

1. D	9. B	17. A
2. C	10. A	18. C
3. A	11. D	19. A
4. B	12. E	20. A
5. C	13. D	21. B
6. C	14. A	22. E
7. D	15. C	23. D
8. A	16. E	24. B

Critical Reading Timed Drill 2 Answers

1. B	9. C	17. D
2. E	10. B	18. A
3. E	11. E	19. A
4. A	12. D	20. B
5. E	13. B	21. B
6. B	14. B	22. E
7. E	15. C	23. A
8. D	16. B	24. B

Critical Reading Timed Drill 3 Answers

1. D	8. D	15. A
2. A	9. E	16. D
3. E	10. B	17. C
4. D	11. B	18. E
5. A	12. A	19. B
6. E	13. D	
7. A	14. C	

Writing Timed Drill 2 Answers

1. D	13. E	25. D
2. B	14. B	26. B
3. E	15. C	27. C
4. E	16. A	28. C
5. D	17. E	29. B
6. C	18. A	30. D
7. A	19. E	31. E
8. E	20. D	32. E
9. C	21. B	33. B
10. E	22. A	34. C
11. B	23. E	35. D
12. B	24. A	

Writing Timed Drill 3 Answers

1. B	6. E	11. E
2. C	7. A	12. C
3. A	8. A	13. C
4. E	9. C	14. B
5. D	10. B	

FINAL ASSIGNMENTS

Well, we've done it all. Covered everything you need to significantly improve your SAT score. Here are a few final assignments as the clock winds down to SAT-Day.

THE WEEK BEFORE THE SAT

There are several things you should do in the week before the SAT. Here are some suggestions:

- **Do a drive by.**

    If you're not familiar with your test site, get familiar with it. Figure out how long it will take you to get there, where you need to park, the room in which the test will be given (if possible), where the closest and second closest bathrooms are, etc.

- **Practice in the room.**

  If at all possible, take a 30-minute practice section in the room in which the test will be given just to get the feel for the chairs, the desks, etc.

- **Monday through Thursday...**

  ... work at least 30 minutes per day on timed sections, and at least 15 minutes per day reviewing vocabulary. It's a good idea to practice in the morning since you'll be taking the real test in the morning.

THE FRIDAY BEFORE THE SAT

- **Don't study.**

  Really. If your parents are freaking out about cramming at the last minute, show them this. If you haven't learned it by Friday, cramming isn't going to work.

- **Do something fun.**

  Go to a movie, take a bike ride, or hang out with your friends. Relax. Moderate exercise in the afternoon is a great idea. Whatever you do, make sure it's mellow. Just don't stay out late.

- **Set out your "SAT Pile."**

  It should include your admission ticket, acceptable identification, #2 pencils, a big eraser, your calculator (with fresh batteries) and a watch or timer that doesn't beep.

- **Set out a snack.**

  You can't eat or drink during the test, but you should be allowed to nibble during the break. Don't fill up on sugar or other carbohydrates. A snack with some protein, and maybe a banana, would be good. And perhaps a sports drink to replenish those electrolytes. You don't want to stuff yourself. Just eat enough to keep your body-machine running at peak performance.

- **Set out your clothes for the morning.**

  Remember, the room might be very hot or very cold, so dress in layers that you can easily peel off. If you're uncomfortable, you won't be able to focus on the test as well.

- **Get a good night's sleep.**

  Don't stay up too late, but don't try to go to sleep too early either. Everybody's sleep needs are different, but a good number to shoot for is 8 hours.

SATURDAY, SAT-DAY

- **Eat a decent breakfast.**

  Nothing too heavy, nothing too light. Have some protein. Don't try anything new. If you don't drink coffee every day, don't start now. But if you can't see straight without the java, don't stop now. (Just fill up your travel mug… you can always quit on Sunday.)

- **Arrive early.**

  You don't want to get all worked up about being late. Panic caused by tardiness is not at all helpful. Don't be dilatory. (Look it up!)

- **Warm up with some easy SAT questions.**

  The first question on the SAT shouldn't be the first question you do on Saturday. Take a couple of pages of a real SAT, one you've done before, and redo some easy or medium questions just to get your brain in gear. Do them in the car before you go into the test.

DURING THE SAT

- **Don't panic.**

  You know everything you need to know about this test. Have faith in yourself, and you'll be fine. Take a couple of deep breaths and dive in.

- **Don't get bogged down.**

  If a question seems too hard, skip it and move on. You can come back to it later if you have time, and if you don't have time, then it would have been foolish to waste it all on a question that was giving you trouble.

- **Forget about the section you just took.**

  Focus on the section you are taking now. If you felt you had a really bad section, tell yourself it was probably the experimental section and move on.

- **Turn it all in.**

  At the end of the test, make sure you turn in all your test materials in the appropriate places. You're not allowed to take the test materials with you, and if you do, ETS will cancel your scores and possibly start a criminal investigation. So carefully follow all directions after the test — *and turn everything in*.

IF THERE ARE TESTING PROBLEMS

We hope this section never applies to you, but sometimes situations make testing unfair for some test takers. There may be a power failure, or a marching band might plant itself outside the window, or a proctor may not give you the allotted time. Anything that can detrimentally affect your test score is a serious issue, and if ETS thinks it's reasonable, the company will cancel scores and let the entire test site retake the SAT. In some extreme cases, they've even allowed students to hear their scores first and then decide if they want to cancel, but they'll try to avoid this. It's definitely not an ideal situation, but retaking the test is better than living with a score you got sitting under a busted water pipe.

Keep in mind, however, that you may be able to solve the problem immediately. Speak up if the proctor doesn't give you enough time. If a proctor is hovering above you or staring over your shoulder, let him or her know it is distracting you and ask the proctor to move. It's your test, after all, and you shouldn't be disadvantaged in any way.

If you can't solve the problem at the test site, and you seriously believe your performance was diminished by factors outside your control, make sure you keep a record of everything. Write down the test location and date, the proctor's name, exactly what happened, the names of some other students who were affected, etc. Contact ETS and see if the company is willing to listen to you and offer a suitable solution. If you find ETS is reluctant to help you, contact us, and we'll try to assist you, if we can, by steering you in the right direction.

After the SAT

Reward yourself, go have some fun and release all of that nasty SAT pressure.

Then, on Sunday, or sometime in the next few days, send a report on your test experience to:

SATreport@MaximumSAT.com

We want to hear anything you have to say about your test: if you felt you were well prepared, if there were any questions you weren't expecting, etc.

Finally, when you get your scores, email them to:

SATscores@MaximumSAT.com

Be sure to include your previous scores on any real SATs you've taken, or your score from the first diagnostic test you took. We'd love to know how much you improved.

VOCABULARY LISTS

The following vocabulary words are grouped together according to definition and subject matter, which makes learning the words a little bit easier for most students. You should use as many techniques as possible to get these words into your head: lists, flashcards, audio cds or iPod files, etc.

Remember to pick up a copy of the American Heritage Dictionary or Merriam-Webster's Collegiate Dictionary, and use it whenever you see a word you aren't sure about.

Energy

aggregate	adj.	constituting or amounting to a whole; total; collective; clustered in a dense mass or head
ardent	adj.	passionate; eager, zealous; fiery, hot
arduous	adj.	hard to accomplish or achieve, difficult; painstaking; steep, hard to climb
attrition	n.	gradual wearing away; a natural or expected decrease in size or number usually by resignation, retirement or death; sorrow for one's sins
dearth	n.	a shortage or scarce supply of something; lack
dominant	adj.	most powerful; commanding, controlling or prevailing over all others
enervate	v.	to lessen the strength or vitality of; to reduce the mental or moral vigor of
enhance	v.	to make better or stronger; improve; increase
fervent	adj.	having intense feeling, enthusiastic, zealous; fervid; very hot, glowing
impetuous	adj.	characterized by sudden energy or passion; impulsive
indolent	adj.	averse to activity, habitually lazy; causing little or no pain; slow to develop or heal
pique	v.	to arouse anger or resentment in; to excite; to arouse an emotion or provoke to action
potential	adj.	existing in possibility, capable of actually occurring
prolific	adj.	abundantly productive, fruitful, or fertile
quiescent	adj.	motionless; at rest; still; causing no trouble or symptoms
saturnine	adj.	cold or steady in mood; slow to act or change; gloomy or surly
smidgen	n.	a very small amount; a small bit
somber	adj.	serious or grave; depressing, dismal, gloomy; melancholy
soporific	adj.	causing sleep or sleepiness
sufficient	adj.	enough to meet needs; adequate
temperate	adj.	moderate, mild; restrained
unfettered	adj.	set free from restrictions or bonds; liberated
vapid	adj.	dull, spiritless; uninteresting, insipid
vestige	n.	a remaining bit of something, a last trace; footprint
wane	v.	to decrease in size, strength or intensity; to fade away; to decline in power; dwindle
wizened	adj.	shriveled; withered; shrunken; dried out

Think Happy Thoughts

adage	n.	a wise, old saying; a saying often in metaphorical form that embodies a common observation

affable	adj.	easy to talk to, friendly; being pleasant and at ease talking to others
amiable	adj.	good-natured and likable; friendly, sociable; generally agreeable
augury	n.	divination from omen, esp. a good omen; portent
avuncular	adj.	kind, helpful, generous, like a nice uncle; of or relating to an uncle
benefactor	n.	one who gives a gift or bequest; one that confers a benefit
blithe	adj.	carefree, cheerful; happy and lighthearted; casual; heedless
candor	n.	sincerity, honesty; lack of prejudice or malice, fairness; whiteness, brilliance
coterie	n.	a group of close associates; a circle of friends or associates
curmudgeon	n.	a greedy, irascible, crotchety, cantankerous old person
ebullient	adj.	bubbling with excitement, exuberant; boiling, agitated
euphonious	adj.	pleasant to the ear; melodious
exonerate	v.	to clear from accusation or blame; to relieve of a responsibility or hardship
expiate	v.	to make amends for, to atone
fortuitous	adj.	accidental, occurring by chance; fortunate, lucky
gastronomy	n.	the art or science of eating well; culinary customs or style
humanist	n.	one who has great concern for human welfare, values, and dignity; a student of the classics or humanities
ideal	n.	a standard of perfection, beauty, or excellence; lacking practicality
idyllic	adj.	simple and carefree; pleasing or picturesque in natural simplicity
kudos	n.	prestige; honor, glory, acclaim, compliment; fame resulting from achievement
lampoon	v.	to harshly satire; ridicule
lampoon	n.	a harsh satirical piece
mirth	n.	gladness or happiness as shown by laughter
rapport	n.	a relationship of harmony, mutual accord or affinity
sanguine	adj.	blood red; ruddy; cheerful, optimistic, hopeful
serendipity	n.	accidental good fortune, discovering good things without looking for them
sublime	adj.	of great intellectual, moral, or spiritual value; lofty or grand; splendid
tolerance	n.	ability to endure pain or hardship; sympathy or respect for the beliefs or practices of others
values	n.	beliefs of a person or social group, morals; the monetary worth of something

wry	adj.	dryly or grimly humorous, often with a touch of irony

Actions

afford	v.	to permit or allow, to enable, to make available; to be able to bear the cost of; to manage to bear without serious detriment
application	n.	the act of using something; a request or a petition
catalyst	n.	a substance that initiates a chemical reaction without changing itself; one that provokes significant change
coalesce	v.	to grow or come together as one, to fuse, to unite
consequence	n.	a result that follows from an action or condition; significance, importance
dehydrate	v.	to remove water from; to deprive of vitality
depict	v.	to represent by or as if by a picture; to describe
desalinate	v.	to remove salt from something
desiccate	v.	to dry up; dehydrate; drain of emotional or intellectual vitality
draft	n.	a preliminary sketch or version; the act of drawing; the act of pulling
excavation	n.	the act of digging; a cavity formed by cutting, digging or scooping
exhibit	v.	to display or show outwardly or publicly
forge	v.	to advance steadily or with a sudden increase in speed; to form (a metal) by heating and hammering; to make or imitate falsely with intent to defraud
furrow	v.	to form grooves, wrinkles, or lines, often in the face
gaffe	n.	a social or diplomatic blunder, an embarrassing mistake, a faux pas
galvanize	v.	to startle into sudden activity; to revitalize; to subject to electrical current or shock
generate	v.	to create, to bring into existence; produce
importune	v.	to beg, urge, or insist persistently and troublesomely; to annoy or trouble
itinerant	adj.	traveling from place to place
jettison	v.	to throw or cast off; discard; to drop from an aircraft or ship
liquid	adj.	flowing readily; neither solid nor gaseous; smooth and unconstrained
passive	adj.	not active; lacking energy or will
persist	v.	to go on resolutely and stubbornly; to remain unchanged or fixed; to continue to exist
preempt	v.	to take for oneself; take precedence over; to seize something by prior right
thwart	v.	to prevent the occurrence of; contravene; to successfully oppose

Adventure

ford	n.	a shallow place in a body of water, such as a river, where one can cross by wading or riding on an animal or in a vehicle
ford	v.	to cross or wade across a body of water at a ford
impromptu	adj.	not planned in advance; spur of the moment, improvised
jaunt	n.	a short trip for pleasure
quest	n.	a pursuit or search, often adventurous

Easy Does It

accessible	adj.	able to be reached or used; capable of being understood
assuage	v.	to lessen the intensity of, to ease; to soothe, pacify, or relieve; to put an end to by satisfying, appease, quench
compromise	n.	an agreement which partially satisfies each side
compromise	v.	to give up something in order to reach an agreement
demure	adj.	modest and reserved; affectedly shy, modest or reserved; coy
facile	adj.	fluent; poised, assured; easily accomplished or attained
implacable	adj.	impossible to appease or mitigate
latent	adj.	in a dormant or hidden stage; inactive but capable of action
mere	adj.	only; being nothing more than; pure
mitigate	v.	to make less harsh, hostile, severe or painful; mollify; alleviate
mollify	v.	to soften, soothe or pacify; appease; assuage

Hatred and Anger

acerbic	adj.	bitter, sour, severe; acid in temper, mood or tone
anathema	n.	something or someone loathed or detested; one that is cursed by ecclesiastical authority; a curse
cantankerous	adj.	difficult or irritating to deal with; ill-natured, contentious
carp	v.	to complain or find fault with someone or something
castigate	v.	to criticize severely, to chastise; to subject to severe punishment or criticism
censure	v.	to condemn or criticize severely for doing something worthy of blame
choleric	adj.	hot-tempered, quick to anger, irritable
contempt	n.	lack of respect, scorn, haughty disdain; the state of being despised; willful disobedience of authority
crude	adj.	raw; rude or tactless; unrefined; roughly made
cynical	adj.	distrustful of people's motives as selfish
divisive	adj.	creating conflict, disunity and disagreement

effigy	n.	an image or representation of a person, usually a hated person
exasperation	n.	the state of being annoyed or irritated
execrate	v.	to declare to be evil; to curse, denounce
flout	v.	to treat with contempt and disregard, scorn; insult
glower	v.	to look or stare with sullen dislike or anger
harsh	adj.	rough; coarse to the touch; causing physical discomfort; crude
ignominy	n.	deep personal humiliation, shame, disrepute, disgrace; dishonorable or disgraceful conduct
inane	adj.	silly, senseless; empty, insubstantial; pointless
indignation	n.	moral outrage; anger aroused by something unjust, mean or unworthy
lambaste	v.	to attack violently with words, censure; to attack violently, beat, whip
misanthrope	n.	one who hates or distrusts people
pander	v.	to cater to or exploit the tastes and desires of others
rebuke	v.	to criticize sharply; reprimand
resentment	n.	a deep feeling of ill will at something considered wrong or insulting
sardonic	adj.	disdainfully or skeptically mocking or scornful
undermine	v.	to remove support from under; to weaken

War and Aggression

annihilate	v.	to destroy completely, rout; to make ineffective, nullify
arsenal	n.	a storehouse of weapons; a place where weapons are manufactured; store, repertory
beleaguer	v.	to surround with an army to prevent escape, besiege; trouble, harass
bellicose	adj.	warlike, belligerent; inclined to start quarrels or wars
capitulate	v.	to surrender, give up, or give in; to negotiate
captious	adj.	ill-natured, quarrelsome; inclined to stress faults and raise objections; critical
competition	n.	a contest between opponents
conquer	v.	to defeat or subdue an opponent; to overcome
conscript	v.	enlisted, drafted, or enrolled, usually refers to mandatory military service
fracas	n.	a big fight; a noisy quarrel; brawl
imperious	adj.	commanding, dominant; urgent; pressing or overbearing
jingoist	n.	someone who shows extreme chauvinism or nationalism, especially by a belligerent foreign policy; warmonger
perfidy	n.	treachery; the state of being unfaithful or disloyal

polemic	n.	a powerful attack on the opinions or principles of another
pugnacious	adj.	quarrelsome, combative, always ready to fight; truculent; belligerent
raze	v.	to completely destroy or level something; demolish
recalcitrant	adj.	defiant of authority; stubborn; not easily managed; not responsive to treatment
revolution	n.	a political overthrow; a sudden, radical or complete change; completion of one circle around something
semaphore	n.	a system of signaling, usually through the use of flags
subterfuge	n.	deceptive strategy used to conceal, escape, or evade
truculent	adj.	fierce, cruel, savagely brutal; deadly or destructive; belligerent
usurp	v.	to take power and hold it by force; replace by force; supplant
xenophobe	n.	one who greatly fears foreigners

Bad to the Bone

abysmal	adj.	extremely hopeless or wretched; bottomless, having immense or fathomless extension downward, backward or inward; profound
apostate	n.	one who deserts or renounces his or her professed principles or faith; one who abandons a previous loyalty
debacle	n.	a great disaster; a violent disruption; a complete failure, fiasco
draconian	adj.	severe, harsh, cruel
egregious	adj.	extremely bad, flagrant
insidious	adj.	treacherous, waiting to entrap; harmful but enticing, seductive; having a gradual and cumulative effect
malevolent	adj.	having or exhibiting intense ill will, spite or hatred; wishing harm to others; hateful
maverick	n.	a nonconformist; a rebel; an independent individual who doesn't go along with a group
milk	v.	to draw or extract profit or advantage from; exploit
pernicious	adj.	deadly, highly injurious or destructive
plebeian	adj.	common, vulgar, low class; crude or coarse in manner or style
recidivism	n.	a tendency to repeat an offense, especially criminal
renege	v.	to go back on a bet or promise; to make a denial
scrupulous	adj.	having moral integrity; strict, careful, hesitant for ethical reasons; painstaking
squalor	n.	a filthy condition or quality, usually from neglect or poverty
vilify	v.	to say vile, abusive things about, to defame
wanton	adj.	malicious, unjustifiable, unprovoked, egregious; merciless; lewd or bawdy; lustful

Death and Sadness

bequest	n.	something left to someone in a will; the act of handing down
exhume	v.	to dig out of the ground (a grave); disinter; to bring back from neglect or obscurity
forensic(s)	n.	the art or study of argumentation and formal debate, often legal debate
inexorable	adj.	relentless, inevitable, unavoidable; not to be persuaded or changed
lugubrious	adj.	exaggeratedly mournful; dismal
maudlin	adj.	weakly and overly sentimental; drunk enough to be emotionally silly
moribund	adj.	in the state of dying; approaching death
morose	adj.	sullen, gloomy, sad and dreary
sympathy	n.	compassion marked by sharing of feelings or interest

Contrary

antithetical	adj.	in direct opposition, contrary to; opposite
brusque	adj.	blunt, abrupt, rough and short in manner or speech
contradiction	n.	a situation in which two things do not make sense together; a state of contrasting qualities
contrary	adj.	opposite; disagreeing; counter to
controversial	adj.	causing debate, dispute or argument
conventional	adj.	following accepted customs; normal; ordinary; using weapons or power that is not nuclear
corroborate	v.	to confirm, back up, strengthen or support with evidence
demur	v.	to object or take issue with; delay or hesitate
dither	v.	to vacillate between choices; to tremble with excitement or nervousness
idiosyncratic	adj.	quirky, peculiar, eccentric; hypersensitive (to a food or drug)
inconsistent	adj.	not compatible with another fact or claim; lacking consistency
obdurate	adj.	stubborn, persistent in wrongdoing; insensitive; unyielding, resistant to persuasion
relatively	adv.	somewhat; in comparison with something else
stymied	v.	thwarted; stumped; blocked

Lies and More Lies

beguile	v.	to lead by deception; to delude by guile or craft; to mislead, divert; charm
belie	v.	to give a false impression; to contradict; to prove (something) false

cabal	n.	a secret group of conspirators; the acts of such a group; a clique
chicanery	n.	trickery, deceitfulness, artifice, subterfuge
debunk	v.	to expose the falseness of; to show to be untrue
derived	adj.	taken from a different source; not original; inferred or deduced
ersatz	adj.	describing an artificial or inferior substitute or imitation
feign	v.	to pretend; to make a false representation of; to assert as if true
furtive	adj.	characterized by stealth; sneaky; secretive; sly
goldbrick	v.	to swindle, to sell something worthless as if it were valuable; goof off
mendacious	adj.	given to falsehood and deception, dishonest, often not intended to genuinely mislead or deceive
misleading	adj.	deceptive; leading in the wrong direction
refute	v.	to prove wrong by argument or evidence; to deny the truth of
specious	adj.	deceptively plausible or attractive; misleading; having a false look of truth
unscrupulous	adj.	without honor or morals; unprincipled

Amazing

awe	n.	an emotion combining fear and wonder; dread, terror
bizarre	adj.	very strange; unusual; strikingly out of the ordinary
deft	adj.	very skillful

Beginners

archetype	n.	an original model or pattern, prototype; a perfect example
neophyte	n.	a novice, beginner or tyro; a new convert
novel	n.	a book that tells a fictional story, usually long and complex

Body and Soul

chagrin	n.	humiliation; embarrassed disappointment
humanity	n.	the quality of being humane, kindness; mankind
hybrid	n.	formed, bred, or composed from different elements, races, breeds, varieties, or species
impulse	n.	a sudden force or urge; motivation, incentive
incarnate	adj.	in the flesh; invested with human or bodily form; made understandable
insouciant	adj.	nonchalant, lighthearted, carefree
portrait	n.	a picture or painting of a person showing the face
pulchritude	n.	physical beauty or comeliness

| quixotic | adj. | idealistic to a foolish or impractical degree; extravagantly chivalrous; from "Don Quixote de la Mancha" by Cervantes |

The More Things Change

adapt	v.	to adjust or make usable
behest	n.	an authoritative command or order; an urgent prompting
cajole	v.	to persuade with flattery or gentle urging, coax; to deceive with soothing words or false promises
capricious	adj.	unpredictable, likely to change at any moment, changeable, impulsive
circumvent	v.	to avoid or get around; to entrap or overcome by ingenuity
compel	v.	to force; constrain
conform	v.	to act in accordance with prevailing standards or customs; to be similar; to be in agreement
devise	v.	to imagine or create; invent; to plan to bring about, to plot; to give by will, bequeath
eclectic	adj.	drawn from various sources
expunge	v.	to strike out, obliterate, to blot out; to destroy
fragile	adj.	easily broken or destroyed; frail
illumination	n.	decorative lighting; the act of lighting; spiritual or intellectual enlightenment
immutable	adj.	not capable of or able to be changed
influence	n.	ability to persuade or affect; an emanation of spiritual or moral force
influential	adj.	exerting or possessing influence or power
persuasive	adj.	able to move people to act or believe by argument, entreaty or urging
plastic	adj.	easily bendable, pliable, capable of being molded

Dumb and Dumber

prosaic	adj.	dull, unimaginative; everyday, ordinary
stupor	n.	a state of reduced or suspended sensibility; daze
vacuous	adj.	empty of content; lacking in ideas or intelligence; stupid, inane

Government

abdicate	v.	to cast off, discard, to formally give up power
abrogate	v.	to abolish by authoritative action, repeal, or nullify, annul
allocate	v.	to distribute, assign, or allot; to set apart or earmark
appropriate	v.	to take without permission; to take exclusive possession of, annex; to set aside for a particular use

canon	n.	a rule or law, especially a religious one; a body of rules or laws; an authoritative list; the set of works by an author
canvass	v.	to campaign; to seek or solicit orders, votes, etc.; to examine in detail to determine authenticity
corruption	n.	dishonesty; immoral or depraved behavior; openness to bribery
demagogue	n.	a leader of the common people; a leader who uses false claims and common prejudice to gain power
diplomatic	adj.	tactful and conciliatory; of or relating to diplomats
hegemony	n.	leadership or authority, especially of one nation over another
oligarchy	n.	government by only a very few people, usually for selfish purposes
poll	v.	to receive and record the votes of
poll	n.	a survey of people's opinions, the recording of the votes of a body of people; the place where votes are cast
potentate	n.	a person who possesses great power; ruler, sovereign
promulgate	v.	to publicly or formally declare something; proclaim; to put (a law) into action
unilateral	adj.	involving one side only; done on behalf of one side only; done by one person

Who's the Greatest?

capacious	adj.	roomy; spacious; containing or capable of containing a great deal
extent	n.	the range over which something extends; scope; the amount of space something occupies
glut	n.	surplus, overabundance, excessive quantity
grandiloquent	adj.	using fancy, lofty words to sound impressive; pompous eloquence, bombastic
hedonism	n.	the pursuit of pleasure as the main good in life
paucity	n.	smallness of number, fewness; an extreme lack of, dearth
predominant	adj.	having superior numbers, strength, or importance; being the most common
primarily	adv.	for the most part; chiefly; in the first place, originally
principle	n.	a rule or code of conduct; a comprehensive or fundamental law or assumption
prominence	n.	the state of being noticeable or conspicuous; a projection (something that sticks out)
purist	n.	one who is particularly and often excessively concerned with maintaining tradition, especially language
quintessential	adj.	relating to the essence of a thing in its purest form; being the most typical example

| vital | adj. | important, necessary for life; full of life; of the utmost importance |

Health and Caring

ameliorate	v.	to make better or more tolerable
deleterious	adj.	harmful, often in a subtle or unexpected way
hypodermic	adj.	beneath the skin; relating to injection beneath the skin
inoculate	v.	to protect against disease; to introduce a microorganism to
liniment	n.	a medicinal liquid or salve applied to the skin as an anti-irritant
olfactory	adj.	pertaining to the sense of smell
palliative	adj.	making something less severe without getting rid of the problem; reducing the violence of; cover by excuse or apology
panacea	n.	a remedy for all ills, cure-all
salutary	adj.	promoting good health; curative

That's Interesting

broach	v.	to open up a subject, often a delicate one, for discussion; to break into
equine	adj.	relating to or resembling horses, horse-like
farce	n.	an absurdly ridiculous situation; mockery; a light, funny dramatic work marked by highly improbable plot and satirical comedy
piquant	adj.	pleasantly sharp in flavor, spicy; engagingly provocative or stimulating
predilection	n.	a natural preference for something; a taste for
queue	n.	a waiting line
queue	v.	to line up
trenchant	adj.	keen, incisive, perceptive; forceful, effective, and vigorous; clear cut

Life, Sweet Life

aesthetic	adj.	relating to beauty; artistic
anthropology	n.	the study of human cultures; the science of human beings especially distribution, origin, classification, relationship of races, culture, etc.
anthropomorphic	adj.	described or thought of as having human form or characteristics; ascribing human characteristics to non-human things
burgeon	v.	to grow and expand rapidly; to flourish; to send forth new growth; sprout

catharsis	n.	purification that brings emotional relief or renewal
cultivate	v.	to help something (ideas) to grow, foster; to prepare land for growing crops
fecund	adj.	fertile, fruitful in offspring or vegetation; intellectually productive or inventive
halcyon	adj.	peaceful, serene; carefree; prosperous, affluent
organic	adj.	derived from plants or animals; produced without chemically formulated fertilizer, hormones, etc.
poignant	adj.	painfully effecting the feelings, extremely moving, being to the point
pristine	adj.	not spoiled by civilization, pure; being fresh and clean
verdant	adj.	covered with green plants; leafy; inexperienced
vivid	adj.	bright or lively; sharp, intense

Losing Out

annul	v.	to make legally invalid or void, usually refers to marriage; to reduce to nothing, obliterate
retrenchment	n.	reduction, especially of expenses; curtailment
supplicate	v.	to ask or beg humbly and earnestly
incensed	adj.	extremely angry or indignant
indignant	adj.	angry or insulted, especially as a result of something unjust, mean or unworthy
irascible	adj.	easily angered or provoked, irritable, hot tempered

Money Money Money Money

avarice	n.	greediness, excessive desire for wealth or gain
closefisted	adj.	stingy; not willing to spend money
fund(ing)	n.	financial resources set apart to make some project possible
liquidate	v.	to get rid of; to settle a debt; to convert assets to cash
ornate	adj.	elaborately or excessively decorated; marked by elaborate or flowery style
parsimonious	adj.	excessively cheap, frugal or stingy
patron	n.	a wealthy or influential supporter of an artist or an artistic institution; a special guardian, protector or supporter
penurious	adj.	extremely stingy, poor, or miserly
skinflint	n.	one who would save, gain or extort money at any expense; miser
subsidy	n.	a grant or gift of money
threadbare	adj.	worn so the thread shows through; shabby; worn out, hackneyed

| usury | n. | the practice of lending money and charging interest, usually very high or illegally high interest |

Music to My Ears

laconic	adj.	using a minimum of words; concise to the point of seeming rude or mysterious
mellifluous	adj.	flowing sweetly, usually refers to sounds or voices; filled with something that sweetens
redolent	adj.	fragrant, aromatic; suggestive
reticent	adj.	reluctant to speak; reserved

Pat on the Back

accolade	n.	an award or honor; a ceremonial embrace; an expression of praise; a ceremony conferring knighthood
auspices	n.	protection, support; sponsorship, patronage; a prophetic sign, especially a good one
laudatory	adj.	expressing praise
luminary	n.	a person who has attained prominence in a field; a celestial body that gives off light
meritorious	adj.	deserving praise, honor or esteem
obeisance	n.	deep reverence; a bow or curtsy; deference, homage
obsequious	adj.	marked by fawning attentiveness; subservient, servile, excessively deferential
panache	n.	flair, verve; dashing style; an ornamental tuft on a helmet
paragon	n.	a model of excellence
urbane	adj.	notably polite and elegant in manner; suave; polished
validity	n.	truth; correctness; legal effectiveness

Rituals and Religion

anomaly	n.	an aberration, deviation, or irregularity; something different or not easily classified
contrite	adj.	penitent for sin or shortcoming; repentant
heresy	n.	an opinion that disagrees with established, dearly held beliefs; adhering to religious beliefs contrary to church dogma
homily	n.	a sermon; an inspirational catchphrase
incantation	n.	a chant; spells or verbal charms that are part of a magical ritual
moral	n.	the significance or practical lesson of a story or event
moral	adj.	relating to principles of right and wrong in behavior; ethical
sacrosanct	adj.	most sacred or holy; reputedly but not genuinely sacred

tenet	n.	a principle or belief held to be true

School, Learning and Academics

analysis	n.	the process of looking at something carefully and methodically
ascertain	v.	to determine with certainty; to find out definitely
cartography	n.	the science and art of making maps
characterize	v.	to describe the qualities of
cite	v.	to quote or refer to a person's speech or writing; to commend deserving action
cogitate	v.	to ponder; to meditate; to think carefully about
colloquial	adj.	characteristic of ordinary, informal speech or writing
conceive	v.	to imagine, think; to form in the mind, devise; to become pregnant
consideration	n.	careful thought
convey	v.	to express; to carry, transport; to communicate or impart
critical	adj.	tending to call attention to flaws, inclined to judge severely; crucial or decisive
deliberate	v.	to think about or discuss issues and decisions carefully
deliberate	adj.	carefully considered and intended; slow, unhurried and steady
demography	n.	the statistical study of human populations
endemic	adj.	belonging to or native to a particular region or people, indigenous
epiphany	n.	a sudden grasp of reality or understanding, usually simple and striking
etymology	n.	the study of words, their origins and their meanings
evince	v.	to demonstrate convincingly; to prove; to reveal
feasible	adj.	possible; capable of being accomplished; reasonable, likely
florid	adj.	very fancy; excessively flowery in style, ornate; tinged with red, ruddy
generalization	n.	a statement or judgment about all based on a few particulars; a general statement
imply	v.	to lead someone to believe something without directly stating it; to express indirectly
infer	v.	to conclude or figure out; to conclude from facts or premises; guess, surmise
insightful	adj.	exhibiting clear and deep perception; able to clearly see into a situation; seeing or understanding intuitively
jurisprudence	n.	the study of law; a system or body of law
lexicon	n.	a glossary or dictionary; the specific vocabulary of a person or subject; inventory

neologism	n.	a new word or phrase, a new usage of a word, often disapproved because of its newness
numerology	n.	the occult study of numbers for the purpose of predicting the future
pedantic	adj.	unimaginative; boringly scholarly or academic; narrowly and ostentatiously learned
pictorial	adj.	consisting of pictures; relating to a painter, a painting or the drawing of pictures
playwright	n.	someone who writes plays
prose	n.	the ordinary language people use in speaking or writing; writing or speaking without steady rhythm or rhyme, as opposed to poetry
recapitulate	v.	to review or summarize; repeat the main points of
rhetoric	n.	the study or art of using language effectively; insincere or grandiloquent language
semantic	n.	pertaining to the meaning of words
standard	adj.	common or ordinary; regular
standard	n.	a generally accepted model, example or rule used to judge or compare; a banner
terse	adj.	brief and to the point; concise; smoothly elegant
verify	v.	to establish the truth or existence of
vernacular	n.	language specific to a region, place or country; everyday speech, slang, idiom

Self Love

aloof	adj.	standoffish, uninvolved, keeping one's distance; reserved
ascetic	adj.	hermit-like; practicing self-denial especially as a measure of spiritual discipline; austere in appearance, manner or attitude, severe
esteem	n.	respect or admiration
esteem	v.	to respect or admire; think, believe; set a high value on
garrulous	adj.	pointlessly or annoyingly talkative; given to excessive, rambling talk
headstrong	adj.	bold; not easily restrained, ungovernable; stubborn; unruly
hubris	n.	excessive or exaggerated pride, often resulting in retribution
narcissism	n.	excessive love of one's body or oneself; egoism, egocentrism
narcissist	n.	one who excessively loves oneself or one's body; egoist
philistine	n.	a smugly ignorant person with no intellectual or artistic appreciation; one guided by materialism rather than intellect or artistic values
priggish	adj.	offending or irritating by being very fussy or self-righteous
profligate	adj.	extravagantly wasteful, prodigal; wildly immoral

| supercilious | adj. | haughty, patronizing |

Spirits and Ghosts

chimerical	adj.	imaginary, unreal; given to fantasy
consciousness	n.	the state of being aware and awake; a sense of one's personal identity
craven	adj.	cowardly, afraid
detached	adj.	standing by itself; separate, unconnected; exhibiting an aloof objectivity
ethereal	adj.	lacking material substance; delicate and refined; related to the regions beyond earth, celestial, heavenly
harbinger	n.	a forerunner, a signal of, precursor; one that foreshadows what is to come
ineffable	adj.	incapable of being expressed or described in words, indescribable; unspeakable
karma	n.	good or bad emanations generated by a person's actions (Hinduism and Buddhism); good or bad vibrations
limpid	adj.	transparent; clear and simple in style; absolutely serene and untroubled
mythical	adj.	fictional; unreal; based on myth; legendary
portend	v.	to serve as an omen or a warning of; bode
portent	n.	an omen, something that foreshadows a coming event
prescient	adj.	having knowledge of things before they exist or happen; having foresight
prophetic	adj.	foretelling or predicting future events
transparent	adj.	clear, obvious; see-through; free from deceit or pretense, frank
uncanny	adj.	extraordinary, mysterious, uncomfortably strange, supernatural; eerie
zeitgeist	n.	the intellect, morals, mood or spirit of an era

Strength and Weakness

adamant	adj.	extremely stubborn; unshakable or unmovable especially in opposition; unyielding
assent	v.	to agree, especially after thoughtful consideration, concur
assert	v.	to put forth as true, to state positively, forcefully and aggressively
assiduous	adj.	diligent, hardworking, busy; marked by careful, unremitting, persistent application
buttress	n.	a projecting support for a wall, building or structure; something that supports or strengthens
flaccid	adj.	not firm or stiff; soft; lacking vigor or force

| hermetic | adj. | airtight, impervious to external influence |
| timid | adj. | lacking self-confidence or boldness |

What's that Stuff?

commodity	n.	something bought or sold; something useful that can be used for commercial advantage
inchoate	adj.	incomplete, only partially formed; imperfectly formed or formulated
indigenous	adj.	originating and living in a particular region or environment; innate, inborn
stand	n.	a group of trees or plants; the place a witness testifies in court

Success

acumen	n.	keenness of judgment, depth or perception, mental sharpness; shrewdness
apotheosis	n.	elevation to divine status, deification; the perfect example of something, quintessence
conclusive	adj.	putting an end to any uncertainty or doubt; final
determined	adj.	committed; certain; firmly resolved
perseverance	n.	the act of persisting or continuing without quitting; steadfastness
prosperity	n.	the state of being successful or thriving; economic well-being
resolution	n.	something settled or resolved; the outcome of a decision
strive	v.	to struggle in opposition; to devote serious effort or energy
tenable	adj.	valid, capable of being argued successfully; reasonable; defensible
zenith	n.	the highest point; peak; pinnacle

Time

anachronistic	adj.	out of place in time or history; chronologically misplaced
current	adj.	up-to-date; at the moment; prevalent; a flow of electricity, liquid or gas
diurnal	adj.	occurring every day; occurring during the daytime
ephemeral	adj.	lasting a very short time; lasting one day only
evanescent	n.	fleeting, tending to vanish like vapor
expeditious	adj.	prompt and efficient
immediate	adj.	direct; instant; current; without anything in between, next in line; nearby
outdated	adj.	old-fashioned, outmoded; no longer current

Tools and Instruments

apt	adj.	suitable; appropriate; unusually fitted or qualified; having a tendency, likely, inclined; keenly intelligent
barometer	n.	an instrument that measures atmospheric pressure; one that indicates fluctuations
caliper	n.	an instrument with two legs or jaws used for measuring thickness, diameter or distance between two surfaces
capacitor	n.	a device which stores electrical energy, usually between two plates or foils
furrow	n.	a trench made in the ground by a plow; a deep wrinkle
implement	n.	tool, utensil, instrument
impractical	adj.	not usable or effective; not practical
odometer	n.	instrument that measures the distance traveled
practical	adj.	concerned with actual use or practice; useful
jejune	adj.	lacking nutritive value; devoid of substance or significance; insipid
lax	adj.	not strict; careless or negligent; slack

Unimportant or Unclear

abstruse	adj.	difficult to comprehend, recondite
ancillary	adj.	subordinate, subsidiary; providing assistance; supplemental
cavil	v.	to quibble; to raise trivial and frivolous objections
chaos	n.	great disorder or confusion
coy	adj.	shy, especially flirtatiously; reluctant to make a commitment; unforthcoming
discomfit	v.	to frustrate, to thwart; to confuse or disconcert
elliptical	adj.	oval in shape or manner; relating to extreme economy of speech or writing; deliberately obscure
equivocal	n.	ambiguous, intentionally confusing, capable of being interpreted many ways; undecided
germane	adj.	relevant, applicable, pertinent, appropriate, fitting
gratuitous	adj.	given freely; free; uncalled for, unjustified, unwarranted
hackneyed	adj.	overused, trite, stale; lacking freshness or originality
impenetrable	adj.	incapable of being understood; incapable of being penetrated or pierced
indifferent	adj.	impartial, unbiased; without feeling; not caring; lack of interest or enthusiasm; apathetic; neutral
irrelevant	adj.	having no connection to a subject; inapplicable
nebulous	adj.	vague, hazy, indistinct
nuance	n.	a subtle difference or distinction; a subtle quality

obfuscate	v.	to darken or confuse, to make obscure
overlook	v.	to look past, miss or ignore; to look over, inspect
paltry	adj.	inferior, trashy; insignificant, worthless, trivial; mean, despicable
peccadillo	n.	a minor offense or error
perfunctory	adj.	unenthusiastic, careless; routine or mechanical
quotidian	adj.	daily; occurring everyday; ordinary, commonplace
skeptical	adj.	doubtful; disbelieving
subtle	adj.	hard to detect; not obvious; elusive; delicate; expert; artful
turbid	n.	thick or opaque with mud; lacking clarity or purity

Workplace

colleague	n.	a coworker; a fellow member of a profession
conscientious	adj.	careful and principled; guided by one's conscience
labor	n.	work; physical or mental effort; workers
perquisite	n.	a privilege that goes along with a job, a "perk"; gratuity or tip
yeomanly	adj.	dependable, sturdy, loyal

Yuck!

noisome	adj.	offensive or disgusting to the senses; stinking, noxious, unwholesome
noxious	adj.	physically harmful or destructive to people; offensive, obnoxious; morally corrupting
repugnant	adj.	causing disgust or aversion; incompatible

INDEX

ABOUT THE AUTHOR:

Pete Edwards is the founder and president of Achieve Tutorials. He is a graduate of Princeton University and holds a Master of Professional Writing degree from the University of Southern California. Pete has been helping students maximize their SAT scores in the classroom and through individual tutoring for 16 years. He also tutors academic subjects ranging from calculus to English and history to physics. His passion for teaching is equaled only by his passion for the ocean. Pete is an avid surfer, and has sailed half way around the world.

[1] "Is-ought problem" *Wikipedia: The Free Encyclopedia.* 26 Dec 2004, 00:26 UTC. 5 Jan 2005 <http://en.wikipedia.org/wiki/Is-ought_problem>

[2] "Actual Idealism" *Wikipedia: The Free Encyclopedia.* 22 Nov 2004, 19:52 UTC. 5 Jan 2005 <http://en.wikipedia.org/wiki/Actual_Idealism>

[3] Thoreau, Henry David. "Walking", 1851

[4] "Fungus" *Wikipedia: The Free Encyclopedia.* 29 Dec 2004, 14:47 UTC. 5 Jan 2005 <http://en.wikipedia.org/wiki/Fungus>

[5] "Ancient Olympics" *Wikipedia: The Free Encyclopedia.* 24 Dec 2004, 23:25 UTC. 5 Jan 2005 <http://en.wikipedia.org/wiki/Ancient_Olympics>

[6] "Papuan Languages" *Wikipedia: The Free Encyclopedia.* 15 Nov 2004, 00:59 UTC. 5 Jan 2005 <http://en.wikipedia.org/wiki/Papuan_Languages>

[7] "Native American languages" *Wikipedia: The Free Encyclopedia.* 31 Dec 2004, 05:17 UTC. 5 Jan 2005 <http://en.wikipedia.org/wiki/Native_American_Languages>

[8] "Aleatoric music" *Wikipedia: The Free Encyclopedia.* 11 Nov 2004, 02:27 UTC. 5 Jan 2005 <http://en.wikipedia.org/wiki/Aleatoric_music>

[9] "Mayapan" *Wikipedia: The Free Encyclopedia.* 30 Dec 2004, 15:25 UTC. 5 Jan 2005 <http://en.wikipedia.org/wiki/Mayapan>

[10] Eliot, George. "Adam Bede" 19 Dec 2004 <http://www.princeton.edu/~batke/eliot/bede/bede_04.html>

[11] Gaskell, Elizabeth. "Wives and Daughters", 1866, 19 Dec 2004 <http://www.online-literature.com/elizabeth_gaskell/wives_daughters/1/>

[12] Emerson, Ralph Waldo. "Art", *Essays*, 1841

[13] "A priori" *Wikipedia: The Free Encyclopedia.* 12 Nov 2004, 13:28 UTC. 5 Jan 2005 <http://en.wikipedia.org/wiki/A_priori>

[14] "Coventry Cathedral" *Wikipedia: The Free Encyclopedia.* 19 Dec 2004, 21:37 UTC. 5 Jan 2005 <http://en.wikipedia.org/wiki/Coventry_Cathedral>

[15] "Gene therapy" *Wikipedia: The Free Encyclopedia.* 21 Dec 2004, 09:12 UTC. 5 Jan 2005 <http://en.wikipedia.org/wiki/Gene_therapy>

[16] "Reconstruction" Frederick Douglas, Atlantic Monthly 18 (1866): 761-765

Printed in the United States
59567LVS00001B/145-154

9 781411 623859